Well Made in America

WELL MADE
IN
AMERICA

*Lessons From Harley-Davidson
on Being the Best*

PETER C. REID

McGRAW-HILL PUBLISHING COMPANY

*New York   St. Louis   San Francisco   Auckland   Bogotá   Caracas
Hamburg   Lisbon   London   Madrid   Mexico   Milan   Montreal
New Delhi   Oklahoma City   Paris   San Juan   São Paulo
Singapore   Sydney   Tokyo   Toronto*

Library of Congress Cataloging-in-Publication Data

Reid, Peter C.
    Well made in America : lessons from Harley-Davidson on being the
best / Peter C. Reid.
        p.   cm.
    Bibliography: p.
    Includes index.
    ISBN 0-07-026500-3
    1. Harley-Davidson Motor Company—Management.   2. Motorcycle
industry—United States—Management.   3. Corporate turnarounds—
United States—Management—Case studies.   I. Title.
HD9710.5.U54H376   1990
658.4'063--dc20   89-12138
                                                                                      CIP

1234567890   DOC/DOC   89432109

ISBN 0-07-026500-3

The editors for this book were Martha Jewett, Barbara B. Toniolo, and Jim
Halston, the designer was Mark E. Safran, and the production supervisor
was Richard A. Ausburn. The book was set in Palatino by Techna Type.

Printed and bound by R. R. Donnelley and Sons

A sixty-minute audio program to accompany this book is now available. Ask
for it at your local bookstore or phone toll-free 1-800-2-MCGRAW.

For more information about other McGraw-Hill materials, call 1-800-
2-MCGRAW in the United States. In other countries, call your nearest
McGraw-Hill office.

Contents

Part 2 How Your Company Can Do What Harley-Davidson Is Doing / *139*

About the Author

Peter C. Reid is a writer, editor, and journalist who specializes in business topics—and loves motorcycles. He is the author of *The Motorcycle Book, The Employer's Guide to Avoiding Job-Bias Litigation,* and coauthor of *Corporate and Executive Tax Shelters* and *How Successful Managers Manage.*

Foreword

When Vaughn Beals first suggested a book about Harley-Davidson's recovery, the more I considered it, the better I liked it. At last, an outside observer would describe all the elements in our company's turnaround.

It's a true story about people, spirit, pride, and a fierce determination to succeed in the face of some incredible odds. Many thought Harley-Davidson didn't stand a chance against some very formidable foreign competition. And indeed, without the sacrifices of a lot of people, we wouldn't have made it.

Today's senior management team is keenly aware of what it took to stay alive and prosper during the past decade: Vaughn Beals, Jim Paterson, Jeff Bleustein, Tom Gelb, and I did not turn Harley-Davidson around on our own. We weren't the only people lying awake at night, worrying about the company's survival.

For example, when we had to cut our work force by more than 40 percent, the 1600 people we laid off made a tremendous sacrifice for Harley-Davidson. So did the 2200 who remained. Some bargaining-unit employees agreed to freeze their wages, forgo cost-of-living increases, and work reduced schedules; salaried employees took major pay cuts; and everyone worked long and arduous hours to improve the product and develop innovative programs to sell it.

The State of Wisconsin Investment Board and the United States government helped, too. The State of Wisconsin Investment Board invested money in Harley-Davidson when we needed it most to make changes in our financial structure, and the

United States Trade Representatives and President Reagan leveled the playing field while we got our competitive act together.

Our suppliers invested in new manufacturing techniques such as just-in-time inventory and statistical operator control to accommodate our needs. And then they waited weeks, sometimes months, for us to pay them, because our cash flows were almost nonexistent.

Our customers bought motorcycles that were a far cry from the less expensive, high-quality motorcycles our competitors offered. They stuck with us despite problems that would have sent other buyers elsewhere.

Much of the credit for retaining our customers' loyalties belongs to Harley-Davidson's dealers. They continued to buy our motorcycles even when they already had large inventories of them. They repaired our manufacturing deficiencies before a Harley motorcycle was ever presented to a customer. And finally, they maintained their enthusiasm for the product and the company, even when their better business sense dictated otherwise.

Those days are behind us now. But the struggle isn't. Yes, we've been successful in the initial phases of implementing advanced manufacturing techniques, and we've developed innovative marketing programs that keep us close to our customers. But we have much to do to complete the process. We have dedicated ourselves to continuous improvement throughout the total organization, from top to bottom, administration through manufacturing. That's our way of remembering and rewarding the pain and anguish suffered by everyone who believed in Harley-Davidson.

RICHARD F. TEERLINK
Chief Executive Officer
Harley-Davidson, Inc.

Introduction

Today for thousands and thousands of Americans their relationship to their motorcycle is directly akin to the way the cowboy of yesterday's West related to his horse. Those two roamed the Great Plains and moved from roundup to roundup on one vast ranch after another. With coffee and grits around campfires, they contemplated sunsets and sleep. Rugged independent souls moving to their own beat, treasured as key parts of the nation's heartbeat.

The spirit that moved those two inseparable companions is as alive today as yesterday, only the motorcyclist's steed has two wheels instead of four legs. It's geared to horsepower in a teeming civilization no longer gaited for horses.

For heart-and-soul bikers, their dream's reality is saddling up their machines, whether it's to go down the block for a beer and a look or to reach the farthest corners of the country and sometimes the globe.

For many of us and perhaps most, Harley-Davidson seems to embody that spirit of freedom more than other machines. A good part of the feeling, of course, stems from the fact that Harleys are the only U.S.-made motorcycles in an industry overwhelmingly dominated by Japanese models.

But there's far more to it than that. For instance, there's the intense satisfaction of knowing from the action, the feeling, and the sound when you've shifted gears. The husky Harley engine sounds could never be confused with those of a sewing machine or a lawnmower. Harley saddles fit better. Your own seat lasts longer, tires less after hours on 'em.

Today's durably handsome Harley visibly embodies a colorful past in its powerful present. The Harley mystique is a reality to its rider. If Harley had gone belly up, as it damnear did a few short years ago, a real part of our heritage, an American tradition, would have gone with it.

The following pages grippingly tell how that near-tragedy was avoided. It's an American success saga, describing the inspired efforts of Vaughn Beals and a handful of colleagues. Often hanging by a fiscal thread that came perilously close to parting more than once, the Beals–Willie Davidson team have put this vital segment of Americana robustly back on the road.

This book reaches out far beyond the motorcycle business. In *Well Made in America* are powerful, straight-from-the-shoulder lessons and wisdom for every business manager and everyone who yearns to be his or her own boss.

If you want to ride safe in business as well as on the road, here's how.

MALCOLM S. FORBES

Acknowledgments

T he idea for this authorized account of Harley-Davidson's dramatic business turnaround originated with people both in and outside of Harley-Davidson who believe its story can inspire and inform other U.S. companies facing the challenge to become world-class competitors. Many Harley-Davidson people and others gave generously of their time to provide me with a rich vein of material on which to draw. Among them were:

Harley-Davidson: Vaughn Beals, Jeff Bleustein, John Campbell, Bennie Carter, Frank Cimermancic, Bob Conway, Willie G. Davidson, Al Dean, Trevor Deeley, Kathleen Demitros, Tom Gelb, Timothy K. Hoelter, Randy Horning, Roger Hull, Michael J. Kami, Mike Keefe, Jerry Knackert, Milt Kornburger, Jim Marcolina, Bob Miller, Kathryn Molling, Liz Morgan, Jim Paterson, Linda Peavy, George Schroeder, Jeff Sipling, Harry Smith, Richard Teerlink, Pat Thomson, Ann Thundercloud, Don Valentine, Tom Veigh, and Jerry Wilke, as well as Robert Rohrer and F. T. Swain (now retired) and the late Charlie Thompson.

Harley-Davidson dealers: John F. Brinkworth, Armando Magri, Philip S. Peterson, Emil Schott, Nathan F. Sheldon, Orville Sheldon, Howard L. Whittington, and Ray Worth.

Other contributors: Joe Anthony, Del Austin, Lou Bacig, Tim Carpenter, Steve Deli, Wendell Edwards, Rodney Gott, Stan Groner, Dawn Hardies, Ron Hutchinson, Thomas Rave, Ray Tritten, Jack M. Sands, and Jack Werner.

My special thanks go to Patricia Haskell for her major contribution to this book.

And to those at McGraw-Hill whose enthusiasm never flagged and whose guidance was invaluable: Martha Jewett, William Sabin, Alison Spalding, Barbara Toniolo, Jim Halston, Mark Safran, and Jane Palmieri.

I would also like to thank USAV Communications Group, Inc., and Purcell *Imaging,* Ltd., for the use of some of the photographs that appear in the book.

Finally, thanks to my wife Carol for letting me wear her Harley T-shirt as I revved up my word processor every day.

PETER C. REID

1

Winning the Race for Competitive Survival

chapter 1

"If We Can Do It, Any Company Can!"

To understand why Harley-Davidson's executives make this claim with total conviction, consider this scenario: You're a senior manager in a U.S. company that makes big-ticket leisure products and belongs to a conglomerate seeking to shift its focus *away* from leisure products to industrial products. When the parent puts your company on the block, you and other top managers see an opportunity to purchase it in a leveraged buyout (LBO). You're looking at the following facts about your company's current situation:

- You are losing sizable chunks of market share to your much bigger Japanese competitors.
- The economy is beginning to slide, and many blue-collar workers—your core customers—are facing layoffs.
- Sky-high interest rates are also making it hard for people to buy your product.
- Your manufacturing systems and product quality are inadequate to meet world-class competition.
- Your product line is seriously out of date.
- Your product has been stereotyped with a rough, tough image.
- Your Japanese competitors are unloading thousands of products on American shores that compete directly with yours.

- The Japanese products not only have higher quality, but they also have lower prices.

Sound like a good deal? Few observers thought so in 1981 when the Harley-Davidson Motorcycle Company was put up for sale by American Machine & Foundry (AMF), the conglomerate that had owned it for 11 years. It looked like just another sad case of an old-line U.S. manufacturer being hammered into oblivion by Japanese competitors whose basic strategy was to invade American markets with high-quality products at substantially lower prices. All of AMF's worldwide attempts to sell Harley-Davidson were unavailing. No one wanted it.

Next, consider what happened after 13 Harley-Davidson managers—despite all these negatives—still went ahead and bought the company in an $81.5 million LBO:

- The market for heavyweight motorcycles declined by 20 percent within a year.
- Harley lost more market share as the Japanese flooded the United States with Harley look-alikes at discounted prices.
- For the first time in almost 50 years, Harley lost money.
- Harley had to lay off more than 40 percent of its work force.
- Saddled with a staggering LBO debt, Harley had to borrow even *more* money just to service its debt and keep going.
- Harley's major lender, Citicorp, seriously considered withdrawing its support and taking steps to liquidate the company for whatever the assets would bring.

Small wonder that industry observers concluded that Harley-Davidson was not long for this world.

"There's Something About a Harley"

Why did 13 apparently astute executives buy a company that the Japanese were literally blowing away? Like many business decisions, this one was both rational and emotional.

On the practical level, Harley-Davidson did have solid business assets: an extraordinarily loyal customer base, a well-established dealer network, a high added-value product, and a strong, in-place management team.

But those factors aren't enough to explain the buyout. The buyout team was also motivated by strong feelings about Harley-Davidson, and to understand them it is necessary to understand the Harley-Davidson "mystique." Or as one Harley rider, an investment banker, calls it, "the value of intangibles."

From its first appearance in 1903, the Harley motorcycle has been unique, one of the few U.S. consumer products destined to evolve into an "American institution" with a committed constituency. To Harley owners, Harleys have heart, Harleys have soul. Harleys have raw power and a "voice": a basso-profundo thump that makes other motorcycles sound like sewing machines. To many riders, Harley-Davidson is the *real* "heartbeat of America."

These Harley riders run the gamut. About half are supervisors, machine operators, and other skilled workers. But Harley riders also include lawyers, doctors, bankers, entertainers, engineers, and scientists. Perhaps 1 percent belong to the Hell's Angels end of the spectrum.

Despite their diversity, Harley riders all have something in common: a fanatical dedication to their Harleys. It's a feeling that many cannot articulate, and for them there's a Harley T-shirt inscribed: "Harley-Davidson—If I Have to Explain, You Wouldn't Understand." Actor Mickey Rourke says, "It's a personal thing that can't be described. It's part of you."

One thing is certain: This incredible brand loyalty is emotional. It is based on a pattern of associations that includes the American flag and that other American symbol, the eagle (which is also a Harley symbol), as well as camaraderie, individualism, the feeling of riding free, and pride in owning a product that has become a legend. On the road, one Harley rider always helps another in distress—even though one may be a tattooed biker and the other a bank president.

Some of these feelings obviously spilled over into the decision of Harley's managers to buy the company in 1981. Though not all were motorcyclists, they all shared the Harley rider's emotional commitment to Harley-Davidson—and they had an intense desire to see the last U.S. motorcycle manufacturer live to fight again. They had the greatest incentive in the world to improve: survival. They firmly believed that Harley-Davidson would go under at the hands of its Japanese competition unless they assumed ownership of the company and turned it around—no matter how much sweat it took.

And Now the Good News

In the five years following the LBO, Harley-Davidson again became a thriving company. Shortly thereafter, it recaptured its market-share lead from Honda, its major Japanese rival, and Honda has since sharply cut back its participation in the U.S. heavyweight motorcycle market.

Harley quality is at an all-time high. The company sells every motorcycle it can make—at the premium end of the market—and at this writing is failing to meet market demand.

By going public, Harley was able to pay off its heavy LBO debt, with enough money left over to acquire a leading maker of premium recreational vehicles.

Now Harley is on full throttle.

The first section of this book, a behind-the-scenes account of how Harley-Davidson came back from the dead and achieved its remarkable turnaround, is a classic story of the little guy against the big guys, of a small company that fought a fierce battle against industrial giants with far greater financial, technological, production, and marketing resources—and survived. Much of this story has never been told before.

At another level, however, the Harley-Davidson saga carries some clear lessons for all U.S. companies on what it takes to become a world-class competitor in today's global economy—and a strong message of hope to those who fear that U.S. competitiveness may be finished and done with.

The most important lesson, says Harley-Davidson chief executive officer Richard Teerlink, concerns people:

> Without the dedication of all its employees, no company
> can have long-term success. Top management must
> recognize that it has the responsibility and obligation to
> provide an environment in which an employee feels free

to challenge the system to achieve success. Once the employee is committed, the techniques become easy. For Harley-Davidson, the techniques involved *all* functional areas of the business.

Harley-Davidson learned many other lessons—often the hard way—along the road from the euphoria of independence in 1981 to the brink of bankruptcy in 1985 to market leadership today. These lessons have a major theme: To survive in today's competitive world, U.S. manufacturers must make customer satisfaction their ultimate goal and must adopt (1) the Productivity Triad techniques of employee involvement (EI), just-in-time inventory (JIT), and statistical operator control (SOC); (2) a "close to the customer" marketing approach; and (3) a "cash is king" financial strategy.

Supporting this theme, the following key conclusions can be drawn from Harley-Davidson's turnaround:

- Competitive success requires a corporate strategy based on continuous improvement in *all* areas of company operations.
- Quality-improvement programs do not require large cash investments; on the contrary, they *generate* cash.
- The key to finding out what the customer perceives as "quality" is to create occasions and opportunities for customers to tell you what they think about your product and then to *listen* to the customers carefully. And "close to the customer" should be a way of life for top management and all employees, not just the marketing department. (Harley senior executives make a point of riding and talking motorcycles with their customers.)
- Particularly in this era of heavy LBO debt, a company must focus on having enough cash to operate on a daily basis; otherwise, it will not survive long enough to become a world-class competitor. Having cash doesn't ensure success, but not having it can ensure failure. Harley-Davidson learned several key techniques for improving its cash flow in difficult times: (1) understand the terms of a loan agreement better than the lender does, because loan terms can reveal hidden opportunities to maximize

cash flow; (2) know a lender's objectives, which makes it possible to negotiate more effectively; (3) sell off assets that don't fit the company's long-term strategy; and (4) exploit untapped profit opportunities that exist within the business.

- The secret of continuous improvement in manufacturing quality does not lie in high technology but rather in the development of three major programs in unison: EI, JIT, and SOC (also known as statistical process control). The potential of these programs that make up the Productivity Triad can only be realized if they are adopted together: (1) There can be no quality improvement without full *employee involvement*. Employees can no longer be asked to check their brains at the door. They must be trained in new skills and new ways of thinking about their jobs so they can make timely decisions on the shop floor instead of bucking them up to a supervisor. When the employee is given the right tools and is listened to, problems start getting solved. (2) High inventories are simply an excuse for inadequate systems and production processes. *Just-in-time inventory* not only generates cash, it also increases quality. (3) With *statistical operator control*, employees can focus on reducing variability instead of on conforming to specifications.

- There can be no quality improvement without the involvement of *management*—first-line to the top. Managers must forgo certain management prerogatives they may have previously taken for granted and let employees make more and more decisions.

- The Japanese work processes and methods can be adapted to any work force, anywhere, regardless of culture. That has been proved by Harley-Davidson—an All-American culture if there ever was one—as well as by the growing number of other U.S. companies that are providing useful models for any company willing to commit itself to meaningful change.

The second section of this book, "How You Can Do What Harley-Davidson Is Doing," translates these lessons into practical recipes. There you will find the nuts-and-bolts strategies and techniques that Harley-Davidson used to achieve striking gains in quality, productivity, employee morale, market share, and profitability. This valuable information comes from the people who work for Harley-Davidson, both managers and non-

---

 PORTRAIT OF A SURVIVOR

Since its founding in 1903, Harley-Davidson has made it through five major crises that threatened its very existence. That it overcame the first four—all brought on by external events—can be credited to the ability of its tough-minded founders, who simply refused to let it succumb.

- *Survival Crisis 1.* After zooming from 150 motorcycles in 1907 to 28,000 in 1920, production drops precipitously to 10,000 because of an economic downturn and a consumer switch from motorcycles to cars for basic transportation.
- *Survival Crisis 2.* The Great Depression hits just as the company is regaining previous production levels. In 1933, production collapses to a meager 3700 motorcycles. (As one Harley-Davidson senior executive says today, "One can only have admiration for a management group that figured out how to adjust to the almost 80 percent drop in shipments the company suffered from 1929 to 1933!")
- *Survival Crisis 3.* With the military's need for motorcycles in World War II, production reaches 1920 levels once more—only to nose-dive when the war is won.
- *Survival Crisis 4.* Postwar demand from returning veterans takes production to record levels temporarily, but the market sags again as veterans turn their attention to housing and other necessities. Indian Motorcycle Company goes out of business in 1953, leaving Harley as the only motorcycle company in the United States.

All of these crises were externally generated. The fifth was generated by the failure of Harley-Davidson—and its parent, AMF—to answer the Japanese motorcycle invasion of the 1970s with better quality, increased productivity, and fresh new products. Instead, production was expanded so fast that it flew out of control, and product development was neglected, throwing Harley-Davidson into a crisis that few thought it would ever survive.

managers, and from the Harley-Davidson training seminars, which, thus far, management teams from over 650 U.S. manufacturers have attended—at $300 a head.

Surmounting the "Insurmountable"

Can the United States reverse its industrial slide? Can it compete in a global economy? The Harley-Davidson story answers those questions with a resounding yes. Will it be easy? An equally resounding no.

No for a lot of reasons, which have to do with both the internal and external environments that U.S. companies must deal with in trying to improve their competitive position.

Internal Environment

In 1980, Harley-Davidson's internal environment was fairly typical of many U.S. manufacturers. The company had:

- A corporate management that focused mostly on short-term returns
- A management that didn't listen to its employees or give them responsibility for the quality of what they made
- High inventories of parts that gobbled up cash and reduced productivity
- Inefficient production systems that generated poor quality, low productivity, and excessive costs
- A "meeting specifications is good enough" attitude toward quality, rather than a constant drive toward higher standards
- A belief in quick fixes for problems—such as throwing in computers and state-of-the-art machinery to improve productivity
- Slow design and development time that allowed foreign competitors to reach the market first with new products
- A high breakeven point that left the company vulnerable to unpredictable market fluctuations

- A management that woke up too late to the threat of foreign competition because of the "it can't happen here" syndrome

For the most part, you won't find these conditions and attitudes in Harley-Davidson today. But that's not true of a majority of U.S. manufacturers—it is difficult to change beliefs and systems that have been entrenched so solidly for so many years. What does it take? Most of all it takes top management's total commitment to change. It takes tremendous energy and dedication from the whole management team. And it takes the full involvement of every employee in the organization. Add patience, perseverance, and obstinacy and you have the necessary ingredients.

Easy it is not—but it can be done. Look at what Harley accomplished:

- Productivity improvement   +50%
- Inventory reduction   −75%
- Scrap and rework   −68%
- Increased U.S. revenue   +80%
- Increased international revenue +177%
- Increased U.S. market share   +97%
- Increased operating profit   +$59 million

External Environment

It is tempting for U.S. corporate chieftains to blame their difficulties on the many advantages enjoyed by their foreign competitors, particularly the Japanese. As James C. Abegglen and George Stalk Jr. point out in *Kaisha: The Japanese Corporation*, Japanese concerns live in an environment characterized by

- A free, competitive domestic market in Japan
- Plenty of low-cost funds for investment, provided by a high savings rate and a supportive financial system
- An educated, disciplined labor force at moderate wages
- A government that nurtures the private sector

Yes, it would be easier for U.S. companies to become world-class competitors if we could transfer these economic benefits to our shores. But waiting around for that happy day will be self-defeating.

Harley-Davidson's position is: Our environment may not be ideal, but we must learn to improve our competitive position despite it. We must focus on the Japanese advantages we *can* transfer to our own operations: better management methods, more effective production systems, faster product-development cycles, and full employee involvement.

Making It Against Your Competition— Anywhere in the World

The manufacturing revolution now going on in the United States was forced on us by the Japanese, so it is natural for us to consider them our major competitors. But as the quality and productivity revolution spreads throughout the world, your competition can come from anywhere—including your competitor down the street. Those who join the revolution will become the survivors, while those who prefer the status quo will be the casualties. If foreign competitors don't get you, a domestic competitor will.

So the story of Harley-Davidson's resurgence is both a warning and a promise. The warning is that companies in your business are right now adopting progressive systems and methods that will give them a competitive edge. The promise is that if a small, underfunded U.S. company like Harley-Davidson can meet and beat the toughest competitors in the world, you can, too.

chapter 2

Eye-Opener

"At first, we found it hard to believe we could be that bad—but we were," says Vaughn Beals, Harley-Davidson's chairman of the board.

It was 1982, eight months after their leveraged buyout. Some Harley-Davidson managers, engineers, and leaders from the largest unions had just returned from a mind-boggling tour of a Honda motorcycle assembly plant in Marysville, Ohio, and were trying to absorb what they had seen as they went through a painful and depressing audit: comparing their own manufacturing operations with those of their chief competitor, Honda.

Just what had they learned on this plant tour? For Tom Gelb, senior vice president of operations, one scene was memorable: "The assembly line was neat and uncluttered with hardly any material at the line—unlike our operation, where the line was always littered with parts and material. There was minimum paperwork, and things flowed very smoothly." Adds Beals, "Sure, they'd put some effort into dressing the place up before we arrived, but the condition of the plant was clearly far better than anything we could have done, even with the greatest preparation."

Labor relations also seemed excellent—whenever workers looked up from the line and saw Harley's Japanese hosts they would smile broadly, wave, and call them by name.

But what hit the visitors hardest were two things they *hadn't* seen: The Honda plant had no computer and practically no overhead staff. Here was a company doing mixed-model assembly at 50,000 units a year (about what Harley was doing) *without a computer*. Harley managers found this incredible since they used a computerized materials requirement planning system that would have won an award in any contest for complexity.

Honda's total overhead staff at Marysville (president, secretaries, personnel department, accounting, material planning, etc.) numbered 30 out of 500 employees. There were no squadrons of engineers and planners stashed in the back room. This was also startling to Harley managers—they couldn't even conceive of how to do such a thing. It was a sobering lesson that the basic difference between Honda's costs and theirs was not in direct labor but rather in overhead staff.

 A FACE SAVER—JUST IN TIME

When we assembled in the Honda conference room after the plant tour, one of our materials people said that he hadn't seen a computer. They didn't have one, our hosts said, and they actually seemed embarrassed, as if they were losing face. We couldn't believe it, so we asked the question several times. We thought we might be having a language problem. Finally, with a sigh of relief, one of our hosts remembered that a local bank used a computer to do their payrolls.

Observations from a member of the Harley-Davidson team on viewing a Honda assembly plant in Marysville, Ohio, in 1982.

Why was the Marysville tour so traumatic? After all, Harley's new owners had already begun to realize that there were significant differences between their manufacturing methods and those of the Japanese (they had visited motorcycle plants in Japan back in 1980). And the Milwaukee engine plant had been experimenting with some Japanese methods for a few months.

But the visit to Marysville showed Harley executives in very stark terms that the vast gap in competitiveness between them and their Japanese rivals was a difference in *management*.

Here was a plant right in the smokestack belt of the United States—with American employees—that was demonstrating that Japanese superiority could not be attributed to its culture or to any other exclusively Japanese factor. This fact brought it all home. Harley-Davidson management had discovered the enemy, and it was themselves.

Two other guests on that tour, Jerry Knackert, president of AIW Local 209 (Milwaukee, Wisconsin), and Eric Burkey, president of IAM Lodge 175 (York, Pennsylvania), noted that Harley-Davidson engineers from York were busily sketching the procedure that workers were using to "bleed" the brake lines (that is, to force air out of a hydraulic system), because the Japanese would not allow cameras. Knackert thought it was curious that Harley engineers were paying so much attention to this method when it was the identical method that his union members had used to bleed Harley brakes before the company had moved its assembly operation to York. Evidently, the technology had not survived the move, and it became one more lesson that Harley-Davidson had to learn or relearn from the Japanese.

Jeff Bleustein, senior vice president of parts and accessories, points out that it was easy for U.S. companies to misread the source of Japan's competitive superiority. He quickly admits that he had missed the main point when he visited Japan in 1975 to find out what the Japanese bike makers were doing about noise and emissions technology. He recalls:

> When I saw the Japanese manufacturing operations, I had the feeling there was a tremendous gap separating us. But I didn't realize what it was. I was thinking in terms of culture, technology, capital investment, government assistance, and so on—the way we all were then.

> Those things were important, of course, but they were maybe 20 percent of the story. The other 80 percent was that they were just better managers than we were and they understood how to do manufacturing a hell of a lot better, with less inventory and much higher quality. It took us seven years to understand that.

The Marysville Honda plant tour brought Harley's grow-

"THEY MUST BE DOING SOMETHING RIGHT—BUT WHAT?"

In 1980, two years before their tour of Honda's Marysville plant, Harley and AMF executives spent 10 days in Japan visiting the four companies that, combined, were clobbering Harley in the U.S. market: Yamaha, Suzuki, Kawasaki, and, of course, the biggest, Honda.

What they saw startled them. True, there was more automated equipment than they used at home. They expected that. But there were no robots. No exotic machine tools. And no hidden magic. Only crowded plants and diligent workers whose activities were meticulously scheduled and organized and who paid great attention to detail.

But, as in the visit to Honda's Marysville plant two years later, what Vaughn Beals and his colleagues did not see was as important as what they did see: They didn't see factory floors littered with huge supplies of parts waiting to be used on the assembly line. They didn't see complicated, time-consuming paper systems governing the flow of materials. And they didn't see hordes of inspectors and production-control people weeding out defective parts and straightening out scheduling screwups. In other words, they didn't see what they probably would have seen in almost any U.S. manufacturing plant.

Later they would come to understand the significance of what they hadn't seen. But then, in 1980, their Japanese trip showed them only what was going on, physically, in their competitors' plants and gave them some disturbing production data to carry home and mull over:

- Only 5 percent of Japanese machines coming off the assembly line failed to pass inspection, compared with 50 to 60 percent of Harleys.

- The amount of Japanese production in "float"—that is, needing additional work between the end of the assembly line and the beginning of the crating line—was two to three hours, compared with two to four *days* at Harley-Davidson. This disparity was a significant measure of the difference in quality between the Japanese and the U.S. motorcycles as they came off the line.

- Japanese productivity seemed to be substantially greater than Harley-Davidson's, although it was difficult to achieve an accurate comparison because much of the Japanese production consisted of simple, small mopeds and motorcycles in highly automated plants. However, visiting Harley executives estimated that Japanese productivity was 25 to 30 percent higher than theirs. Later, when they were able to observe the stripped-down overhead structure at Honda's Ohio plant, they realized that the productivity gap was even wider.

ing awareness of its manufacturing problems into sharp focus. The major problem was quality.

Vaughn Beals got his first inkling of the depth of Harley-Davidson's quality problems in 1976, the year after he arrived in Milwaukee. One of the mechanics in Harley's service shop who handled warranty returns came into Beal's office one day, and, a bit timidly, asked if Beals would come down to the shop and look at some of the motorcycles that were coming back for repair. Beals says:

> I did, and it was a shock to see the poor quality that was being sent out to our dealers. I resolved to do something about it. So after a fairly intense meeting with some of our line management, I chose a new product that was about to roll off the assembly line as the place to take my stand. It was the Cafe Racer, the first major new heavyweight motorcycle to come out of Harley-Davidson since 1971. I decided that if the Cafe Racer could arrive at our dealers with a visibly higher level of quality than its predecessors, it might be viewed as the start of a new quality era at Harley-Davidson.

Beals then appointed an ad hoc team of engineering, manufacturing, and service supervisors to go down to the assembly plant and inspect the new bikes before they were shipped but *after* the manufacturing division said they were *ready* to ship. Any bikes that didn't pass inspection had to be fixed before they were shipped.

"To give you an idea of the quality problems," Beals says, "the first one hundred Cafe Racers that came off the line 'ready to ship' cost us over a hundred thousand dollars to fix before they could pass inspection."

Expanded to all Harley motorcycles, this inspection-and-correction approach became the Quality Audit Program.

"It definitely helped us improve quality by catching product problems before we had expensive recalls and warranty problems, and we're still using this tool today," Beals concludes. "But it's an awkward approach with definite limitations—and it's expensive. After three years we found that our quality audit scores were stagnating. We had stopped improving."

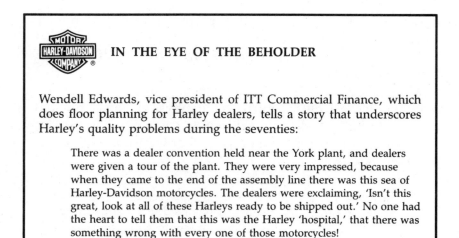

IN THE EYE OF THE BEHOLDER

Wendell Edwards, vice president of ITT Commercial Finance, which does floor planning for Harley dealers, tells a story that underscores Harley's quality problems during the seventies:

> There was a dealer convention held near the York plant, and dealers were given a tour of the plant. They were very impressed, because when they came to the end of the assembly line there was this sea of Harley-Davidson motorcycles. The dealers were exclaiming, 'Isn't this great, look at all of these Harleys ready to be shipped out.' No one had the heart to tell them that this was the Harley 'hospital,' that there was something wrong with every one of those motorcycles!

So what does any reasonable U.S. manufacturing company do? Come up with another program. This time it was the "I Make the Eagle Fly" program, complete with speeches and banners aimed at giving every employee they had a stake in quality. Again there was some improvement in quality, but manufacturing variances shot up $5 million in three months, overtime went crazy, and production dropped. Beals says:

> We started to realize that no matter how intense they were, conventional efforts to improve quality—more inspection, banners, speeches, and T-shirts—would not give us the results we needed to compete effectively with the Japanese. We were trying to work within a production system that was basically flawed. In this system, we gave the worker responsibility for quantity, not quality. Then we set up a whole police force for quality and a battalion of accountants to measure the errors made in production.

So despite some quality improvement, the level of quality compared with the Japanese remained dismal.

Nowhere was the wastefulness and inefficiency of Harley's approach demonstrated more vividly than in the area of production control. Because of missing parts, more than 50 percent of new motorcycles came off the assembly line incomplete. Then they sat on the factory floor, mute and useless, in areas dubbed "hospitals." Eventually they were completed, but sometimes not for days later.

It wasn't that they had no parts. Stock rooms and factory floors were jammed with parts. But—many were the wrong ones, obsolete, rusting, or not made to specifications. Production was dictated by the availability of usable parts, not by a planned schedule.

"It was a nightmare," says one manager, "like a wartime MASH unit."

And what did it all add up to? Production shutdowns, costly overtime, exorbitant scrap, and, worst of all, poor quality and poor customer and dealer relations.

And yet Harley-Davidson's manufacturing methods were no different from those of most U.S. companies.

"The trouble was," says CEO Richard Teerlink, "we weren't competing against U.S. manufacturers; we were competing against the Japanese, and their methods were light-years ahead of ours."

chapter 3

Invasion

But how had Harley-Davidson's Japanese competitors established a U.S. beachhead in the first place?

It had started early and small—very small. Just a modest advertisement in motorcycle magazines in late 1959: Honda Motor Company of Japan was introducing a minuscule motorcycle into the United States. Nobody—including Harley-Davidson, then family-owned—paid much attention. If anything, Harley-Davidson management concluded, sales of these buzzing little Japanese machines might even help sell Harleys to buyers who would buy Japanese bikes and then want to move up to faster, heavier bikes. The idea that the Japanese might also build quality heavyweight bikes—at a time when "Made in Japan" still meant cheap junk—was inconceivable.

But with hindsight, the strategy of the Japanese motorcycle makers is clear:

- Invade the market segment least threatening to Harley-Davidson with a product that also has a strong home market: lightweight motorcycles.
- Go for high volume by keeping prices low, even if it means sacrificing short-term profits.
- Increase volume further by selling products at less than fair market value.
- After securing a beachhead, expand product lines to include heavyweights.
- Then go head-to-head with Harley by marketing Harley

look-alikes that copy almost everything unique about Harley machines.

- Finally, consolidate market position by again flooding the market with heavily discounted inventory.

Most companies invading a foreign market use strategies with a similar approach: Start with an area that does not directly attack the home industry and, after establishing a beachhead, move into direct competition. But in 1959, Harley-Davidson management was not worried about losing the company's virtual monopoly of the heavyweight market. Its major concern was with the substantial imports of British middleweight motorcycles that had become popular in the United States after World War II. In response to this threat, it had introduced the

---

 HOW HARLEY-DAVIDSON HELPED START THE JAPANESE MOTORCYCLE INDUSTRY

It is said by some that Harley-Davidson turned the Japanese on to motorcycling.

In the 1920s, a low ebb in Harley-Davidson's fortunes, help came from an unlikely source: Japan, which had no motorcycle industry to speak of and where the few machines ridden were imported. By 1923, Harley-Davidson's chief U.S. competitor, Indian, already had a foothold in Japan, selling about 800 bikes a year. To bolster its own sagging domestic sales, Harley-Davidson entered the Japanese market in 1925 and within a year was outselling Indian.

However, the Japanese export market turned sour in 1929, when the yen suddenly dropped half of its value against the dollar and made Harleys prohibitively expensive for the Japanese.

What Harley-Davidson did next was done very quietly. Through its field representative in Japan, it agreed to sell manufacturing rights for producing Harleys to a Japanese pharmaceutical company called Sankyo. For around $30,000, Harley-Davidson turned over blueprints, tools, and dies to the Japanese company, which eventually produced Harley look-alikes with the nameplate *Rikuo*: "King of the Road."

Thus, Harley-Davidson had a role in starting the Japanese motorcycle industry—a role that came back to haunt the Milwaukee firm 40 years later.

competitive Sportster model in 1957, a now-legendary machine that became the best-selling motorcycle ever produced by Harley-Davidson.

As the sixties began, Harley continued to revamp its product line, after phasing out its smallest machines, which had never found favor with Harley dealers. To bring its line back to full strength, the company bought 50 percent of Aermacchi, the motorcycle subsidiary of Aeronautica Macchi, an Italian company that had made military aircraft until its plants were destroyed by Allied bombs during the war. With the help of technical consultants from Milwaukee, Aermacchi built motorcycles to Harley-Davidson specifications, starting with a mid-range size model.

But it was late in the day. The Japanese were now sending in heavier forces: bikes that competed directly with Harley's Italian-made models. The Aermacchi machines sold reasonably well for some years, but they eventually succumbed to Japan's counterparts, which were faster, less expensive, and more technically advanced in electric systems and engine designs.

Too Much, Too Fast, Too Bad

Harley-Davidson began to be like the little Dutch boy who scurried around sticking his finger into the dike as more leaks appeared. To compete with Japanese and Italian scooters, the Milwaukee company introduced one of its own called the Topper. Bad timing. The scooter fad began to evaporate just as production got under way, and the Topper lasted only a few years, until 1965.

Hoping to cash in on the popularity of Honda's smallest bike, Harley-Davidson offered its own version, made by Aermacchi. The tiny machines sold for a few years, but then inventories built up and they were phased out at disaster-sale prices.

In 1965, Harley-Davidson was at a crucial crossroads. Honda was throwing millions of dollars into a massive ad campaign that said "You meet the nicest people on a Honda" and showed middle-class suburbanites having good clean fun on their immaculate Japanese machines. This was boosting not only Honda's sales but also the popularity of motorcycling in general among white-collar professionals and students. More and more of these "closet" bikers were being lured into motorcycle showrooms. Motorcycling was joining the mainstream of American life.

Harley-Davidson's problem was that it wasn't cashing in on this phenomenon. True, its volume was going up, but its market share remained static (see Figure 3-1). It still relied mainly on a basic core of loyal Harley riders. New motorcycling converts were buying British and Japanese machines.

Harley-Davidson needed an infusion of capital to take advantage of the burgeoning motorcycle boom. Capital demands were also increasing because the company had started a golf-car and snowmobile business in the early sixties. These pressures forced Harley-Davidson to go public in 1965, after almost 60 years of private family ownership. During the next three years, more than 1.3 million shares in Harley-Davidson were sold.

But other problems loomed. In 1968, Harley-Davidson ex-

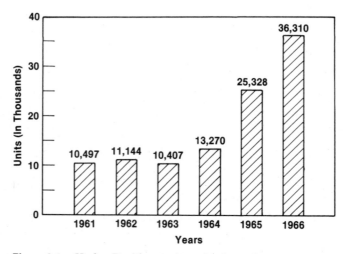

Figure 3-1.   Harley-Davidson unit production volume 1961–1966. As the sixties began, Japanese motorcycle makers boosted the popularity of motorcycling and broadened the market. Harley-Davidson's volume kept going up, but, significantly, it was attracting far fewer new riders than the Japanese competition. (Source: Harley-Davidson Motor Co.)

ecutives noted with alarm that Bangor Punta, an eastern company with roots in the railroad business, was acquiring sizable amounts of Harley-Davidson stock. "You can't blame the H-D people for getting nervous," said Roger Hull, then editor of *Road Rider* magazine. "Bangor Punta had a reputation for acquiring a company, squeezing it dry, and then scrapping it for the salvage." So Harley-Davidson now faced the unpleasant prospect of a hostile takeover.

 THE OLD LESSON: DO WHAT YOU DO BEST

Between 1968 and 1978, Harley-Davidson marketed an assortment of lightweight and middleweight motorcycles, but all met the same fate: defeat by Japanese makes that offered better quality for less money. Many Harley-Davidson dealers—who wanted to sell bigger bikes with bigger profit margins—pointed out to the factory that people just did not associate Harley-Davidson with smaller motorcycles.

Today, the Harley-Davidson motorcycle division makes nothing but super-heavyweights. Some observers say that the Milwaukee company never should have deviated from that market in the first place. They cite the case of Indian, Harley-Davidson's one-time U.S. competitor, which rushed poorly designed smaller machines onto the market after World War II—and went down the tubes in 1953. The British motorcycle industry also tried to meet the Japanese challenge head on, by building smaller bikes with electric starters, but they could not match Japanese designs or quality. Today, there is no British motorcycle industry.

Enter the White Knight

For Rodney Gott, CEO of American Machine & Foundry (AMF), Harley-Davidson was high on the list of possible acquisitions for building up AMF's leisure-products business. But until he heard about Bangor Punta's hostile tender offer, Gott did nothing about it. Then, he says, he moved into action:

> I decided to play the good guy and went out to
> Milwaukee to make friends with Harley management. I

showed them how to combat hostile takeovers—the last thing I should have been doing since I was after them myself. But Bangor Punta was the bad guy and we were the good guys, so it was pretty easy to work out a deal. We offered them less than Bangor Punta did—about $22 million against Bangor Punta's $23 million—but they took our deal because they saw an opportunity to expand their production.

Because Harley-Davidson wanted to share in the current motorcycle boom (and to avoid being gobbled up and spit out by Bangor Punta), William H. Davidson, who was president at the time, urged stockholders to accept AMF's offer, assuring them that the deal would "give the stockholders of H-D participation in a large and more diversified enterprise with greater financial resources for further development and growth."

Gott's plans for Harley-Davidson seemed to justify William H.'s words to the stockholders. Asked recently about those plans, Gott gave an emphatic, one-word reply: "Expansion."

But this was a miscalculation, as Rodney Gott soon found out. Harley-Davidson was simply not geared up for mass production because its factory equipment was antiquated. But the pressure was on to produce more and more Harleys. "There was a motorcycle craze," says Gott. "You could sell anything you could produce. We wanted to meet the demand."

To do so, AMF directed an explosive expansion of Harley production that the company's systems and people couldn't keep up with. Volume shot up from 27,000 units in 1969 to 60,000 in 1972, including the lightweight models.

But quality was going down just as fast as production was going up. And this was just when the Japanese companies were flooding the United States with competitive heavyweight machines that were reaching new standards of performance and features—and were selling for less than Harleys.

Gott takes some of the blame for what happened. He says, "I'm afraid we concentrated too much on expanding production and not enough on quality. Our only concern was to get the motorcycles out as fast as we could. We felt that if we took time out to redesign the product at that point we could have kissed goodbye to the motorcycle boom. So we got it out, and it was a rough, noisy motorcycle."

But Gott faults Harley-Davidson management, too: "Trouble number one was that we didn't have the right people in charge in Milwaukee."

The viewpoint of a few Harley-Davidson people remembering this period is that if AMF had *listened* to the experienced Harley employees, instead of "dictating," many of the problems could have been dealt with. But there was no question that Harley-Davidson had a tradition-bound family-management style totally incompatible with the kind of dynamic growth that Gott envisioned. However, Gott's zeal for quick expansion perhaps blinded him to the fact that Harley's appeal was based on legend and uniqueness—it was not a mass-market item to be stamped out by the millions like Hondas. What helped Harley to turn around eventually was that it brought its production methods into the twentieth century without sacrificing the historic Harley mystique.

In addition to modernizing Harley's production systems, AMF should have been investing more in research and development and product development, says a Harley senior executive. "The bottom line was that quality went to hell because AMF expanded Harley production at the same time that Harleys were getting out of date and the Japanese were coming to town with new designs and reliable products at a low price."

Despite Gott's belief that Harley's family management was the problem, the parade of nonfamily presidents (many from AMF) who followed the departure of President William H. Davidson in 1971 did not produce better results. Eventually, William H.'s son, John A. Davidson, was appointed president in an attempt to recapture some of the loyalty to the family that still existed.

Meanwhile, AMF pressed on with ambitious expansion plans. To make more bikes to meet the demand, more assembly space was needed. In York, Pennsylvania, AMF had a huge plant for making military and bowling equipment. The plant was virtually idle because AMF's military business had almost disappeared and its bowling-machinery cash cow was beginning to run dry. So AMF decided to convert the York plant to

chassis manufacturing and final assembly of Harley motorcycles, while leaving the production of engines and transmissions
in Milwaukee. When the first Harley, a Sportster, rolled off the
new, modern York assembly line in February 1973, one Harley
fan asked Rodney Gott with some bitterness whether "those
of us who call our cycles a 'Milwaukee hawg' will have to call
future models 'York pork.' "

The shift to York was traumatic. One AMF executive said
that the labor union and people at Milwaukee were completely
alienated by the way the move to York was handled. They were
promised there would be no great disruption and no layoffs,
but there was, in fact, a substantial reduction in the work force.
Consequently, labor relations in Milwaukee deteriorated.

Worker resentment was far from being the only problem
created by the York move. AMF spent millions to move the
fabrication and assembly operation to York to boost motorcycle
production but did nothing to increase the production of engines and transmissions in Milwaukee. Nor had plans been
made for operating two separate plants 700 miles apart and
there was no system for forecasting, coordination, or operation.
Each plant was on its own. Annual forecasts were made for
each model, with York calling Milwaukee daily to find out
when—and how many—engines and transmissions were being
produced.

This deadly combination of intense production pressures,
heavy-handed AMF management style, labor hostility, and inadequate systems resulted in motorcycles that constantly deteriorated in quality.

So it wasn't surprising that while Harley-Davidson was
selling more bikes than ever, it was rapidly losing market share
to higher-quality, cheaper Japanese machines. Alarmed, AMF
fired its group executive in charge of the Motorcycle Products
Group and replaced him with Ray Tritten, a manufacturing
specialist who had been successfully turning around ailing AMF
divisions since 1970, starting with the Ben Hogan company, a
faltering golf club maker. Tritten's new challenge: making Harley-Davidson profitable.

Tritten's initiation was not auspicious. He had been in his
new job for only a few months when the seeds of work-force
hostility, sowed by AMF's refusal to meet with the union on

THE AMF CEO WHO LOVED HARLEYS

Rodney Gott is a spare, bluntly outspoken man living in retirement in a traditionally furnished house on a Mt. Kisco (New York) hilltop. In 1968, as CEO of American Machine & Foundry (AMF), he was mainly responsible for the purchase of Harley-Davidson, a company that had been independent for more than 60 years. Behind that purchase was an odd mixture of business strategy and sentiment.

The business strategy: Gott was trying to move his company from a mostly industrial base to 50 percent recreational. In 1968, AMF, which had headquarters in White Plains, New York, was a conglomerate with most of its divisions making industrial products such as tobacco machinery and bakery equipment. Its first step toward leisure products was automatic pin-setting equipment for bowling alleys, which soon became AMF's cash cow. Eventually, AMF acquired divisions making leisure products that included golf clubs, tennis rackets, skis, yachts, and motorcycles—Harley-Davidson motorcycles.

Gott's theory about balancing industrial and consumer products was based on studies showing that in a recession the consumer market goes down first, followed by the industrial market. By the time the industrial market starts sinking, the consumer market begins to recover. Gott reasoned that a company with a good mix of consumer and industrial products would thus be protected from fluctuations in the economy.

The sentiment: Gott was, in the words of one observer, a "Harley freak." He first rode a Harley in the 1930s when, as a recent West Point graduate, he joined a topographical battalion assigned to explore Washington State's Olympic Peninsula. With his wife quartered in a town 72 miles from where the battalion operated, he found it difficult to make it there for weekends and be back for Sunday mess. Then he discovered that a Harley-Davidson motorcycle had been assigned to the battalion. A complete novice, he taught himself to ride and used the bike to visit his wife on weekends.

"I loved it," he says now, "but I didn't touch a bike again until we bought Harley-Davidson in 1969. The bikes looked so great I couldn't resist, and I started riding steadily. I guess I could claim as an excuse that I was field-testing the product."

the issue of coordinated bargaining, bloomed into a bitter 100-day strike in Milwaukee. When the 1974 strike finally ended and Tritten began picking up the pieces, he had his work cut out for him.

How Bad Can Things Get?

The litany of problems that Tritten discovered seemed endless:

1. Although Harley-Davidson had only one competitor, Kawasaki, in the super-heavyweight class, and sold every motorcycle it could make, it was losing substantial amounts of money almost every month.
2. The Harley-Davidson people disliked AMF intensely because many AMF staffers had no respect for the Harley people's business experience and no interest in motorcycles. Harley people blamed all their problems on the parent company.
3. Harley-Davidson was unresponsive to complaints from its dealers and from Harley customers, who remained remarkably loyal to the company considering that nearly every motorcycle delivered to dealers had to be thoroughly serviced before it would run.
4. There were no marketing forecasts by region or by district, no sales incentives for district managers, no quotas by district. The district sales managers were underpaid.
5. The engineering department was not only understaffed, but it also included very few professional engineers. Most Harley engineers were fine technicians who knew motorcycles because they'd grown up with them. But without professional know-how, they initiated engineering changes that drove manufacturing up the wall.
6. The spare parts department carried millions of dollars in inventory but lacked the systems for shipping required parts on time.
7. Harley-Davidson had its own finance company for dealers,

with interest rates pegged at one-half of a point over the prime. That meant that the dealer was actually charged less than AMF paid for borrowing money, and the process tied up some $20 to $30 million in working capital.

8. Harley-Davidson top management was still not convinced that it faced any threat from the Japanese in its super-heavy-weight niche (an attitude toward Japanese competition that was typical of many U.S. manufacturers at that time).

Tritten attacked these problems vigorously: Production bottlenecks were isolated and eliminated, cost reduction programs established, production forecasts refined, the marketing program overhauled, and Harley-Davidson's internal financing of dealers replaced with a dealer finance floor-planning program provided by ITT Commercial Finance.

 **EXERCISE IN FUTILITY**

Although the company worked hard to solve its many operating problems, it made one major mistake, says a top Harley manager.

"We retained one of the Big Eight accounting firms and spent $6 million to install new corporate systems on a crash basis. Nothing came out of this effort because no attempt was made to involve the people who really understood how the place worked. From that we learned a key lesson: Don't try to put systems in from the top down."

Improvements, yes—but not enough. Market share was not improving. And there was still the nagging problem of the engineering department which, according to Tritten, was composed of motorcycle buffs. Dedicated, absolutely, but lacking professional engineering qualifications. Tritten's answer was to bring in Jeffrey Bleustein, AMF's chief mechanical engineer and a former associate professor of engineering at Yale.

As vice president of engineering, Bleustein set about to build an engineering department that eventually would make a major contribution to Harley-Davidson's resurgence. But it took time—two years—and the willingness to go against Harley's traditional way of doing things. He brought in professionally trained engineers who knew nothing about motorcycles but had good track records in other industries and could look at Harley's problems from fresh viewpoints.

chapter 4

Struggle

Until Vaughn Beals came to Milwaukee late in 1975, Jeff Bleustein had felt like a lone voice trying to wake up Harley-Davidson management to the engineering realities they had to face.

Harley-Davidson motorcycles have always been prized by their riders for the integrity of their design and their reliability. To many Harley riders, the problem lay in the quality of the assembly of the motorcycles, but the Harley design was still preferable to the design of Japanese motorcycles. While perhaps not as fast as the competition's motorcycles, Harleys could easily be improved in performance by riders after being delivered from the showroom. Harley owners often disassemble, then reassemble, their motorcycles in their garages.

But newcomers to the Harley franchise didn't share the fanatical devotion or didn't have the mechanical knowledge needed to make the bikes right. So if Harley-Davidson was to continue to attract new customers and expand its market base, it had to improve the quality of its machines and update the design of their engines.

Compared with the state-of-the-art, smooth-running, oil-tight engines on Japanese bikes, Harley engines were primitive. It was commonly said that you could always tell where a Harley had been parked by the puddle of oil it left behind. Vibration made long trips distinctly uncomfortable. Some riders accepted these burdens as part of the Harley "experience"—but others were defecting to the "nice people" amenities of Japanese motorcycles.

Unsympathetic motorcycle magazines were no help. Some magazines refused to road test Harley-Davidson motorcycles, claiming that since there were no new models being introduced, there was no valid reason for a road test. In so doing, they gave their readers the impression that Harley-Davidson machines were not worth considering. But these magazines also hurt themselves by alienating loyal Harley riders, who had no interest in reading about Japanese motorcycles and felt that the magazines were demeaning their favorite machines because they were seeking Japanese advertising revenues. (In the mid-seventies, one motorcycle magazine went so far as to declare the legendary V-twin engine dead. They ended up with a lot of egg on their faces when, within five years, the Japanese were introducing V-twin engines of their own.)

Harley's only ongoing effort to come up with a badly needed new engine was an 1100cc V-twin (see box). However, the newly developed engine was in big trouble before it even reached the production stage. Bleustein's evaluation had found it wanting in two critical respects: First, it could not achieve its

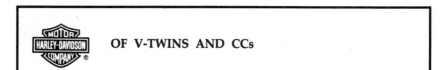

OF V-TWINS AND CCs

Most motorcycle engines have one or two cylinders and are known as "singles" or "twins." (Some bikes have four or six cylinders—as many as a car.) Harley-Davidson's distinctive engine, which it introduced in 1909, is the *V-twin*, so-named because its two cylinders are set at a 45° angle opposing each other. The V-twin is a legendary engine, both for its look and its low-torque power. The V-shaped juxtaposition of its two cylinders somehow conveys the image of immense power more than any other engine configuration.

Motorcycle engine size is commonly measured in cubic centimeters, shortened to "cc." For example, Harley's largest bikes feature a 1340cc engine, meaning that these motorcycles have an engine displacement of 1340 cubic centimeters, putting them in the super-heavyweight class. Middleweight motorcycles range around 500cc's and lightweights around 250cc's and lower.

performance objectives and still meet noise regulations and second, it had basic structural problems which he did not believe could be solved without a major redesign. With this engine obviously headed for the scrap heap (after an investment of $10 million), Harley-Davidson's new-product picture was bleak.

What made the picture even bleaker was that the Japanese *were* bringing new products on the U.S. market—bikes that competed directly with Harley's super-heavies. One was Honda's Gold Wing. Introduced in 1975, the Gold Wing represented Japan's first attempt to knock out Harley's big V-twin touring bikes, massive machines used for long-distance traveling by those who considered cars too tame. Harley-Davidson had owned this niche for more than 25 years. Then came the Gold Wing. With its smoothly purring 1000cc four-cylinder engine, Honda's new entry was the biggest, heaviest, most sophisticated and complex motorcycle ever produced in Japan, and Harley-Davidson had nothing to throw in against it.

Unknown to Bleustein, Ray Tritten had also been looking for ways to wake up the Harley-Davidson management. (An impossible undertaking, say some, because in the wake of AMF's continual disregard for Harley management's recommendations, an impenetrable apathy had set in.) After five years of trying to solve Harley-Davidson management problems long-distance from corporate headquarters in White Plains, New York, AMF had given up. Now Tritten was determined to have an AMF deputy group executive on the spot in Milwaukee, someone with years of experience in rebuilding an operation from the ground up and in all phases of management—engineering, manufacturing, marketing, personnel.

"We needed a top-notch business executive," says Tritten. "The requirements were stringent, and it took us a year of headhunting before we came up with Vaughn Beals."

Beals seemed to fit the requirements perfectly. He was an incisive, tough-minded manager with energy and drive, tenacious in pursuing his objectives—and he had a wealth of hands-on experience in building and restructuring organizations.

Beals knew nothing about motorcycles; he'd never even been on one. But the problems of the Milwaukee company were exactly the kind that sparked his interest.

One of Beals's first major challenges as AMF's deputy group vice president in Milwaukee was to prepare a long-range strategic plan for the company. Comments Beals:

> Obviously, this was urgent. Harley had grown explosively after AMF bought it in 1969. Basically, Harley was a company that had been successfully managed by a small group of family members for many years. Its systems were adequate for an intimate management group but grossly inadequate for a scaled-up operation. With low volume, craftsmen were able to build the product satisfactorily, even though the drawings weren't necessarily up to date, because in that kind of environment changes could be made on the shop floor by the chief engineer. But at higher volumes the company lost control.

In April 1976, Beals assembled a group of Harley-Davidson senior managers and took them off to Pinehurst, North Carolina, for a concentrated week-long session on long-range product strategy. The Pinehurst meeting was to set Harley-Davidson's product policy for the next 10 years. This was the first time in the company's history that it had looked so far ahead.

All participants agreed on one thing: To beat its Japanese competition, Harley-Davidson had to develop new, top-quality products. At the top of the list was the need for technologically improved engines that would provide better performance and yet conform with impending noise and emission rules. Next came the need to attract new riders by offering them a line of bikes with the high-performance characteristics of the Japanese machines that were doing well in the American market.

Thus, the Pinehurst meeting developed a two-pronged attack on Harley's urgent new-product needs. The first part of the strategy was to improve Harley's existing engines in gradual stages. Appropriately enough, these improved engines were to be called the V^2 Evolution engines. The goal was to bring them up to date technologically but at the same time keep the original look and sound of the traditional V-twin engines.

Sound was an important consideration, says Jeff Bleustein.

"There's good sound and bad sound. Good sound is opera and a Harley-Davidson. Bad sound is noise."

The second part of the strategy was to design a whole new family of engines. This project—which eventually came to be known as the NOVA program—was aimed at competing directly with Japanese high-performance bikes, which were much faster than Harley's.

"The NOVA bikes were going to have a totally new look for Harleys, sleek and streamlined," says Bleustein. "They were going to have state-of-the-art water-cooled engines ranging from two to six cylinders, and from 500cc's to 1500cc's. And they were going to be fast—although not the fastest, because over the long haul, someone can always make a faster motorcycle. Being 'the fastest' just isn't a tenable 'product position.' "

Says Vaughn Beals, "For us, the advantage of developing a family of engines was that we only had to do the combustion development once and we could get the cost down and the quality up by having common valves, pistons, gears, and other parts."

And in the early days of the NOVA project, neither Beals nor Bleustein had any complaints about AMF's willingness to put money into the new-engine program. "AMF was very good in those first years," Bleustein acknowledges. "Anything I asked for in engineering we got—a new piece of equipment, whatever. They understood we had a lot to do in a short time. We had emissions control coming up on us in very short order

---

 MOTIVATION

Jeff Bleustein's wife, Brenda, gave him an extra personal incentive to improve Harley's V-twin engines. "I remember when we first moved to Milwaukee and bought a house and I came home with a new Harley one day and parked it in our garage. The next morning there was a big puddle of oil on the garage floor. Brenda said, 'Jeff, I know you want to ride a motorcycle, but you'd better fix those oil leaks—because there will be no motorcycles in our garage until you do.' "

and nobody in Milwaukee even knew what an emission was. And Vaughn Beals had the same kind of mandate. They said, 'Look, Vaughn, tell us what you need and you're going to get it.' "

This happy situation would change very shortly, but for a while AMF put its money where its mouth was (overall, the conglomerate poured $10 million into the NOVA project). Porsche, in Germany, was given a contract to develop the NOVA family of engines, because Harley-Davidson didn't have a large enough or an experienced enough engineering staff to carry out both engineering programs.

Meanwhile, work began in-house on the V^2 Evolution project that would bring Harley-Davidson's line of antiquated engines up to date.

Willie G. and His Magic Crayons

The one drawback of the Evolution and NOVA programs was that they were long-range. It would be years before new engines could actually be brought to market. Meanwhile, what was Harley-Davidson going to do to offset Japanese technological superiority?

The answer was to be found in a large, airy room that constituted the styling department of Harley-Davidson, presided over by William G. Davidson. The design changes he inaugurated, many observers say, kept Harley-Davidson alive until it was able to develop up-to-date engines that could compete with the Japanese technologically.

Known simply as Willie G., this grandson of one of the company's founders is an almost mythical figure in the motorcycling community—and is considered by many to be the "soul" of Harley-Davidson. He's not the only Harley-Davidson executive who goes to motorcycle events and mingles with riders, but he's the most convincing, the one who establishes the closest rapport with riders of all varieties. And he looks the part, with full beard, black leather, and jeans.

It was not always thus. A 1969 picture of Willie G. at his office desk shows a strictly executive type: clean-shaven face, neatly trimmed hair, horn-rimmed glasses, conservative business suit. Shortly thereafter he doffed his business uniform, grew a beard, and got into his jeans and leathers. He says it was a spontaneous transformation.

Some skeptics claim that Willie G. is a product of Harley-Davidson's marketing department. But to meet Willie G. is to be convinced that he's the real thing. It's obvious that he loves motorcycles and everything associated with them. (In fact, some refer to him as Willie G. "I Love to Ride" Davidson.) His office is a virtual motorcycling museum, packed with memorabilia, including a statuette of a distinctly slovenly rider and a photograph of a 1912 Harley that Willie G. has sitting on an Oriental rug in the family room of his home. And he not only gets a kick out of being with Harley owners, he also gets a firsthand understanding of what they want in a motorcycle.

"Harley riders are kind of folk artists," he explains. "A lot of them are untrained designers who'd rather talk about their motorcycle than almost anything. And I'm happy to listen because I'm of the same breed."

With one notable exception. Willie G. is a *trained* designer, a graduate of the Art Center College of Design in Pasadena, California. He started out doing automotive design for Ford and then general industrial design for Brooks Stevens Associates in Milwaukee, but in 1963 he got a call from his father, William H., then president of Harley-Davidson.

"We need a full-fledged styling department at the company," William H. told his son. "Will you run it?"

Willie G. didn't hesitate; he had grown up with motorcycles. "Give me five minutes to pack my crayons and I'll be right over."

Willie G. turned out to have an instinctive understanding of what riders wanted. And in 1971 he came up with what one writer has called "a true watershed in U.S. riding." Called the Super Glide, this model was Willie G.'s response to what bike customizers in California were doing to Harley's big, heavy touring model, the Electra Glide. Bike customizers were removing the Electra Glide's saddle bags and windshield and replacing the massive front forks with lighter, extended forks that pushed the front wheel farther from the motor. (Peter Fonda rode such a bike in the film *Easy Rider*.)

To simulate this chopper look, Willie G. married a modified

Sportster front end to an Electra Glide engine and chassis. He produced a totally new motorcycle design by simply combining components already on hand, thus minimizing both time and expense.

The Super Glide was a milestone machine because it offered customers a bike right from the factory that already had the individualistic look that riders had always had to achieve themselves through their own modifications. Thus, this was the first of the factory "custom" bikes which were to provide Harley riders with a far greater choice of styling differences than they had ever enjoyed before. The Super Glide was also the first of a type which became known as the "cruiser"—a big, powerful machine that fell somewhere in between a full-dressed touring bike and a high-performance sport bike.

The Super Glide was an early example of Willie G.'s uncanny ability to combine already existing components to come up with a new design. One Harley executive says: "Many designers have the talent to draw pretty pictures that are difficult to translate into hardware. Willie's real genius is in keeping it simple and producible and working with what he has available. That's something that saved us when we just didn't have the capital to produce completely new designs."

The Super Glide was followed by a variety of custom cruiser models with individual touches. One was the now-legendary Low Rider, which Willie G. created in 1977. It is basically a Super Glide with special paint and trim, low bars, and a lower seat that brought the rider closer to the ground—a popular manifestation of the *Easy Rider* look.

Another was the Wide Glide, a bike that took the chopper look even further than the Super Glide, with a bobbed rear fender, stepped seat with sissy bar and backrest, tool pouch, extended forks, and high bars.

Then there was the Fat Bob ("fat" because of the dual fuel tanks and "bob" for the bobbed fender), which was simliar to a Low Rider but with spoked wheels and higher bars.

Through these and other styling variations, Harley-Davidson managed to stimulate its market with a range of factory-customized models that differed mainly in cosmetics.

Not all of these designs were willingly accepted by Harley-Davidson's then-conservative management.

The story of the Wide Glide, in particular, illustrates the image dilemma with which the Milwaukee company has always had to deal. The Wide Glide design was based on popular modifications that individual customizers in California were making on Electra Glides. It was enthusiastically pushed by the general sales manager at the time, Robert Rohrer. But Harley's Product Planning Committee balked at approving it because they were apprehensive about the bike's image—the modified Electra Glides were ridden by an undesirable target audience: the bike outlaws or "one-percenters."

It took more than a year-and-a-half for Rohrer to persuade senior management that this design was what the other 99 percent, the mainstream Harley riders, also wanted. In the end, he was proved right: the Wide Glide became one of the company's biggest sellers.

The Wide Glide eventually led to another model, the Softail, which is currently enjoying great success and has been described as Harley's "ultimate" custom bike. Incidentally, the Softail is an interesting example of how important a bike's image is to Harley aficionados—even if the image isn't real. This model's name comes from its shock absorbers and springs, which soften the ride but which are artfully concealed under the gear box so that the bike retains the "hard-tail," no-rear-suspension look of older Harleys. This look is considered to be more macho by many riders.

All of Willie G.'s styling changes were—and still are—based on a simple but profound principle: Understand your customer. Says Willie G.:

> Our customers really know what they want on their bikes: the kind of instrumentation, the style of bars, the cosmetics of the engine, the look of the exhaust pipes, and so on. Every little piece on a motorcycle is exposed, and it has to look just right. It's almost like being in the fashion business. Harley riders see their bikes as art objects, and they want them to look a certain way. Often the difference is extremely subtle. A tube curve or the shape of a timing case cover can generate enthusiasm or be a total turnoff.

So what is the Harley look? "It's a certain raw look that

we deliberately try to maintain. The bike conveys a mechanical forcefulness—it's not totally tamed. We don't cover up the nuts and bolts because they're part of the mechanical beauty of the bike."

Willie G. espouses evolutionary styling changes rather than radical ones—mainly because he thinks that's the way Harley riders want it. "They rank the Harley look right up there with motherhood and God—and they don't want us to screw around with it. They'll talk about changing this curve here or maybe a piece there. But they'd get nasty if we turned the Harley into a Star Wars rocket ship."

Not all of Willie G.'s creations have been commercially successful. His one major miscalculation was the Cafe Racer, perhaps because it represented his only sharp departure from Harley tradition. Although it had a Sportster engine, the rest of the Cafe Racer resembled a racing motorcycle: faired rear fender with integrated seat, small fairing, and race-inspired gas tank and handlebars. The all-black Cafe Racer had a unique racing-bike look that made it something of a cult classic.

But although it had its fans, it was ahead of its time and not profitable. As Allan Girdler pointed out in *The Illustrated Harley-Davidson Buyer's Guide* (Motorbooks International, Osceola, Wis., 1986, p. 93): "The Cafe Racer was a good answer, but the question was never asked. It wasn't part of the day's fashion, that is, stock bikes that looked like mild choppers."

The Cafe Racer (the name comes from European riders who, traditionally, race their bikes between open-air cafés) was produced for only two years, but Willie G., who owns one, as do his two sons, thinks of it fondly.

"Some day," he says, "I want to do another design that is strictly at the performance end of our market. The timing wasn't right for the Cafe Racer, but I think there's a niche out there for something in between a cruiser and a performance bike."

Despite this one market failure, everyone agrees that Willie G. did a superb job in bringing excitement to the product line while Harley-Davidson was working on the future Evolution and NOVA engineering projects.

"The guy is an artistic genius," says Jeff Bleustein. "In the five-year interim before we could bring the Evolution engines on stream, he performed miracles with decals and paint. A line here and a line there and we'd have a new model. It's what enabled us to survive during those years."

"We've Been Dumped On"

While Harley-Davidson was struggling with its many problems in the mid-seventies, the Japanese bike makers were flying high—and right into Harley's niche known as "Hog Heaven."

But as the seventies wound down, the worldwide motor-cycle market began to level off. The Japanese big four—Honda, Yamaha, Kawasaki, and Suzuki—were making more bikes than they could sell and sending most of their excess production to the United States. Since the Japanese came out with new bike models every year, they heavily discounted earlier models that hadn't been sold. Often the carryover of last year's models amounted to almost a year's supply.

In April 1978, Harley-Davidson filed a dumping suit against the Japanese bike makers, charging that they were selling their machines at less than fair market value. This was the second time that the Milwaukee company, with the support of union leadership, had applied to the federal government for protection against what it considered unfair competition in the motorcycle industry; in the fifties it had asked for tariff relief mainly to thwart the postwar invasion of British motorcycles and had been turned down cold.

This time Harley seemed to be getting a better reception—at first. The U.S. Treasury agreed with the dumping charge. But in addition to proving dumping, Harley had to prove to the International Trade Commission (ITC) that it had been *injured* by the dumping. It failed to do this, ruled the ITC after hearings.

Vaughn Beals believes the decision was political; the Carter administration was not keen on imposing tariffs. Says Beals: "I believe a study of most of the tariff cases at that time would show that the government's criterion for injury was terminal illness. If you weren't dying, you weren't injured."

Perhaps. But there is little doubt that the ITC was also heavily influenced by what it heard when it interviewed Harley's own dealers. One of Harley's injury claims was that Japanese dumping was killing the firm's efforts to compete in the lightweight field with Italian-made Aermacchis. But at this point, Harley dealers—who have never been enamored of lightweight bikes—were fed up with Aermacchis. Admits Ray Tritten:

> They had a point. Coordination between the Milwaukee marketing department and design and manufacturing in Italy was even worse than between Milwaukee's engine plant and the York assembly plant. Always the wrong motorcycle at the wrong time, and generally a lack of service parts when the right motorcycle was finally delivered to the customer. And the Harley heavyweight dealer organization had absolutely no interest in trying to market an Italian lightweight—it went against their grain.

So it was a few disgruntled dealers who delivered the coup de grace to Harley-Davidson's dumping suit, by testifying that the Aermacchis were obsolete and could not compete with state-of-the-art Japanese lightweights. As a result of this testimony, the ITC ruled that Harley had injured itself by failing to keep its products up to date.

With this decision, the ITC virtually signed the death warrant for Harley's Aermacchi operation. It was closed down shortly after the ruling, and since then Harley-Davidson has never ventured from its super-heavyweight niche.

However, Harley did gain one solid benefit from its Washington foray. Because the Japanese makers had been found guilty of dumping, they were forced to end their excessive discounting (for the moment) and prices were stabilized—giving Harley-Davidson a better competitive shot.

A "Harley Freak" Retires

Harley-Davidson's failure to get relief from Japanese dumping was followed by another blow in 1978: Rodney Gott's retirement as AMF's chief executive. As the man mainly responsible for purchasing Harley-Davidson in 1969, Gott had had a vested

interest in seeing the company succeed. He was further motivated by his personal enthusiasm for the Harley hog.

Some of those involved during the AMF years have said
that Gott became disenchanted with Harley-Davidson in the
mid-seventies and started looking for potential buyers so he
could unload the company. Gott vigorously denies this. While
not entirely satisfied with the company's family management,
he says he never wavered in his determination to help the
company solve its problems. "There was not a single point at
which I felt we had made a mistake in buying H-D," he says.
"I was confident that Harley was going to make it."

As his successor, Gott selected Tom York, a choice he now
calls "one of the major mistakes of my career." No motorcycle
nut, 44-year-old York came up through the accounting end of
the business.

"York's succession had two impacts on Harley," says
Vaughn Beals. "First, Tom was not a motorcyclist and didn't
really understand the subtleties of the business the way Rodney
did. Second, when he finally articulated a direction for AMF,
it was toward the industrial side and away from the leisure side
of the company. That, obviously, did not mean good things for
Harley-Davidson."

York also lacked rapport with Harley customers. When
Beals invited him to Daytona, Florida, for the annual Motorcycle
Week—the biggest bike bash of the year—York showed up in
a black stretch limo wearing a business suit, something not
likely to endear him to Harley riders.

Although York soon became intrigued by motorcycling
and even ordered a Harley for himself, he still did not weaken
his strategic resolve to emphasize the industrial side of AMF's
business. This became obvious every time Beals and Charlie
Thompson, Harley-Davidson's president at the time, brought
up the subject of funding for Harley's long-term NOVA engine
project. Both Beals and Thompson were alarmed by York's lack
of enthusiasm. Unless AMF kept its financial muscle behind
NOVA, they foresaw disaster. Explains Beals:

> In Milwaukee, we felt that time was running out for us
> to live off our old engines because the Japanese were
> coming on strong with state-of-the-art engines. We

strongly recommended that they fund NOVA on a more aggressive schedule. There were only two choices that we could see: to develop the product as quickly as we could without being technically reckless or to do nothing. Unfortunately, AMF chose the middle ground, which was to "pace" funding. By early 1980 we should have been moving aggressively into the manufacturing planning. But since this is where the capital demand was, their timidity was not hard to understand.

While AMF waffled on the NOVA project, Harley-Davidson's sales remained strong, but at the same time its market share was still eroding badly. By 1980, the company's share of its once uncontested super-heavyweight niche had dwindled from almost 80 percent in 1973 to a mere 30.8 percent—just slightly ahead of oncoming Honda (see Figure 4-1). And Honda was increasing the pressure with still more super-heavyweight models, such as the GL-1100 and the CB-900, while Suzuki was getting a piece of the action with its GS-1100.

But as the Japanese motorcycle giants mounted a stronger and stronger attack, AMF showed less and less interest in doing anything about it. One reason was that Harley-Davidson's bottom-line results were far from inspiring. Although sales of Harley motorcycles and other travel vehicles accounted for 17 percent of AMF revenue, they provided only 1 percent of the conglomerate's profits. There were other pastures that looked

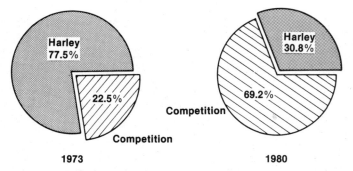

Figure 4-1. Harley-Davidson's share of the U.S. 851+cc market 1973 versus 1980. In the seventies, Harley's once undisputed market—the super-heavyweight class—eroded steadily. (Source: R. L. Polk & Co.)

much greener to Tom York, such as the oil business and the electronics business.

His attitude was not altered by an evaluation of Harley-Davidson done at his request by the Boston Consulting Group (BCG). Much of the BCG's report was positive. It concluded that Harley-Davidson could continue as a viable organization, but *only* if AMF invested in the new Porsche-designed NOVA engine family to the tune of $60 to $80 million. The catch was that for two or three years Harley-Davidson would be faced with a "valley of death" as capital investment exceeded its ability to generate cash.

Tom York showed no inclination to follow the BCG's recommendation to speed up the NOVA project and get the new engines on stream. It became increasingly clear to Vaughn Beals that the interests of AMF and those of Harley-Davidson were miles apart. For AMF to throw millions into Harley-Davidson's new-engine program would certainly not promote the AMF goal of strengthening its industrial side—and it would be a high-risk venture as well.

Harley-Davidson, on the other hand, was committed to the development and manufacture of its new products. The new-engine program had been widely rumored in the motorcycle press, and to abandon it would generate a devastatingly negative reaction. In fact, concluded Beals, a decision not to make the engines might very well lead to the company's early demise. (Beals is quick to admit he was wrong on that score. Harley-Davidson is thriving, even though it aborted the NOVA project in 1983 for lack of capital and is still keeping it on the shelf because (1) the company is doing well without it, (2) it would require a $20 million investment to resurrect, and (3) the high-performance motorcycle market is weak.)

When Beals sees a threatening situation he likes to move on it as fast as possible. Late in 1980, he acted. Over a September weekend, he labored long hours to draft a "white paper" addressed to Tom York. Although the paper did not exactly have a zingy title—"Analysis of Motorcycle Strategic Alternatives"—it definitely had a provocative conclusion: AMF should sell Harley-Davidson to another company. The seeds of the leveraged buyout had been planted.

chapter 5

Buyback

When 13 Harley-Davidson executives met at Harley-Davidson's International Division offices in Stamford, Connecticut, in early 1981, only one of them knew that the subject of the meeting would be buying their company from AMF.

Beals had organized the meeting, but he had not told his associates what he was going to propose. When he recommended that they buy their company with an equity investment of $1 million, their jaws dropped.

The idea seemed outlandish. Some of them thought he had flipped his lid to think they could buy a $300 million company for that little cash. But they listened intently as he reviewed the past six months and told them why he was convinced that a buyback was the only way to keep Harley-Davidson alive.

He first reminded them that AMF top management had agreed to his recommendation that it sell Harley-Davidson and had retained Goldman Sachs to handle the sale on a crash basis. There were no takers.

That wasn't too surprising, he said. Nobody could be expected to jump at the opportunity to buy a capital-intensive company involved in a life-and-death struggle against aggressive Japanese competition. But with these avenues seemingly closed, the AMF man in charge of the Harley-Davidson sale, Gary Ward, had turned to the possibility of a leveraged buyout. He and Beals had had an exploratory meeting with Harvey

Appelle, a senior loan officer for Citicorp Industrial Credit, to discuss how such an LBO could be financed.

That meeting, Beals now told his associates in Stamford, had convinced him that all signs were positive for a buyback. He restated his belief with feeling: the 78-year-old Harley-Davidson Company—the last motorcycle maker in the United States—could survive only if it were owned and run by people who understood the motorcycle business and were dedicated to preserving a legendary institution.

In retrospect, Beals says now, the events that followed confirmed his conviction that Harley-Davidson had to become independent:

> We suffered serious losses in 1981 and 1982. If we had still been under AMF's wing, it would have done what any corporate parent would do—replaced Harley-Davidson's senior management—perhaps not an unreasonable decision, but one that probably would have been fatal to Harley's long-range interests. An experienced, closely knit management team would have been replaced by people who didn't know the motorcycle business at all—and the long-term values of the company would have gone down the drain.

Beals strongly believes that short-term management lies at the root of problems in many U.S. companies, that business managements have become transient, "either because of upward mobility through promotion or a conglomerate's policy of replacing management when things don't go well. Having your own money in the game clearly has a positive influence on your responsibility as a manager."

Some Harley executives at the Stamford meeting were still unconvinced. But Beals's fervor made them feel it was worth trying. Given a green light, Beals opened serious negotiations with Citicorp Industrial Credit. He assumed it would be tough going, he says now, because he was no sophisticate in the world of finance. "I thought we were asking the bankers to do us a favor by lending us so much money against so little equity."

But no arm-twisting was necessary. Beals found to his surprise that far from having to be talked into financing a LBO, Citicorp was actually excited about doing the deal.

In view of Harley's problems with quality, productivity, and Japanese competition, some observers did not believe this excitement was justified. However, Citicorp saw some strong positives. Most LBO's in the early eighties were based on expectations that the leveraged company would pay off its debt through profitable operations rather than through sale of assets as is often the case today. Lenders looked for companies led by a strong management team with a good track record who would stay on, thus assuring a continuity of operations. Harley-Davidson met these specifications. Citicorp also felt that Harley-Davidson's hard assets provided a solid collateral package, so it could still get its money out even if the company did fail.

Beyond this, there were the intangibles: the name *Harley-Davidson* and the fantastic loyalty of its customers. A Citicorp executive says, "What hit me was that this was the only product I'd ever seen that people had tattooed on their bodies."

Despite these positives, the LBO deal did not receive a favorable reaction from Todd Slotkin, the Citicorp loan officer first asked by Harvey Appelle to handle it. (Slotkin was to be a key figure in Harley-Davidson's cliff-hanger survival crisis four years later.) After hearing Slotkin's misgivings, Appelle handed the package to another loan officer, Jack Reilly, who reacted positively. Reilly eventually cut the deal with Harley management and became the senior loan officer on the account. He played a strongly supportive role in the Milwaukee company's turnaround until he moved off the account in 1984. This was a serious blow for Harley-Davidson because it reversed the climate completely, but that story comes later.

Negotiating With the Boss

During the spring of 1981, the Harley management team was totally consumed in negotiations on two fronts: the sale-and-purchase agreement with AMF and the financing package with Citicorp.

It was an uncomfortable time. "Like walking a tightrope," Beals says. "How can you be a tough negotiator against a senior officer of the company that employs you? AMF didn't like the situation either and hinted that we should resign or at least take a leave of absence. But since the whole Harley-Davidson management team was involved in the buyout, this didn't seem very practical."

So the difficulties continued. One example: Beals approached a potential backup lender, General Electric Credit Corporation (GECC), not only as insurance in case the Citicorp loan fell through but to put himself in a better bargaining position with Citicorp. He got a receptive initial response from GECC. However, shortly after Beals's second meeting with GECC, his negotiations with it came to a screeching halt. The reason: AMF Vice Chairman Merlin Nelson, who was handling the LBO for the conglomerate, ordered Beals to break off talks with GECC. Nelson felt that negotiating with two bankers at once was unethical. While Beals expressed his strong disagreement (but politely, since he was still an AMF employee), he had no choice but to go along with Nelson's demand and pray that the Citicorp deal would go through.

This kind of discord set the tone for the lengthy negotiations between the Harley-Davidson buyout team and the AMF conglomerate. Beals found Merlin Nelson to be stiff and formal.

For his part, Beals tried to lighten up the atmosphere as much as possible. One late night the negotiations had reached the point of signing a letter of intent—but the parties were still half a million dollars apart on the purchase price. "We were all pretty tired," Beals says. "Since the total purchase price was around $80 million, I didn't think the half-million gap was worth any more haggling over, so I finally suggested to Merlin Nelson that we flip a coin for the difference. He looked pained by the idea, but he gave his assent."

Beals pulled out a quarter, which was tossed by AMF general counsel John Johnson, with Nelson calling heads. Beals lost. "But at least we got to go home and have a good night's sleep," he says ruefully. He later had the unlucky quarter encased in plastic to make sure he never used it again.

With the letter of intent signed, Beals and AMF Group Executive Ray Tritten hopped on the AMF company jet to fly to Milwaukee and tell Harley-Davidson employees the news. On the plane, they were jolted by an article in that day's issue of *The Wall Street Journal* about plans for the sale of Harley-

Davidson. According to the *Journal* story, AMF was negotiating not with Harley-Davidson *but with its archrival Honda* for the sale of the Milwaukee company.

Based on this report—which Beals and Tritten knew was untrue—the story quoted one analyst as saying: "Harley-Davidson celebrated its 75th anniversary in 1978 with a major bike bash in Milwaukee. Without a doubt, the next anniversary will be a Japanese affair."

Beals was appalled. "The *Journal* had been explicitly told that AMF and Honda had *never* been involved in any negotiations for buying Harley-Davidson. To our employees, who had been fighting Honda and the other Japanese makers tooth and nail, it would have been anathema for Honda to have even a minority interest in Harley-Davidson. This story created problems for us for months afterwards because a lot of people assumed that somewhere in our financial structure Honda owned a piece of us."

Despite the *Journal* story, the announcement in Milwaukee that Harley-Davidson would become independent once more was received enthusiastically. The AMF logo alongside "Harley-Davidson" on the gas tanks had never sat well with most Harley-Davidson employees. To many, the news meant that Harleys were going to be Harleys again.

But before that could happen, there was a long road of tough bargaining ahead over the definitive terms of the sale-and-purchase agreement. The three months of negotiations that followed were characterized by Beals as "long periods of boredom with occasional brief periods of confrontation."

During these months, Harley's problems grew worse, and with senior management totally preoccupied with closing the deal, there was almost no one left to mind the store. As the buyout team's head negotiator, Vaughn Beals had no time to run the business. He delegated management of the company entirely to Charlie Thompson, sixth president of Harley-Davidson in eight years. Thompson was faced with an almost impossible responsibility. With his whole management team's attention diverted elsewhere, operating problems became severe. And the members of the Harley negotiating team watched helplessly as the motorcycle market turned sour under the pressure of a recession and high interest rates. No doubt they spent some sleepless nights wondering why they were breaking their backs to take over an enterprise in this predicament.

But the buyout team's confidence that it could turn things around prevailed, and the negotiators hung in, even as the negotiations became increasingly combative.

"At one point Merlin made some comments that were a big mistake," says Beals. "I'm a pretty even-tempered guy, but what will always blow me away is somebody impugning my integrity. I went right through the ceiling and told him I was ready to bolt the deal."

But Beals stayed cool enough to realize that Nelson had given him an opportunity to get a better deal than AMF had offered so far. A main sticking point was that AMF wanted $2 million in equity whereas the Harley-Davidson team felt it could go no higher than $1 million without bringing in more investors, which it didn't want to do.

Beals's angry response to Nelson's comments had apparently put Nelson on the defensive. His job was to sell Harley-Davidson, and if Beals walked out now, it would mean failure. When Beals now toughened his position on the amount of equity, Nelson caved in.

Beals says, "There's one very basic rule of negotiating: don't get your adversary ticked off at you personally. Merlin forgot that rule and it cost him a million dollars."

After that episode, the $500,000 coin toss didn't seem so painful.

The Market Heads South

Negotiations with Citicorp on a financing package also had bumpy moments. Things started smoothly enough as arrangements were made for three other banks to participate with Citicorp in the LBO loan: Girard Bank of Philadelphia (now Mellon East), First Wisconsin National Bank of Milwaukee, and New England Merchants National Bank (now Bank of New England). But to the consternation of the Harley LBO team, the motorcycle market picked the spring of 1981 to take a calamitous nosedive, completely vaporizing the sales projection figures they had supplied to Citicorp as a basis for the loan package. They were forced to replace these with sharply lower figures, and then, as the market continued to fall apart, they had to replace those with even gloomier numbers.

"I was sure we could kiss the deal goodbye," says Beals now. "I wouldn't have been surprised if they'd walked away after the first reduction—but after we downsized the forecasts a *second* time I figured it was a certainty."

Fortunately, Beals was wrong. Citicorp stuck with the deal. But there was a condition: AMF had to provide a $10 million subordinated debenture, in addition to taking back a $9 million preferred issue that had been set in the original deal.

"Naturally AMF wasn't too happy about that," says Beals. "But they finally agreed because they were so far into the deal and it was so well-known publicly that for them to pull out then would have been embarrassing."

As negotiations ground to a close, there was a last-minute resignation from the ranks of the Harley-Davidson buyback team. John A. Davidson, who was president of the firm's golf-car division, withdrew from the buyback and ended his relationship with the company that his grandfather had helped to found almost 80 years before. His brother, William G. Davidson, the company's styling genius, remained.

Ending the AMF Era

June 16, 1981, York, Pennsylvania. A large pack of Harley bikers roars out of a gas stop, led by a leather-jacketed, bushy-bearded rider. Are they Sinners . . . Saracens . . . Hell's Angels? No, they're the new owners of Harley-Davidson Motor Company. With spiritual leader Willie G. at the front of the pack, they are off on a ceremonial buyback ride from York to Milwaukee, where it all started back in 1903.

En route, they are greeted by Harley dealers and riders with a fervor reminiscent of the Allies' liberation of Paris. At the Pittsburgh dealership, a Harley rider climbs to the roof with a can of black spray paint and obliterates the AMF logo from the big Harley-Davidson sign. Jubilant yells from the crowd. Arms thrust upward in V-for-victory signs.

The celebration reaches its climax in Milwaukee. Elation and optimism fill the air. "The Eagle soars alone."

AMF: Damned With Faint Praise—or Praised With Faint Damns?

Was AMF good or bad for Harley-Davidson? Eight years after the buyback that question still creates plenty of heat and fire in the Harley subculture. The most positive appraisals come from management, the most negative from Harley-Davidson customers and employees.

At one extreme is Rodney Gott, who headed AMF during most of the years it owned Harley-Davidson. He gets irate if you say that some Harley people don't think back too fondly on the AMF years:

> You can put it down in blood, if we hadn't bought Harley they would have gone under, because they weren't prepared to meet the market demand. We saved them. The people who are griping now about AMF are the people who hate to take orders. Hell, if we paid for the thing, we had the right to put AMF on anything they built. We didn't take the H-D logo off, we just added ours. And I would do it today, and anybody who disagreed would get the gate.

Despite Gott's ire at AMF-bashing, the fact is that many Harley-Davidson people take a balanced view of the AMF years. Listen to Frank Cimermancic, director of business planning:

> I think that AMF gets kind of a bum rap. If you consider the funds they invested in Harley, the management talent they hired, I don't see how they can be faulted as much as a lot of people would lead you to believe. Sure, sometimes they zigged when they should have zagged, but they really did Harley-Davidson a lot of good. They turned it around from a basically very low-volume producer to a much higher-volume producer. They systematized many things and brought the company forward in many areas.

Chairman Vaughn Beals's view of AMF is also tempered— perhaps because he came on board in 1976, just when the conglomerate was realizing that it had to address the motorcycle company's serious engineering and manufacturing problems. But he believes that AMF itself had contributed to those problems with its total "quantity focus" at the price of quality, labor realtions, and new-product development. He says, however, that any management probably would have fallen into the same trap of trying to catch every sale that went by.

Beals's main beef with AMF during his years there was that the conglomerate procrastinated on the NOVA new-engine program. He blames that on the decision of Rodney Gott's successor, Tom York, to downgrade the leisure-product side of AMF's business.

Harley observer David Wright, author of *The Harley-Davidson Motor Company: An Official Eighty-Year History* (Motorbooks International, Osceola, Wis., 1987, p. 248), maintains that AMF had a positive impact on the Milwaukee firm:

> Dealers still hear it: "Harley-Davidson didn't build any good motorcycles while they were owned by AMF." Not only is this statement not true, it is a cheap shot at a conglomerate that poured millions of developmental dollars into H-D, allowing it to produce such significant bikes as the Super Glide and the Low Rider Custom. Harley motorcycles would not be half as good as they are without AMF's willingness to spend money.

Another Harley historian, Allan Girdler, says in *The Illustrated Harley-Davidson Buyer's Guide*:

> There are Harley fans today who sincerely believe AMF set out to gut the fine old firm, take the money, and run. This is neither fair nor accurate. AMF had grabbed more than it could handle. It takes a while to learn how to build things, especially complicated ones like motorcycles . . . AMF invested literally millions of dollars in Harley-Davidson. Production facilities were improved beyond description.

AMF's most severe critics are Harley-Davidson's plant employees and Harley riders. Workers who were with Harley during the AMF years speak bitterly of how they felt they had to sacrifice quality to AMF's relentless demand for more output.

And then there were the customers—Harley's loyal fans. As a roving goodwill ambassador for Harley-Davidson, Roger Hull keeps his finger on the pulse of Harley riders all over the country. His evaluation of AMF's impact on them:

> AMF's impact was huge—and among customers, mostly unfavorable. Riders began to separate the machines: If it was pre-1969 it was a Harley, while post-1969 models were called "AMFs"—and that was an insult. Customers viewed AMF as a villain with questionable intentions.

Hull felt the same way then, but revised his opinion after the buyback:

> It took several years for me to realize that AMF actually rescued Harley-Davidson. If anything, Harley-Davidson got the best of the deal: a modern assembly plant in York and an updated engine-and-transmission plant in Milwaukee. AMF didn't make that much profit from H-D—what kept Rodney Gott happy about the merger was that he could buy his Harleys at cost.

Regardless of Hull's change of heart, many bikers still feel bitterly negative about AMF. It was even suggested by some after the buyback that the Rodney C. Gott Motorcycle Museum in York be renamed. "Unfair," says Hull. "Without AMF and Gott, it might have been Bangor Punta back in 1969. And if that had happened, I don't think there would be any museum— or any Harley-Davidson for that matter."

At least one former Harley executive believes that AMF was unjustly blamed for all of the company's quality problems. According to Robert Rohrer, who was Harley-Davidson's vice president of marketing, AMF became a convenient scapegoat for the Milwaukee company's own deficiencies. He says:

> The truth of the matter is that the vehicle prior to AMF taking over wasn't all that reliable and suffered from quality problems. Then when AMF took over, quality slipped some more because of the growth pains of

increasing production capacity by thousands of
machines. For Harley-Davidson, it was a good thing that
AMF became the lightning rod for all the dissatisfaction,
because when the company was bought back much
hoopla could be made about removing the AMF logo
from the tank and getting rid of the "bad guys."

Much hoopla *was* made after the LBO. Hog riders every-
where exuberantly hailed the buyback as a rebirth of the Harley
legend. Charlie Thompson, key buyback team member and
president of the now-independent company, cheerfully told the
press he was bullish about the big-bike end of the motorcycle
market.

But the euphoria soon evaporated. Independent or not,
Harley-Davidson was still a company in deep trouble, which
was getting even deeper as the motorcycle market continued
to slide along with the economy—and now the company was
in hock to Citicorp and other lenders to the tune of $80 million.
Would the eagle soar—or would it come crashing to the ground?

chapter 6

Breakthrough

Free at last—but the new owners of Harley-Davidson were now faced with the formidable challenge of figuring out what they had to do to survive on their own.

The competitive environment was ferocious and frightening:

• *The Japanese were winning the motorcycle wars.* First, they were continuously building up U.S. inventories of all their motorcycles and their dealers were discounting prices aggressively to get rid of them. Second, they were invading Harley's turf by exporting heavyweight motorcycles that competed directly with Harley-Davidson bikes. In 1981, the year the new Harley owners took over, Yamaha even introduced the Virago, a big V-twin that looked remarkably like a Harley. This Harley clone had it all: the buckhorn handlebars, the stepped seat, and, most important of all, the big V-twin engine that had been so distinctively Harley for more than 70 years. Moreover, this brash impostor ran better than the real thing and cost 25 to 50 percent less.

The Harley mystique began to lose its hold on those riders who a few years before would have turned violent if anyone had suggested that they consider riding Japanese machines. Japan's combination of higher quality, more advanced technology, and lower prices was weakening a once-fanatical dedication to the only U.S. motorcycle maker. The company now was depending on die-hard fans who wore T-shirts emblazoned with sayings like "I'd rather see my sister in a whorehouse than my brother on a Honda."

Harley-Davidson sales began to plummet. By the end of 1981, Harley's U.S. market share in what had been its very own private preserve—the super-heavyweight class—had dropped to 29.6 percent, *below* Honda's 33.9 percent. For the first time in its long history, Harley-Davidson was no longer king of the super heavyweights.

• *The motorcycle market (which the Japanese had broadened since the sixties) was now eroding.* The economy was in a downturn, while interest rates remained high—like cars, most motorcycles are sold on credit. The blue-collar workers from whom Harley drew a major part of its sales were not exactly lining up to buy $8000 motorcycles. (Almost 96 percent of Harley buyers are male, and even under the best of economic circumstances, they often have to overcome intense spousal resistance before they feel they can make the plunge without serious domestic complications. In a depressed economy with high interest rates, forget it.) On top of that, there were credit restrictions which favored the Japanese: Although motorcycles *under* $3000 could still be financed, credit was unavailable for motorcycles in Harley-Davidson's higher price range.

The result was that in June 1981, when the buyout was completed, Harley-Davidson had almost 6000 motorcycles in finished-goods inventory, while the norm for that time of year was from 200 to 600. To get rid of this merchandise, the company and the dealers cooperated in an "Independence Celebration" and granted large rebates to buyers. "If our rebate program hadn't succeeded," says one Harley executive, "the company would have had to fold six months after the buyout."

• *Harley-Davidson had no capital.* The now-independent company no longer had a parent corporation to turn to for funding that was desperately needed for new-product development and manufacture.

• *Quality was a major problem.* Half the machines coming off the Harley assembly line had missing parts. A bitter joke circulated: "The only way to own a Harley is to own two of them. That way you'll have something to ride while the other one is in for repairs."

DESERTIONS IN THE RANKS

As Japanese quality kept reaching higher and higher levels, some Harley dealers deserted to the Japanese brands. "They took on the Japanese bikes, sang their praises, and put the Harleys in the back room," says Philip Peterson, a dealer who remained loyal to Harley. But, he said, these dealers had good economic reasons for downplaying Harleys in favor of Japanese machines. "At our own dealership, we lost an awful lot of riders to the Honda Gold Wing touring motorcycle, which became popular in the late seventies. It was a really smooth bike, everything we weren't—and cheaper, too. Meanwhile, we had terrible problems— oil leaks, vibration, generally poor quality."

Although there were plenty of loyal Harley dealers such as Peterson, many were bitter about these problems. Missouri dealer Ray Worth, who once carried competitive brands, says, "I used to have a Harley district manager who always told me we were selling the Mercedes-Benz of motorcycles—and my answer was that we had the Mercedes price, all right, but not the Mercedes quality."

Today, Ray Worth carries nothing but Harleys.

Going Back to School

The new owners of Harley-Davidson had to face some hard truths. The Japanese were building better bikes at lower costs. How did they do it? Harley's new owners decided they'd better find out.

In 1981 there was virtually no literature on Japanese manufacturing techniques available to U.S. readers. But Tom Gelb managed to dig up some articles on the subject, and he could hardly believe what he read. The Japanese were using just-in-time (JIT) inventory methods that produced inventory turns of 20 to 30 times a year. The significance of this lies in the impact that inventory turns have on costs and quality. (*Inventory turns* are the number of times a year a company turns over its raw material and work in process. For example, one month's inventory means 12 turns a year. The more inventory turns the better because a company has less inventory on hand at any given moment. This not only lowers the cost of maintaining inventory but also has a positive impact on quality, as we shall see from Harley-Davidson's experience.)

Comparing the Japanese figures with Harley-Davidson's performance showed clearly how dismal that performance was. Gelb was particularly dismayed that against the 20 to 30 inventory turns achieved by the Japanese, Harley-Davidson was doing only 4 (a figure fairly typical of U.S. factories).

After his intensive study of Japanese manufacturing methods, Gelb learned that the Japanese were using three practices that were rarely utilized by U.S. companies. They were:

- *Employee involvement (EI).* Enlisting the full participation of *all* employees in solving problems and controlling quality. (Harley-Davidson had been "fooling around" with employee quality circles since 1978 but not with a real understanding of the concept or a wholehearted commitment to it.)
- *Just-in-time inventory (JIT).* Using a production method that eliminates large parts inventories with all their pitfalls and high costs and instead delivers small quantities of parts to the assembly line as they are needed.
- *Statistical operator control (SOC).* Giving all employees the statistical training for measuring the quality of their own output.

Although at that time Harley-Davidson's new owners failed to recognize the importance of SOC, what they learned about Japanese EI and JIT practices profoundly changed how they looked at the problems they were facing. For years they had attributed these problems to their competitors' cheap labor, dumping practices, cultural differences, and huge outlays for advertising. Now they were being forced to give up these rationalizations and face the uncomfortable truth.

Moreover, like the rest of U.S. industry, Harley-Davidson was not cost-competitive with the Japanese.

"That's basic," says Beals now. "If you're not cost-competitive, you're going to be buried—and we were almost six feet under at this point."

A major point that U.S. companies often overlook, Beals believes, is that *even if a company has no foreign competition* it must be cost-competitive in world markets, as well as in domestic markets. "Otherwise, you can't export, and, domestically, you'll be in a defensive posture. You're practically inviting the Japanese to invade your market—or the Koreans or the Taiwanese."

As with its quality problems, Harley-Davidson's cost problems could only be blamed on itself.

"We discovered that the key reason for our lack of competitiveness was poor management—by worldwide, not U.S. standards," Beals says. "We were being wiped out by the Japanese because they were better *managers*. It wasn't robotics, or culture, or morning calisthenics and company songs—it was professional managers who understood their business and paid attention to detail."

Obviously, it was imperative for Harley-Davidson to shape up if it wanted to stay alive. But, realized Tom Gelb, a conventional improvement program (more inspectors, slogans, automation, etc.) just wouldn't do it. The Japanese were not merely more efficient, they did things entirely *differently* from the way Harley-Davidson and other U.S. companies did them. Turning Harley-Davidson around demanded a radical change in the way it manufactured motorcycles.

In 1981, few U.S. companies had adopted EI, JIT, or SOC, and none had adopted all three together. The irony of this was that these practices originally had been developed by two American quality experts, Dr. W. Edwards Deming and Joseph Juran. The practices were introduced in Japan in the late 1940s as part of General Douglas MacArthur's program to help the defeated Japanese revive their war-shattered industry. Japanese managers responded by enthusiastically adopting and perfecting these practices, while U.S. manufacturers stuck to their "this is the way we've always done it" habits: centralized direction, just-in-*case* inventory, and "inspecting" quality into the product.

It can be argued that the postwar Japanese had nothing to lose: They were not only starting with new methods but also with new factories. Postwar U.S. industry, however, had no incentives to change: It would have had to revamp existing facilities that were already up and running profitably. It had a postwar domestic market hungry for anything it could produce. It had no competitors of consequence.

At the time, Deming and Juran, among others, warned that such shortsightedness and complacency would undermine the future of U.S. industry. But few paid any attention to them.

HARLEY-DAVIDSON   CAUSE AND EFFECT?

Vaughn Beals hypothesizes that Japanese manufacturing methods have their origin in the scarcity and high price of land in Japan. Out of economic necessity, his theory says factories must be small, with machines placed close together, so there is no room for excess inventory. Flow processes, setup reduction, statistical process control, and the resulting improvements in quality all follow from the fundamental need to conserve space.

In 1981, EI, JIT, and SOC were the "magic" weapons the Japanese motorcycle giants were using to improve the quality of their products, add new features, control costs, and gain market share. However, Harley-Davidson's new owners focused on only two of the three practices: EI and JIT. The new owners had not yet realized that SOC was an equally important tool and that for best results it had to be adopted together with EI and JIT.

But the company moved fast on installing JIT. In October 1981—just three months after the buyback—Harley-Davidson's manufacturing team began a JIT pilot program. Their objective: To get cash out of the business to reduce Harley's leveraged buyout debt. ("It was two or three years later before we got it through our heads that JIT was really the engine of quality improvement," says a Harley executive.)

The JIT program got under way in a small section of the Milwaukee engine plant. When the results showed promise, Gelb called a series of meetings with engine-plant employees. He told them bluntly, "We have to play the game the way the Japanese play it—or we're dead." He described the pilot program and announced that the JIT system would be expanded to the whole engine plant. The reaction from a lot of managers was disbelief.

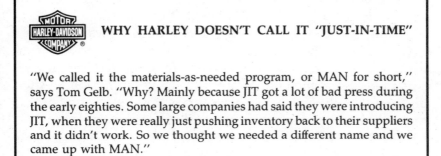

WHY HARLEY DOESN'T CALL IT "JUST-IN-TIME"

"We called it the materials-as-needed program, or MAN for short," says Tom Gelb. "Why? Mainly because JIT got a lot of bad press during the early eighties. Some large companies had said they were introducing JIT, when they were really just pushing inventory back to their suppliers and it didn't work. So we thought we needed a different name and we came up with MAN."

The biggest problem Harley-Davidson had in introducing JIT into the engine plant was lack of understanding and support from middle management and staff professionals. Gelb says this was because the pressures of time and competition made it impossible to build acceptance for the new methods before they were installed. "We didn't take the time we should have to involve the management group that would be implementing change." He points to this as a pitfall that other companies can and should avoid when they change over to JIT. According to Gelb, however,

> The biggest pitfall is not starting JIT at all. People
> agonize over it because it's obviously a big risk,
> especially if you have a successful company with a
> strong balance sheet and financial statements. You ask
> yourself, if I don't have foreign competitors and I'm
> doing really well, why should I take the risk? The
> answer is that if *any* competitor starts a JIT program,
> including the competitor down the street, you're going
> to be in deep trouble.

Harley-Davidson management learned some hard lessons as it tried to introduce JIT methods. One was that the way to gain acceptance for the unfamiliar methods was to *show that they worked.*

"You can put up a banner that says 'Quality is Job One,'" says Vaughn Beals, "but if you don't have a program that actually works to improve quality, people get disillusioned real fast. We learned to do it first, then put up the banner."

One by one, skeptics were converted, but it was not easy. In an article for the book *Execution!* Harley-Davidson's former media liaison Buzz Buzzelli said that when the JIT system was explained at one meeting, employees laughed out loud. After all, they already had a contemporary computer-based control system with overhead conveyors and high-rise parts storage—and this new system proposed replacing all this with *push carts.* In the minds of some, the new owners appeared to be taking the company back to 1930.

Obviously, many Harley-Davidson workers were not convinced that such a simple-sounding system could be that effective. And yet it was the system's very simplicity that made it so attractive. It fit perfectly into a repetitive manufacturing environment. It placed parts control directly on the shop floor. It did not need elaborate planning systems for support. And the beauty of it all was that it required almost no capital investment to make it work—a significant factor for a company that was bleeding red ink by the gallon.

So the push to implement JIT went on. Among other

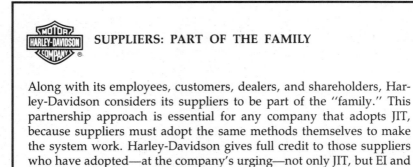

SUPPLIERS: PART OF THE FAMILY

Along with its employees, customers, dealers, and shareholders, Harley-Davidson considers its suppliers to be part of the "family." This partnership approach is essential for any company that adopts JIT, because suppliers must adopt the same methods themselves to make the system work. Harley-Davidson gives full credit to those suppliers who have adopted—at the company's urging—not only JIT, but EI and SOC as well. (For guidelines on changing relations with suppliers, see Part 2, pp. 182–185.)

things, this push required a revolutionary change in the assembly line system at the York plant—a change that led to a giant step toward genuine involvement of the employees.

Ever since the York plant had started assembling Harleys in 1973, parts had been made in large batches for long production runs. These parts were stored until they were needed, then loaded onto a circular, 3.5-mile-long overhead conveyor belt that rattled endlessly around the plant.

Tom Gelb explains some of the drawbacks of this system: "Sometimes we couldn't even find the parts we needed on the assembly line. Or if we found them, they were rusted or damaged. Or there'd been an engineering change since the parts were made, and they didn't even fit. It's no wonder we had high costs and low quality."

Clearly, this system was incompatible with the JIT system and had to go. Management decided to replace it with what came to be known as the "jelly bean" system. No longer would each model be made in long, continuous runs on the assembly line. Instead, the assembly line would make every model, in different colors (hence, "jelly beans"), *every day*. Parts would be made in small batches and used immediately, never getting a chance to rust, be lost, get damaged, or become obsolete. Beautiful.

But how do you do it? How do you gain worker acceptance for a system that is so different, so alien?

By having all employees become involved in actually planning and working out the new system, that's how. This was a superb opportunity to put into practice another one of the three components of the Japanese manufacturing triad: EI. In his book *Trigger Points* (McGraw-Hill Book Co., New York, 1988, p. 108), management strategist Michael J. Kami (who is also a member of Harley-Davidson's board) describes how EI can completely change the way top management decisions are made and implemented:

> A top-management decision in a U.S. company is
> made—after due thought, analysis, and input—in the
> executive suite and is then announced to the
> organization. And nothing happens. That is because
> lower echelons do not understand, do not like, or do not

know how to implement the edict from above. They have to be sold, instructed, and trained before the decision can be implemented.

The Japanese also make the important decision at the top, but they don't announce it. Instead, they sell, discuss, and dissect the proposed action with everyone who will be directly or indirectly involved in it. That takes time and patience and appears to move at a snail's pace. But it also provides feedback and ideas that may modify the decision. Since it has not yet been announced, it can be changed without loss of face.

But when the decision *is* finally announced, all the key pieces are in place and action starts immediately. The Japanese semiconsensus method brings action 30 percent faster than the U.S. decision process.

The "jelly bean" conversion was a perfect illustration of this process. Before announcing the decision to make the change, Harley-Davidson management held meeting after meeting with small groups of employees from all departments that were affected: engineering, manufacturing, maintenance, and more.

"Management at our York, Pennsylvania, plant involved over 250 employees in the change and decision-making process," explains Tom Gelb. "It was only then that we decided what to do and how to go about it. No changes were implemented until the people involved understood and accepted that change. It took two months before the consensus decision was made to go ahead. That was a Friday—we started making the changes on Monday."

About three weeks later, Vaughn Beals visited the York plant and talked to a few employees on the line, asking them how the conversion was going. To his surprise—and delight—the answer was generally, "Well, we have some problems, but it's a lot better than it was before, and we will get those problems fixed."

Says Beals now: "To me, that reaction demonstrated the true value of employee involvement. Normally, it would be the engineers who would figure out how to make the changes. They would have made them with the usual number of errors,

"KICKING ASS AND TAKING NAMES"

It was only after they boned up on Japanese methods that Harley's owners realized that employee involvement in Japan is far more than the public relations gimmick it can be in the United States, where an occasional handshake, a suggestion box, and the annual company picnic are often considered to be employee democracy in action. The Japanese philosophy is that given the tools and the responsibility, workers can solve many of their production problems better than management can.

This concept of employee involvement is ingrained into Japanese managers, but not into their U.S. counterparts. Particularly in the smokestack belt, supervisors and managers are more used to "kicking ass and taking names" than to listening to their subordinates. That attitude had to be changed at Harley-Davidson if any genuine employee involvement was to be achieved.

Today, for example, employee involvement is part of Harley-Davidson's normal day-to-day operations on its assembly lines. Assemblers are asked to meet with suppliers to discuss quality problems, material changes, and packaging changes. Department layout changes are discussed with the operators before implementation. Individual process sheets and work content are reviewed with assemblers before line balance changes are made. New equipment is reviewed with assemblers, and in some cases they are asked to visit the vendor with the production engineer to participate in a preliminary run before delivery.

The result: Disruption from assembly line changes has been reduced, and employees have more interest in their jobs now that their input is listened to and acted upon.

and the reaction then would have been: 'Those dummies screwed up again.' And worse yet, the employees wouldn't have lifted a finger to help solve the problems."

The Drive for Quality

By the early 1980s, "quality" had become a big buzz word in the business world—especially "Japanese quality." And as David Halberstam reported in *Parade Magazine*, many U.S. managers were sick of hearing constant praise of Japanese superiority in achieving high quality. Bitter jokes circulated, such as the following: A Japanese, an American, and a Frenchman were captured by a hostile tribe, and each was given one last request before being shot. The Frenchman asked to sing the "Marseillaise." The Japanese asked that he be allowed to give his standard quality-control lecture one more time. After hearing his request, the American asked to be shot first.

For Harley-Davidson's new owners in the fall of 1982, Japanese quality was no joking matter. In fact, it was killing them. Analysts were saying that the Japanese could put the last U.S. motorcycle company out of business just about any time they wanted to do so.

By now, however, Harley's management team was beginning to understand the Japanese systems that were responsible for the superior quality of Hondas and Yamahas. And the team had a long-range vision: By adopting these systems, Harley-Davidson could beat the Japanese at their own game.

A start had been made, but it was only a start. JIT was producing results and had freed up cash so Harley's borrowing requirements were not as large as they otherwise would have been. Harley had also made strides toward EI.

But while Harley's JIT and EI programs were producing some progress, the progress wasn't good enough or fast enough. There seemed to be a missing ingredient. Although the JIT system flushed cash out of the business, it also demanded top quality. Harley lacked the techniques and tools for achieving such quality.

Harley's top management realized that quality had to improve sharply and that the person in charge of quality assurance would have to be oriented toward making the kind of drastic change that was demanded. Their choice was Ron Hutchinson. Hutchinson had been with Harley-Davidson since 1975 in a variety of engineering and program-management positions, but he had never been directly involved in quality assurance.

This was actually a plus, because Harley's leaders were looking more for a fresh viewpoint than for experience. They wanted someone free from restrictive preconceived notions about quality that could impede the radical changes that had to be made.

Says Hutchinson:

> I did an intensive literature and technology search into
> quality-improvement methods. I interviewed consultants
> and universities. And I investigated the approaches of
> the leading quality gurus. One had too much flag-
> waving and management hoopla without any real
> substance. We didn't need that. Another used a very
> technical project-by-project improvement method. Both
> of these approaches seemed designed to enhance the
> stature and prestige of the quality-assurance department.

What Harley-Davidson really needed, Hutchinson concluded from his research, was a method for providing plant
operators and office employees with statistical tools they could
use to communicate effectively with management. In Harley-
Davidson (and in most U.S. industry) such communication was
based more on emotion than on facts.

The quality approach that Hutchinson felt fit Harley-Davidson's needs best was that of W. Edwards Deming, whose
teachings had been a smash hit in Japan but had been virtually
ignored by U.S. industry. According to Hutchinson:

> If you get past his angry crotchety approach to American
> management, you realize he has the right idea. He's
> saying, 'Hey, management, you have to change and you
> have to provide tools for your people so they can
> change.' Deming's basic philosophy of continuous
> improvement appealed to me as an engineer. And he
> had the key principle that was missing from other
> approaches: that the leadership should come from the
> people with the responsibility for quality, the people on
> the floor.

In Deming's scheme of things that principle has to be implemented through *statistical process control* (renamed *statistical
operator control*—SOC—by Harley-Davidson), which consists of
giving all employees the statistical tools for monitoring and
controlling the quality of their own work. This was the missing
ingredient that Harley-Davidson management had failed to include in the mix when they began to adopt the methods with
which their Japanese competitors were overpowering them.

SOC is the third leg of what Ron Hutchinson later dubbed the "Productivity Triad": EI, JIT, and SOC.

Converting the Managers

Although Harley-Davidson leaders resolved to adopt SOC, they knew it wouldn't be easy. It required nothing less than totally reshaping the work and manufacturing culture of an old-line Midwest company with hundreds of veteran workers and managers who had been doing things virtually the same way for 30 years.

The initial concern was with plant managers and middle managers. Unless they supported—or at least didn't resist—the major changes that had to be made, SOC would never become a reality. This was the first hurdle to be overcome.

"To give credibility to the SOC program," says Hutchinson, "we decided to use an outside source to train managers in the Deming philosophy and SOC methodology. We turned to the University of Tennessee, which had achieved a leadership position in the quality field with its Institute of Productivity and Quality."

During a visit to the Great Smokies in the spring of 1983, Hutchinson went to the University of Tennessee to discuss Harley's quality problems with Tim Carpenter, then program coordinator at the institute. Carpenter and his colleagues primarily taught statistical analysis to managers and supervisors as the basis for a continuous quality improvement system similar to that used by Japanese industry.

Carpenter recalls that Hutchinson gave him a grim picture. "Slide in market share, quality problems, warranty costs through the roof, 35 percent of everything they made had to be scrapped. Who in hell could be competitive and go head-to-head with the Japanese with a situation like that? It didn't take a genius to figure out that if they didn't turn it around fast they just wouldn't be there. Loyalty of hard-core customers was the only thing keeping them afloat."

Carpenter felt that he and his colleagues could help with their three-week statistics training program for managers. But it took until the fall before Harley's skeptical plant managers could be persuaded to spare the time to take the program.

After that, the institute expanded its training to include several hundred middle managers. "Middle managers were taught the basic Deming philosophy and how to crunch numbers," says Hutchinson. "This helped to gain acceptance for the program, but there was still resistance by some managers. We handled that by coaching and having them participate in team problem-solving activities so they would feel like part of the process. Those who just couldn't accept the changes were eased out."

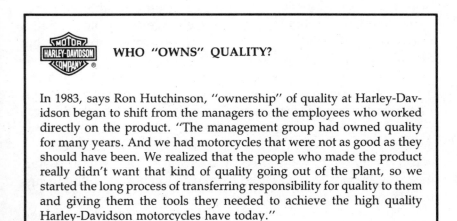

WHO "OWNS" QUALITY?

In 1983, says Ron Hutchinson, "ownership" of quality at Harley-Davidson began to shift from the managers to the employees who worked directly on the product. "The management group had owned quality for many years. And we had motorcycles that were not as good as they should have been. We realized that the people who made the product really didn't want that kind of quality going out of the plant, so we started the long process of transferring responsibility for quality to them and giving them the tools they needed to achieve the high quality Harley-Davidson motorcycles have today."

Tim Carpenter understands why middle managers can feel threatened by SOC. "Their own control is being taken away from them, because the real experts in the SOC system are the operators, not middle managers. The operators understand how the motorcycles are made. So they are the ones who are going to come back and say, 'We have a purchased material that is not meeting our requirements.' Managers' judgment is going to be called into question under this system."

How do you turn managerial resistance around? "It's leadership, hands-on, daily," says Carpenter. "And it's got to come from the top." Carpenter recalls that Beals provided the decisive leadership when it was needed. "He took command—we didn't sit around in a circle holding hands and meditating on the problem. And he didn't exactly use a highly participative approach. When the stress level was up and the pressure was on, Vaughn kind of reverted to the old Theory X management style. We would arrive at the plant in the morning and ask, 'Is Mr. B. in the Magnum mode today?' "

In training employees to control their own quality, Carpenter rates the plant manager's role as the most important key, next to leadership from the top.

"If you can't turn around the plant manager," he says, "you're not going to turn around the employees."

As an example he talks about former York plant manager Jim Lucas, who he says underwent a profound change in his approach to management that made changes possible. Initially, Lucas had been so skeptical about the institute program that he failed to show up for the opening session.

Carpenter remembers a top manager from FMC Corporation being given a tour of the York plant some months after Lucas had taken the program. The FMC manager asked Lucas what was the most important lesson he had learned in his Productivity Triad experience. Said Lucas, "That's easy. I learned that I had to stop being a dictator. That I had to start listening to people. That I had to take action based on the things that they were telling me."

Through 1984, Carpenter and his colleagues continued training Harley managers, although by then they had left the University of Tennessee and formed a consulting group called Tennessee Associates, dedicated to teaching Deming's principles of quality and productivity.

"This disturbed us a bit," says Hutchinson, "because we felt that as part of a university they had more credibility with our managers than they would as professional consultants. Consultants are more suspected of 'hard sell' tactics than universities. (Hutchinson speaks with feeling, since he is now a consultant himself.)

Plant operators were trained in SOC methods internally by Harley-Davidson personnel who in turn had been trained by Ron Hutchinson with the assistance of Tennessee Associates. (For guidelines on introducing SOC, see page 176.)

Completing the Productivity Triad

SOC is based on the simple notion that it pays to make a product right the first time. Traditional manufacturers depend on quality inspectors to discover a faulty product after it's been made but before it gets out the door. This is a wasteful, costly process. By contrast, SOC enables operators to discover problems early on and stop the process immediately, often before any rejects are made.

Because SOC gives employees the opportunity to monitor production and ensure the quality of each manufactured part, it represents a key form of EI. This is perhaps best expressed by plant employees who have bought into the program. One plating department employee, Bennie Carter, says:

> Statistics control and employee involvement go hand in hand in solving quality problems. For example, I had problems with a Sportster sprocket cover. The supplier was delivering them with die marks, and there was also a porosity problem. Being involved in the SOC program, I felt it was my duty to see that these problems were corrected. When parts leave me they go directly into the plater or to the assembly line to be mounted on the motorcycle. And I refuse to send junk to the line.

By using SOC methods, Carter was able to bring the problem part under control. In addition, because of Harley's EI policy, he himself—rather than his supervisor or an engineer—was able to communicate the problems directly to the outside vendor, using the information from his control charts. This led the vendor to improve its manufacturing process and produce a better part.

Carter: "Was I always sold on SOC? No way. I thought, what am I getting into—I never heard of Deming or SOC. But now I'm a believer, because SOC helps me do what I've always wanted to do: turn out a quality product."

Without the contributions of Harley-Davidson employees in all functions and all levels, the company's turnaround would have been impossible. However, it can take years for EI and SOC to become firmly established in a manufacturing culture that has always depended on "inspecting" quality into the product. Carter himself believes that some levels of management could be more responsive toward the program when he has a problem on which he needs help. And Tom Gelb agrees that Harley-Davidson has a long way to go before all its managers wholeheartedly support the program.

Gelb says, "Because this program changes the role of middle managers, and we weren't very sensitive to this in the beginning, some of them really didn't buy into it. Our areas of success are where managers readily saw the value and benefit of the program and went out of their way to nurture it. Now we're having to go back and fill in the educational and training gaps."

 TOM GELB MEETS THE "SUITS"

In the mid-eighties, Big Eight accounting firm Arthur Andersen invited Tom Gelb to talk about Harley's manufacturing process improvements. On the day of the meeting, Tom, as usual, pulled on his leather jacket and got on his XR1000—a motorcycle which is street-legal but is a racing derivative and has a particularly gutsy sound to it. He then drove down to the Arthur Andersen Training Center near Chicago, only to find himself walking into a formidable meeting room filled with three-piece suits looking at him as if he were some kind of alien. His first words: "Is it legal to talk in here?"

There is also much work to be done in gaining support from nonmanagerial employees. Not all are equally enthusiastic about the Productivity Triad program, and its supporters can often be subjected to peer pressure from those who are concerned about jobs that may be changed or lost because of productivity improvements.

Bob Conway, former manager of quality audit, recalls the strange looks he would get from employees when he asked their opinion on an operation:

> I'd say how would you fix this, what would be a better
> way of doing it? In the beginning they'd shrug and say
> nothing. Then word gradually got around that if they
> expressed an opinion we would react to it, do something
> about it, or at least explain why their idea couldn't be
> implemented. Pretty soon some of them would be
> grabbing my arm and giving me their ideas. Of course,
> there were die-hards who'd say, 'I get my paycheck at
> the end of the week, and that's it,' or 'Management is
> just out to screw us.' But even they had to admit that at
> least management was listening. The barriers were
> slowly being broken.

The barriers are not completely down yet. Harley executives describe their progress so far as "islands of success" in
their plants. But in those islands there is now an atmosphere
of continuous improvement, one in which employees are never
satisfied with their results. These employees are pitting their
minds against the process, not against each other.

Harley-Davidson CEO Rich Teerlink believes passionately
in EI but he doesn't think that Harley-Davidson can say it has
achieved full EI until it is established as an ongoing process
that takes place every minute of every day of every week.

"True employee involvement is a process by which you
actually run the business," he says. "It means pushing management responsibility down as far as possible. It means that
the employee accepts the responsibility for saying, 'If there is
something that can help me do my job better or make a higher
quality product then I'm going to do it or tell someone else in
the company about it.' That's employee involvement."

The Triad: More Than the Sum of Its Parts

Harley-Davidson was the first U.S. company to view JIT as part
of an inseparable manufacturing triad that includes EI and SOC.
Using one or two of these programs will produce improve-

ments, but only by adopting all three in an integrated system can their full power be unleashed.

Even now, says Vaughn Beals, too many U.S. companies are forgetting that important principle. "We didn't realize it right away, but we found out through experience that all three of these practices are interdependent, so you must do all of them to achieve the best quality and productivity. I strongly believe that the Productivity Triad is the key to world-wide competitiveness."

chapter 7

Reprieve

A s if Harley didn't have enough on its plate, there was also a Honda-Yamaha war—waged on Harley's turf. Whenever two market leaders lock horns in a struggle for domination, a third party gets hurt, and in this case it was Harley-Davidson. Strangely, it all happened because Honda got into the car business.

For years, Honda had enjoyed the lion's share of the motorcycle market, both in Japan and abroad. In the mid-1960s, Honda produced 65 percent of all motorcycles made in Japan, as compared with Yamaha's 10 percent. But when market growth began to level off, Honda decided to diversify into the car business. By 1975, it was reaping greater profits from its cars than from its motorcycles.

Yamaha saw this development as a perfect opportunity to sneak up on Honda when it wasn't looking. Focused on cars, Honda failed to react quickly enough to Yamaha's aggressive new efforts to grab market share in the motorcycle business. By 1981, Yamaha had pulled up to within one point of Honda, with 37 percent of market share to Honda's 38 percent.

Then Yamaha went too far. Announced Yamaha president Hisao Koike: "In one year, we will be the domestic leader. And in two years, we will be number one in the world."

In their book *Kaisha, The Japanese Corporation* (Basic Books Inc., New York, 1985, p.49), James C. Abegglen and George Stalk Jr. describe Honda's reaction: When word of Koike's statement at the Yamaha shareholders meeting in January 1982 reached Honda's president, Kiyoshi Kawashima, he was incensed. "Yamaha has not only stepped on the tail of a tiger, it has ground it into the earth!" Kawashima issued a battle cry, *"Yamaha wo tsubusu!"*, which can be variously translated as, "We will crush [break, smash, squash, butcher, slaughter, or destroy] Yamaha."

So the slugfest began. Honda counterattacked with all the weapons at its command, which included heavy price cuts, intense promotion, and a proliferation of new models. Under Honda's massive assault, Yamaha wilted. Its market share collapsed to 23 percent, while Honda's rose to 43 percent. After 18 months, a battered Yamaha surrendered. Yamaha's president Koike resigned, and Yamaha chairman Genichi Kawakami admitted, "We turned on the throttle when we should have been applying the brakes."

Caught in the middle of the Honda-Yamaha war, Harley was also battered. Both Japanese makers flooded the U.S. market with a dazzling assortment of new competitive models. Bloated Japanese inventories led to ridiculously low prices for Harley look-alikes that were robbing the American company of sales it might have otherwise enjoyed. In 1982 it needed another rebate program to clear inventory and by midyear it became painfully obvious that Harley-Davidson was heading for a disastrous year-end loss.

Harley-Davidson was now in an almost untenable position. Harley management knew what it had to do to turn the company around: to improve quality, cut costs, lower its break-even point, and regain market share. But the question was whether it would ever get a chance to demonstrate that it could reach these objectives. You need deep pockets to survive a war between your two biggest competitors, and Harley-Davidson didn't have them.

Harley needed breathing room so it could accomplish the ambitious, difficult goals it had set for itself. To get that room, senior management decided there was only one recourse, which was to ask Washington for tariff relief to discourage the Japanese from continuing to build up their U.S. inventories. From 1978 through 1980, Japanese imports closely matched their sales registrations. Then, in 1981, they imported about 30 percent more than they sold and in early 1982 Harley was shocked to see that they were bringing in *twice* their rate of registrations. After running some calculations, Harley concluded that the Japanese had a year-and-a-half's supply of new motorcycles stashed in dealerships and importers' warehouses.

On August 30, 1982, Vaughn Beals—as a courtesy to Harley's two biggest competitors—met separately with officials from Honda and Yamaha to advise them that Harley-Davidson would immediately seek tariff relief under Section 201 of the Trade Act of 1974, a law that had been created for U.S. industries seriously injured by imports.

At both meetings, Beals stressed that Harley-Davidson was asking for temporary relief only—until the company could get its new product line tooled up, improve manufacturing efficiency and quality, and strengthen itself financially. But he also emphasized that the company was forced to take this route because of Japanese actions: building up excessive inventories, aggressively attacking Harley's traditional markets (V-twin engines, custom styling, and fully equipped tourers), and depressing prices.

He pointed out to Honda's representative that maybe he and Yamaha weren't "out to get Harley," but the fact that they were trying to knock each other out of the box by going after the Harley market was causing Harley-Davidson more than a little distress.

When he raised the same point with Ted Kimura, president of Yamaha-U.S.A., Kimura promptly blamed Honda for the situation in which Harley-Davidson found itself. He insisted that he had carefully instructed Yamaha designers to avoid copying Harley's styling, to which Beals replied, "Your designers don't seem to be too good at following instructions."

Kimura explained that Yamaha had a real dilemma: It didn't want to copy the Harley look, but it recognized that this look sold very well. In fact, Kimura said, Yamaha's original V-twin—the Virago—had probably failed to sell because it didn't look *enough* like a Harley.

Kimura also reminded Beals that the Japanese makers had large inventories already in the United States. How would tariff relief solve that problem? While agreeing it was a problem, Beals did not answer Kimura directly. Privately, however, he speculated that the Japanese would raise their prices to maximize profits on the bikes they already had in the country, thus making Harley more competitive. Later, Beals was to find out how wrong he was in expecting higher Japanese prices.

THE FIRST TIME IT WAS *NO*

Harley-Davidson made the first of its appeals for tariff protection against foreign machines in 1951—against the British. Forty percent of U.S. motorcycle sales were of foreign makes, mostly British. Not only did Harley-Davidson want a 50 percent hike in tariff rates, but it also wanted a quota on imported bikes equal to their prewar numbers, which were virtually nothing.

The U.S. Tariff Commission turned Harley-Davidson down cold. Ironically, its decision was largely based on the testimony of Harley-Davidson's former representative in Japan, who was now representing the British exporters. He made a devastating case against Harley-Davidson, charging that actually the Milwaukee company had shot itself in the foot by obstinately refusing to produce middleweight machines to compete with the British. He accused Harley-Davidson of trying to force motorcyclists to buy the kind of machine it made and restraining the sale of any other kind of machine. In fact, however, Harley already had a middleweight motorcycle in the prototype stage and introduced it the following year.

The final matter to be taken up with Honda and Yamaha was their offers of assistance to the Milwaukee company. Both companies had previously proposed to sell advanced V-twin engines to Harley-Davidson, which lacked the capital to develop its own engines. These offers were still on the table, said the Japanese representatives.

Beals's answer was thanks, but no thanks. (He speculates that the Japanese were "playing nice" in an effort to forestall Harley's request for tariff relief—and, as he told colleagues later, he didn't feel he could "make love and war at the same time.")

September 1, 1982. Two days after Beals met with Honda and Yamaha, Harley-Davidson filed its petition with the International Trade Commission (ITC) for tariff relief under the 1974

Trade Act's Section 201—also known as the "escape clause." It was a last-ditch attempt, and prospects for success were bleak. The record on Section 201 was not encouraging: Out of 46 industries that had filed petitions, only 9 had been granted any protection, and that protection hadn't been very meaningful.

Despite these dubious odds, Harley-Davidson management believed it had no other choice but to go ahead with the appeal. It hoped that even if Harley-Davidson were turned down, the Japanese big four motorcycle makers would be sufficiently alarmed to voluntarily curb any aggressive marketing actions when the new season began in the spring of 1983.

In addition to reducing Japanese inventories, another objective for the petition was to get the Japanese makers to boost their prices so that Harley-Davidson could be more competitive. Harley-Davidson management believed that the Japanese were artificially depressing prices as part of their assault on the U.S. heavyweight motorcycle market.

November 30, 1982. The petition was heard in a cavernous hearing room of the ITC in Washington. All four Japanese manufacturers were represented by a single law firm. "Bad politics on their part," says Beals, "because it made it look like little Harley-Davidson against Japan, Inc."

Harley-Davidson's first hurdle was to prove that it was even eligible for relief under Section 201. The law protected industries, not individual companies. Therefore, Harley-Davidson had to show that it was an industry. Its argument: As the only U.S.-based manufacturer of motorcycles, it *was* the U.S. motorcycle industry.

That contention ran into a snag because both Honda and Kawasaki were making motorcycles in U.S. plants. According to the ITC's commissioners, *they* were also part of the U.S. motorcycle industry!

Harley-Davidson's representatives were devastated. This decision seemed to completely destroy their argument that the U.S. motorcycle industry (meaning Harley-Davidson) had been grievously injured by Japanese imports. True, the American company's production had dropped sharply. But Honda's production at its Ohio plant more than made up for those losses.

So if Honda's plant was part of the U.S. motorcycle industry, overall production in the industry had not dropped and had not been injured by imports.

Fortunately for Harley-Davidson, the ITC's reasoning took another curious twist. The commission ruled that the U.S. motorcycle industry *could* be threatened by increasing imports— even though that industry included Honda and Kawasaki.

Although Harley found it more than passing strange to say that Japanese plants in the U.S. were threatened by their own imports, it certainly didn't argue with the ITC's reasoning.

On the other hand, the position of the Japanese representatives at the ITC hearings was, "Who, us?" They did their best to play down any role they might be having in Harley-Davidson's troubles.

"Some of their arguments were really off the wall," one observer recalls. "For example, they said that because Harley's smallest motorcycle was a 1000cc, their 750cc bikes weren't competitive. That drew smiles, but when they topped that by saying that none of their motorcycles competed with Harley-Davidson because Harleys were so different, the commissioners laughed out loud."

Throughout the hearings, Harley-Davidson made it clear that it was not looking for a handout or a free lunch.

"We do not intend to prohibit the Japanese from competing in the American market," Beals testified, "nor are we asking for any kind of financial support from our government. We are only seeking a fair and stable market in which to compete. We recognize the seriousness of the problems the Japanese have created for themselves, but we are determined that they should not become America's problems."

During this time, Harley's loyal supporters jumped at the chance to express their disenchantment with the Japanese manufacturers. Dealers, employees, and union affiliates across the country wrote letters to their congressional representatives. Some circulated petitions on Harley's behalf, and others went to Washington to testify.

Support also came from several members of Congress. The late Representative Clement Zablocki of Wisconsin told the Commission: "There probably is no other company in this country that has made such a substantial effort over such a wide area of operations as Harley-Davidson. As a result, the employees and management at Harley have virtually rebuilt the company from the ground up, making it a potentially strong and viable contender in the motorcycle market."

Added Senator Robert Kasten of Wisconsin (the first U.S. senator ever to testify before the ITC on behalf of an industry): "What has occurred here is a truly massive buildup of Japanese inventory that bears no relationship to U.S. market needs. . . . In essence, the Japanese motorcycle manufacturers—rather than laying off their own workers—are maintaining high levels of production and are exporting the bulk of that production to the United States. In other words, the Japanese are exporting unemployment, and that is not free trade."

Cutting Back: Tough Decisions in Milwaukee

The unemployment Senator Kasten was talking about had hit Harley-Davidson hard. At the end of 1980, the company had 4000 employees. By the end of 1982 it had 2200.

The first cuts came in January 1981, with a 5 percent layoff mainly intended to tighten up the organization. In September of that year, another tightening-up process resulted in similar cuts.

Then came the spring of 1982. When you make motorcy-

 PAIN AND SUFFERING

Harley-Davidson's stringent austerity program lasted for several years. In the spring of 1982, the company eliminated all matching 401(k) contributions, and in the fall the salaried work force took a 9 percent salary cut. In 1983, the unions gave up the 1 percent cost-of-living increase they had negotiated in 1980 and agreed to no increases at all in 1984. In York, Pennsylvania, production was reduced by more than 50 percent, and workers were laid off permanently. In Wisconsin, production was reduced by about 35 percent, and facilities were shut down for extended periods to minimize the number of workers on permanent layoff.

cles, you don't really find out how the year is going until spring-time, because retail sales are so small from November through February that you can't tell a good year from a bad year. In March, you usually start to see the trend.

Unfortunately for Harley that year, spring still hadn't come to the motorcycle business by the middle of May. Senior management realized that it had to make some drastic cutbacks.

Toward the end of May, Harley-Davidson management met with its unions in all plants and told them that substantial financial concessions were necessary if the company was to survive. Their first reaction, of course, was "Let's see your books." When they saw the grim figures, they realized that Harley's problems were real.

In addition to negotiating contract extensions with no increases, the company laid off more than 40 percent of its employees. This was particularly tough, because, as one senior manager says, "We were not dealing with marginal people, we were dealing with the heart of the business. Although many of the terminated employees were young, we also had to terminate employees in their fifties who had joined the company right out of high school and were doing a credible job. But not to have addressed this problem would have meant risking the other 60 percent of the jobs in the company."

Along with plant employees, salaried employees were hard hit by the layoffs. Those who remained took on heavier work loads while enduring pay cuts.

No restrictions were placed on the Harley-Davidson managers who selected employees for layoff, except to be fair and equitable and keep the people who were essential to the future of the business.

With the massive layoffs of their members, it was small wonder that the union heads of both Harley-Davidson plants supported the petition for tariff relief, and one union leader went to Washington with Vaughn Beals to testify before the ITC.

"Essentially, we all had our backs to the same wall," Beals says, "and they fully appreciated the competitive position the company was in. It was us against the Japanese, and in that situation there was no time for internal squabbling."

Now there was nothing for them to do but go back to

Milwaukee and wait for the ITC's decision, which would not come for months. Meanwhile, Harley-Davidson was living on borrowed money from Citicorp—and the bank was becoming increasingly apprehensive about lending it more.

Invasion of the Tariff Busters

Two months later came good news: The ITC ruled that a massive buildup of unsold Japanese heavyweight motorcycles in the U.S. posed a serious threat to Harley-Davidson. The ITC recommended to President Reagan that substantial, temporary tariffs be imposed on imported motorcycles that were 700cc's or bigger. This, said the ITC, would allow Harley to recover from its injuries and give it time to complete a comprehensive program to fully compete with the Japanese.

On April 1, 1983, Ronald Reagan agreed by signing off on the ITC's recommendations. The size of the tariff was a shock to the Japanese bike makers. For the first year, it was 45 percent—and that was tacked on to the existing 4.4 percent. The tariff was to decline to 35 percent in the second year and to 20, 15, and 10 percent in the last three years before 1988, when it was scheduled to expire.

Harley-Davidson was also surprised by the unprecedentedly heavy tariffs, in view of the anemic protection that had been granted in previous Section 201 cases. The most common explanation was that Reagan intended the tariffs to be a warning to Japanese car makers that they were vulnerable to similar action.

But the sizable tariffs looked much better on paper than they worked out in actuality. Stung, the Japanese bike makers reacted swiftly with a concerted counterattack. They quickly downsized their 750cc engines to 699cc's, thus evading the tariff by one cubic centimeter without drastically weakening the power of their heavyweight models. The motorcycle press dubbed these new models "tariff busters."

At first, Harley-Davidson was skeptical that the Japanese had actually reduced their engine sizes. It bought one or two of the new versions just to make sure the engines really did shrink and not just the nameplates, but measurements showed that the changes were genuine.

The incredible shrinking engine eliminated about half the value of the tariff to Harley-Davidson. Then, in another apparent ploy to evade the tariff, Honda and Kawasaki began assembling many more heavyweight bikes in their U.S. plants (Harley had lost its bid to have the tariff applied to power trains, as well as to finished motorcycles, which meant that the Japanese could bring in the larger engines and transmissions without paying extra duty and use them in motorcycles assembled in their U.S. plants).

That left only Yamaha and Suzuki models over 1000cc's subject to the tariff, and these companies were allowed to bring in from 7000 to 10,000 of these heavyweight bikes before they had to start paying the extra duty.

Still, the Japanese motorcycle industry was not satisfied. Yamaha and Suzuki were particularly unhappy with the high tariff because they had no U.S. plants. To bring about a reduced tariff, the Japanese Ministry of International Trade and Industry made an unusual proposal to the U.S. Trade Representative's office. Basically, it was an attempt to buy off Harley-Davidson with a multimillion dollar loan in exchange for reduced tariff rates. Harley's owners took the offer seriously, because they desperately needed working capital. But after extensive discussions in Washington, no agreement could be reached and the deal drifted away.

Disappointing as the tariff results were to Harley-Davidson, one of its important objectives was accomplished, that of stopping the escalation of U.S. inventories by the Japanese and forcing the Japanese to liquidate the large stock of motorcycles already on hand in dealers' showrooms and warehouses. However, even this was not an unalloyed benefit, because the liquidation inspired drastic Japanese discounting. For example, brand-new Yamaha Viragos—Harley look-alikes that were eating away at Harley sales—were being knocked down from $3000 to $1500. Even though these were not current models, the sharp discounts put Harley-Davidson at a serious price disadvantage.

It began to dawn on Harley-Davidson management that beating the Japanese at their own game would require a lot more than adopting their superior manufacturing methods.

chapter 8

Refocus

H aving evened the playing field in manufacturing and engineering, Harley-Davidson now realized it had to shift its focus to marketing. Through the seventies and early eighties, Harley-Davidson had been a technically driven company. It knew what it had to do without the benefit of customer feedback: fix the oil leaks, the vibration, and the generally low quality of its product. It took the market for granted, because in the seventies motorcycle boom it could sell all the machines it could make.

Harley's marketing shift began in the early 1980s when the motorcycle market went into the tank and Harley realized it had to listen to what customers wanted, rather than telling them what they wanted, as it had in the past. But how to do it?

Throwing Out Lines of Communication

Harley could no longer afford even an occasional product bomb such as the Cafe Racer. But neither could it afford extensive formal market research. It needed alternative methods to find out what its customers wanted.

Some say the turning point in customer communications came in 1983 with an industry first, the formation of the Harley Owners Group (that's right, H.O.G.). Staffed by Harley-Davidson, H.O.G. creates riding activities in every region and has become a powerful two-way medium for sounding out customer views and delivering Harley messages. At this writing, it has almost 100,000 members and its own bimonthly publication, *Hog Tales*.

"H.O.G.'s primary goal is to develop a long-term bond with our customers," says Kathleen Lawler-Demitros, vice president of marketing. "We try to run our business by the maxim 'the sale begins *after* the sale.' H.O.G. is one of the ways we differentiate Harley-Davidson from our Japanese competitors."

This appears to be so. Harley's leading competitor, Honda, tried to emulate the Harley owner's club, but its customer group soon faded away. Presumably, the same kind of camaraderie among Honda owners did not exist.

Still another program that brings Harley-Davidson closer to its customers involves individual officers and managers—and their spouses—in the organized "rides" and motorcycle events that Harley-Davidson and H.O.G. sponsor almost every weekend of the year from April to November.

Riding the product with their customers is something that Japanese executives don't do. Lawler-Demitros believes that the obvious enthusiasm that Harley managers take in riding and talking with customers gives the company a distinct "persona." She says, "It humanizes the company and not only gives customers direct access to the Harley family, but also it allows them to *feel* like one of the family. And we try to build on this feeling by letting them hear from us two or three times a year—no hard sell, just friendly letters—with invitations to events and other nonpushy reminders that we're thinking of them."

Both Harley-Davidson's product strategy and its strategy for staying close to the ultimate customer—the rider—are well-grounded on an understanding of rider feelings and what the potential Harley customer is looking for in a motorcycle.

"Buying a Harley is an emotional transaction," says Jim Paterson, president of the Harley-Davidson motorcycle division. He says, for example, that Harley's market share in southern states is smaller than it is in northern states, because in the South motorcycles are more often bought as practical transportation. Harleys sell best in the northern states where you can ride only six months a year, because customers aren't buying transportation, they're buying a riding "experience."

THAT EMPTY FEELING

When Rich and Ann Teerlink were invited—for the first time—to go on a big ride with a group of customers, they were well into the trip before Rich realized that he had forgotten to fill up the gas tank (a common lapse among novice bikers). Since Rich was a Harley-Davidson VIP, he and Ann had been asked to lead the ride, so corporate credibility was clearly at stake. They made it. Barely. Corporate stomachs, however, were reported to be in knots the size of baseballs.

"That's key," Paterson says, "because Harleys don't give you all the comforts of home. What they give you is an intensely exhilarating experience. That's also why we made a mistake when we once tried to target riders of the Honda Gold Wing, a large touring bike. We got nowhere, because most of these riders like the smoothness, comfort, and silence of the Gold Wing. That's not the Harley 'experience' or the experience that Harley riders want."

Slash the Ad Budget? Is That Any Way to Goose Sales?

In 1984, Jim Paterson (then corporate vice president and controller on loan to the marketing department) took a "marketing crisis-management team" of four people to a meeting site far from the day-to-day business pressures at Milwaukee headquarters. There, in two weeks of almost nonstop meetings, the team hammered out a low-cost, short-term strategy for reversing Harley-Davidson's declining market position.

Even short-term, it won no kudos from defenders of space advertising with its recommendation to slash 1985 advertising expenditures from $1.2 million to a mere $180,000. After all, Harley's Japanese competitors were putting plenty of money into advertising that was effectively pulling in nonriders who became first-time buyers—of Hondas and Yamahas, not Harleys. The Japanese were selling their Harley look-alikes with ads that stressed a tough, macho image, featuring riders in black leather tooling down dark alleys. Could Harley really afford to pull out of the media competition?

The crisis-management team's answer was yes, at least temporarily. If Harley-Davidson had to get closer to the customer—which everyone agreed was essential—one customer it had to get closer to was the Harley dealer who bought the product at wholesale prices. This kind of closeness costs real bucks—of which there were none. Hence, the recommendation was to scuttle the 1985 advertising budget and use those funds to increase the field sales force by 50 percent and also to appoint a dealer-relations manager to help solve problems and resolve differences between dealers and the company as they arose.

Why concentrate on improving dealer performance at the expense of advertising? In marketing its product, Harley-Davidson, more than most manufacturers, depends on its dealership network. You can even say that the dealers are the foundation of its business. Buying a motorcycle for thousands of dollars is not like buying a tube of toothpaste. It's not a commodity. In the nadir of the company, when Harley's competitors were selling higher-quality products for lower prices than Harley, it was often the Harley dealers' enthusiasm (and willingness to fix the bikes that arrived from the factory in bad shape) that made the difference in whether a potential customer bought a Harley or went off to a Yamaha or Honda dealer.

Back in the booming market conditions of the 1970s, some industry observers say, *all* you needed to succeed as a Harley dealer was "enthusiasm," but beginning in the 1980s, it was no longer enough. It certainly was no substitute for good business savvy: Harley dealers had to start making it in a highly competitive, maturing market that was also sensitive to economic downturns and high interest rates.

So when Harley-Davidson decided it had to level the playing field in marketing as it had in manufacturing and engineering, it was mindful that the field of combat would now include the retail outlets. That meant that Harley dealers had to become sophisticated marketers who could keep up with changing market conditions.

Harley hoped that by paying greater and closer attention to helping dealers sell product and make money it could raise the level of wholesale shipments to dealers. The pressing need for this was confirmed by the successes—and failures—of Harley's first SuperRide program.

Look Ma, No Oil Puddle

One of Harley-Davidson's marketing problems was that although the Harley motorcycle had improved greatly in quality,

---

 THE HARLEY OWNER'S CUSTOMER PROFILE

Harley owners tend to have higher education and income levels than other motorcycle owners have. They are also somewhat older.

	Harley-Davidson	Industry Total
Median age	34.4 years	29.6 years
Median household income	$35,700	$22,500
Male	95%	90%
Married	57%	49%
Occupation		
Blue-collar	53%	55%
White-collar	40%	31%
Education		
High school graduate	90%	75%
Some college and/or degreed	44%	38%

Some additional information about Harley customers:

- About half of all new Harley-Davidson sales are to people coming off other brands.

- More women are participating in motorcycling. This shows up in sales of the Sportster 883, 9 percent of which are to female riders.

- Harley-Davidson owners remain brand-loyal. Eighty-two percent of current owners have previously owned one or more Harleys.

it didn't look any different because the company wanted to retain its classic styling. So riders figured if it looked like a Harley, it must shake and leak like a Harley. This impression needed to be corrected if Harley was to bring its disenchanted fans back into the fold. The answer that Harley-Davidson and its ad agency, Carmichael-Lynch, came up with was the SuperRide program.

SuperRide offered potential buyers demonstration rides on Harleys at various motorcycle events and its 600-plus dealerships. Launched with TV commercials, the three-weekend event ran demo rides at every Harley dealership in the country and gave 90,000 rides to 40,000 people, half of whom were riding competitive brands.

The program had been set up carefully, with every dealer getting a full day of training in sales techniques, a detailed plan on laying out the shop for the event, and complete instructions on conducting the SuperRides. But of the 40,000 potential customers who took rides, not enough bought Harleys to cover the $3 million investment in the program.

A little first-hand research suggested why. While the SuperRide program was running in Milwaukee, a Harley executive hopped on his motorcycle and visited all four local Harley dealers one Saturday afternoon. When he got to the first store at about 2:30 it was closed. The second store was just about to close. The other two stores were open and busy, but in only one were the demo rides well-organized.

Says Jim Paterson, "That first SuperRide taught us that although we had no trouble bringing people into the dealerships to try out the product, we obviously needed to do a lot of work on closing sales." (Harley's decision to put its marketing chips on getting closer to its dealers was further reinforced by a dealers' revolt that began in 1984, which we'll discuss in the following chapter.)

Today, Harley-Davidson is well-established as "the demo ride company" and SuperRides are such successful sales generators that Harley has a fleet of demo bikes traveling regularly to all motorcycle rallies so that potential customers can try out the Harley motorcycles they desire and tell Harley staff members (drawn from every echelon of the company) what they think of them.

Even the first SuperRide program, although a failure in terms of immediate sales, had a long-range payoff: It showed potential buyers that Harley quality was back, and many participants did choose Harley when they were ready to buy a motorcycle one or two years later.

Product Strategy: Giving Customers a Choice

Now that it was becoming a customer-driven organization, Harley-Davidson learned from listening to its customers that it couldn't continue putting out two or three standard models and still compete with the Japanese big four, which seemed to be introducing new models every other week. So Harley assembly lines began rolling out a broad variety of models (Sportsters, Super Glides, Low Riders, Softails, Sport Glides, Tour Glides, Electra Glides) in an assortment of vivid color combinations ranging from Brandywine and Crimson to Cobalt Candy Blue.

As Michael J. Kami points out in *Trigger Points* (p. 21), an incredible variety of choices for consumers is necessary today.

> Just a few years ago, Coca-Cola sold two cola drinks: Coke and Tab. Today the company markets new Coke, Coca-Cola Classic, caffeine-free Coke, diet Coke, caffeine-free diet Coke, cherry Coke, diet cherry Coke, and Tab with and without calcium, and these products come in cans, glass bottles, and plastic bottles for a total of at least 42 permutations. . . . Henry Ford's successful formula that "You can have any color car you want as long as it's black" is deader than a doornail.

Like Henry Ford and his black cars, Harley-Davidson also had started out with one color: gray. Although Harleys in colors made their entry in the 1930s, the company was still producing only two basic heavyweight models late into the sixties: a touring bike and the Sportster muscle bike. Although customers bought the two standard models, they wanted more distinction in their motorcycles. This desire generated a new business: "chopper shops" that sprang up to provide individual touches to the basic Harleys.

It had taken years for Harley to realize that the money riders spent customizing their bikes—none of which went to the Milwaukee company—was money they would be willing to put into new bikes that had modifications built in right at the factory. As mentioned earlier, it was not until 1971, under the guidance of Harley stylist Willie G. Davidson, that factory custom models began to appear in Harley showrooms, starting with the Super Glide.

The Super Glide was a creative combination of existing parts which produced a motorcycle that had the classic Harley look. It wasn't a market leader but a market follower—a production version of what riders were already doing to modify their motorcycles. It is interesting to note that the differences among Harley models are subtle and, in fact, invisible to a nonmotorcyclist, who would be hard put, for example, to see any difference between the Harley Low Rider and the Harley Low Rider Custom: wire wheels, relocated instrumentation, handlebars at a different angle. But these minor modifications are of major importance for Harley riders. As a Harley catalog puts it: "The Low Rider Custom is not like everything else. It's as distinct as a signature. Which is why it's worth more than all the rubber stamps in the world."

Harley-Davidson has not become an innovation-driven company; its model changes still come gradually, not in rapid succession. The name of the game was and still is tradition, and the Harley philosophy is neatly summed up in the name of the improved engines it introduced in 1983: *V² Evolution*.

"Whenever we design a customized bike," says Jerry Wilke, vice president of sales and marketing, "we always grab something from Harley history. We can borrow from our own history—our major competitors don't have any history to borrow from."

Harley has learned that to keep its loyalist core of riders it must be sensitive to their demand for the legendary Harley look. In fact, to cater to that demand, the company has recently introduced "nostalgia" bikes, based on the beloved models of yesteryear. A typical nostalgia bike is the Heritage Softail which, as the catalog describes it, "wraps the glorious style of the '50s Hydra Glide around a thoroughly modern Harley-Davidson."

LEARNING A LESSON THE HARD WAY

In the mid-1970s, Harley-Davidson received a lot of complaints on its Sportster model—not enough power, poor handling, etc. Based on these complaints, Harley designed a radically improved Sportster and introduced it in the 1979 model year. When members of the Harley-Davidson Dealers Advisory Council saw it, they fell in love with the improved Sportster and ordered a lot of them.

Unfortunately, they were just about the only ones who loved the new Sportster. The customers took one look at it and the market share for that product line dropped 50 percent overnight.

The only good thing the 1979 Sportster did for Harley was to clean out its carryover stock of 1978 models. The customers decided that the 1978s were the last of the real Sportsters.

The problems with the 1979 model were as follows:

- The power increase came from a "Siamese exhaust," which "didn't look like a Harley."
- The softer seat came from more padding that meant a higher seat, which "didn't look like a Harley."
- The better handling came from greater shock "travel" that also produced more daylight between the bottom side of the fender and the top of the wheel, which "didn't look like a Harley."
- The old design had a hot-oil tank protruding from the right side of the motorcycle, which always interfered with the rider's leg (and sometimes overheated it), while the new design tucked the oil tank neatly under the seat and concealed it with a gracefully designed cover. This "didn't look like a Harley," either.

To sum it up, Harley customers thought the whole bike looked like a Japanese design—and they didn't want it.

Harley people say it was the fastest scrambling they've ever done: They took out the seat padding, cut the shock travel down, replaced the Siamese exhaust with classic pipes, and uncovered the oil tank.

And the customers loved it. Harley recovered its sales and learned a lesson it has never forgotten: If you make a radical change, keep the old when you introduce the new. When customers accept the new, take away the old.

The principle has served Harley well ever since.

However, in the mid-1980s Harley knew it couldn't survive on tradition and nostalgia alone. The challenge it still faced was to expand its customer base beyond the intensely loyal but static group of dedicated Harley riders. In a flat heavyweight motorcycle market, it had to get riders off their Japanese machines and into the Harley family. That's why Harley's marketing crisis-management team made the decision to concentrate on helping its dealers develop the up-to-date business skills they needed to sell more motorcycles and accessories.

But Harley's first efforts in that direction were poorly handled and resulted in an acrimonious dealers' revolt that came close to killing the program to improve dealer performance.

chapter 9

Revolt

No one thought it would be easy. Many Harley-Davidson dealers were motorcycle riders first, business people second. They didn't like to be told what to do. But no one predicted it would be as rough as it was.

Vaughn Beals, in particular, was firm in the resolve to move quickly to establish more uniform standards for dealers, improve their business skills, and push them toward smarter marketing efforts, on the grounds that "when you run a McDonald's franchise, you do it McDonald's way. If you don't like arches, you don't run a McDonald's. To get national identity, you have to give up some freedom."

Beals fired the opening salvo of this campaign in August 1983 at the company's dealer meeting held annually to announce the next year's models. The Harley dealers waited expectantly for news about the models they would be selling in 1984, unaware that they were also in for a stern lecture on their marketing deficiencies.

Before chastizing them, however, Beals gave credit where it was due by thanking them for sticking with the company through the troubled late seventies and early eighties. Indeed, most dealers had gone the extra mile for Harley when quality was poor and sales were dropping. They had agreed to buy motorcycles from the factory even when their inventories were already high. They had spent many hours servicing problematic new machines so that they could be sold. Without their loyalty, Beals told them, Harley-Davidson probably would no longer exist.

But that was about the last nice thing he had to say. He then lambasted them for failing to keep up with changing market conditions and pointed out the shortcomings of some dealers:

- They weren't cultivating new riders and Japanese-brand riders; instead, they were catering exclusively to the hardcore Harley loyalists. They would have to reorient their thinking and sales approach: There aren't enough Harley loyalists to support us, so we have to both keep our old customers with our traditional products and reach out to new customers with new products.

- Dealers were perpetuating the bad-guy image of Harley riders: Some of the stores were run-down, located in unsavory neighborhoods, and had a hard-core biker atmosphere—scarcely calculated to make a potential customer want to visit a Harley dealer with his wife and kids in tow.

- They treated riders of Japanese brands with contempt. Potential trade-ins were being lost every time a prospective customer was told to take his "Jap crap" down the street. "If the customer walks through the door and is not welcomed or is outright insulted for owning a Japanese bike, you've lost a sale."

After delivering these brickbats, Beals laid it right on the line:

Now, we must—and will—insist on your full cooperation and support as we work to achieve our common goals. We will insist that *all* our stores meet our standards for proper atmosphere, where *all* are welcome and made to feel comfortable. We will insist that they are properly stocked . . . that they offer showroom sit-ons and demo rides, and take trades. And that the products are properly promoted.

We will first try to do it by persuasion and training—by making sure that you fully understand our common goals and direction. But rest assured, we will do it. Our future—and yours—makes it mandatory!

TICKET TO THE *REAL* FRANCHISE

Harley dealers, criticized for not cultivating new riders, believed that part of the blame lay with the company: It lacked an entry-level bike that would entice first-time buyers, who tended to break into motorcycling with less expensive Japanese makes. Harley's large, heavy machines could be intimidating to new riders—especially women. And buying a Harley required a considerably bigger investment than buying a Japanese machine.

Harley dealer John Brinkworth summed up the problem this way: "All of these years, we didn't have an entry-level motorcycle, which the Japanese did. So if a guy was going to buy a Harley, he had already been a rider and knew what he wanted. But we couldn't get the first-year rider to walk in the door."

In 1985, Harley responded to this problem: It repositioned its 1000cc XLH Sportster as its entry-level bike by downsizing it to a smaller 883cc V^2 engine and pricing it to compete with entry-level Japanese machines. With a few other modifications, it became the ticket into the *real* motorcycle franchise because it was easy to handle (which attracted more first-time riders) and had an engine that was large but not overpowering. Best of all was the price, which was reduced from $4695 to $3995—less than half of what the Sportster's big brothers cost and price-competitive with comparable Japanese machines.

Lacking the capital to develop a new motorcycle from scratch, Harley had in a sense put a new product on the market with minimal expense, simply by incorporating the new V^2 engine into an existing product, repositioning it, and getting buyers to look at it in a different way. In 1987, the company introduced another innovative promotion: When Sportster owners wanted to move up to a larger 1340cc Harley (for around $8000 to $13,000), they could trade in the smaller motorcycle for its full original purchase price. This promotion drove home a key competitive advantage that Harley had always enjoyed over its Japanese competition: traditionally high resale value.

The repositioned Sportster was an instant success. Now Harley-Davidson's best-selling model, it has been a springboard for many riders who have moved up to larger Harleys.

Beals's strong words certainly did not leave Harley dealers in a good mood, but what happened next had them fuming. A Harley speaker announced a new marketing effort called the "Bonus Bucks" program. At first, the dealers were pleased by what they heard: the name sounded good and their impression was that they would be getting an additional 5 percent profit margin on motorcycles they sold over a certain number. But when they understood what the program really involved, they were beside themselves with anger.

Most Harley managers say that the Bonus Bucks program was poorly explained—but they also say that Harley had under-estimated the dealer reaction and that a better presentation would have made no difference. For what Harley had decided to do was to *cut* its dealers' profit margins by 5 percent on all of Harley's big 1340cc V-twins. But, the company told its dealers, you can earn that 5 percent back by taking part in our programs designed to improve your sales and your skills: test rides, advertising, stocking levels, sending personnel to service schools. So you will not only enjoy the same margins you had before, but you will also be improving your operation and stimulating more sales that will actually *raise* your profit.

Dealers saw it differently: what they used to get for no extra effort they would now have to work for. A large number of dealers refused to buy it. Dealer relations worsened rapidly in the months after the meeting. "Those days when you knew you were going to meet with the company the first thing you did was buy some Rolaids," says one dealer. "The Bonus Bucks program was tearing the dealer network apart."

Literally. In a revolt against the program and other Harley-Davidson policies, 32 dealers broke away from the company-sponsored Dealers Advisory Council (DAC) and formed their own dissident group: the National Harley-Davidson Dealers Alliance. According to the Alliance's opening announcement, it was formed to "present a challenge to questionable decisions. of the Harley-Davidson Motor Company that could possibly undermine the very economic foundation of America's sole surviving motorcycle company."

The new Alliance even took a page from Harley's new materials-as-needed (Harley's name for just-in-time inventory) system by announcing a program of their own: Motorcycles as

Needed. Complaining that their inventory levels of new Harleys were too high, the Alliance dealers wrote to their fellow dealers: "We all know that the company is manipulating its Initial Order program to increase your early ordering to force you to comply with franchise requirements. Many dealers have told us they are taking nothing more than they actually *need* to carry them through the winter. . . . As far as we are concerned, we're tired of factory indifference and bullheaded programs, and we recommend that dealers make their own business decisions."

Harley-Davidson management made immediate attempts to mend the breach. Three weeks after the revolt began, the company convened a "let it all hang out" meeting of both the renegade Dealers Alliance and the company-sponsored DAC. The protesting dealers were not shy about expressing their grievances. First, they called the DAC a puppet of the company because it was appointed, not elected.

"To say we were puppets just wasn't true," says John Brinkworth, a dealer in Buffalo, New York, who has served on the DAC since 1980. "Contrary to what a lot of dealers think, the DAC did not agree to the Bonus Bucks program. In fact, we hated it, because it meant dealers had to jump through a whole bunch of hoops before they could get the 5 percent margin that the company was holding back."

Beals told the renegade Dealers Alliance that he would agree to make the DAC an elective organization. But he refused to restore the reduced profit margins. He insisted that if Harley-Davidson were to survive and prosper, its dealers had to change their ways. If they didn't, they and the company would all go down the drain together. Giving dealers the opportunity to earn back the reduced profit margins by improving their marketing was Harley's way of telling them to shape up or ship out.

"We require clearer standards, more factory training for dealers, an intense communication effort between the factory and the dealer," Beals told the recalcitrant dealers. "And sooner or later it will mean that those dealers who can't or won't meet the standards will have to make some new career plans."

Some dealers accepted this blunt talk, but others persisted in their complaints that the new owners of Harley-Davidson had cut dealer profit margins to line their own pockets. This accusation put Harley management in a dilemma. By showing the dealers Harley-Davidson's financial statements since the buyout, it could easily demonstrate that nobody in the company was getting rich at the dealers' expense. However, if it revealed how precarious things really were, it was afraid that most of its dealers would run for the hills.

In the end, even though as a private company it was not obligated to reveal these figures, Harley decided to produce them for senior officers of the Dealers Alliance. The data clearly showed that the company's financial situation was tenuous, although improving. This satisfied some dealers, but a hard-core nucleus was unswayed. To Beals's dismay, he learned that the renegade Dealers Alliance had not only taken its complaints to the union leadership at Harley, but had also informed Harley's lenders at Citicorp that "the company was screwing up."

Despite these hostile moves, apparent progress was made in reaching agreements on some of the issues. But in a Chicago meeting with the Alliance intended to ratify these agreements, it became painfully clear to the company that some Alliance members were intent on widening the gap rather than closing it. The meeting accomplished nothing.

Rather than trying to negotiate further with the Dealers Alliance, the company restructured the DAC to make it an elective organization. At its first meeting in Milwaukee, the newly elected council, which included some Alliance members, discussed the sticky issues with the Alliance members who attended, and once again there was optimism that the wounds had been healed.

Wrong. Shortly before the annual dealer announcement meeting to be held in Reno, Nevada, Dealers Alliance leaders circulated a letter with statements about Harley policies that Beals says were absolutely false—including a charge that the owners of Harley-Davidson had voted themselves a substantial bonus on top of their salaries. Believing that these statements were designed to disrupt the meeting and encourage loyal dealers to desert to the Alliance, Beals decided to tackle the situation head-on.

"To say the atmosphere at the dealer meeting was tense was a gross understatement," he recalls. "On the first night, I met with two of the Alliance directors and confronted them with the fact that untrue statements had been made over their joint signature. One disavowed the letter in front of the entire assembly of dealers and announced his resignation from the Alliance. The other disavowed the letter without resigning."

At the full meeting of dealers, Beals ran through the whole litany of problems he was having with Alliance leaders and charged them with circulating false statements about Harley-Davidson policies toward its dealers.

However, Beals's actions did little to stem the dealer revolt. By 1985, the Dealers Alliance claimed 300 members, and continued to publish letters disparaging Harley-Davidson management. According to a dealer survey conducted by the Alliance, 81 percent of the 300 respondents said they lacked confidence in that management.

Although the 5 percent cut in margins was the main bone of contention, personality conflicts between Vaughn Beals and some dealers did not help. According to one Harley manager, leaders of the Dealers Alliance found Beals overbearing. They were antagonized by what they called his "This is the way it's going to be, guys" approach and what they felt was his failure to listen to them.

"Vaughn had the right answers but not the right presentation," says motorcycle division president Jim Paterson. "You can't just tell someone who's been running a shop for 20 years that they don't know what the hell they're doing and then expect them to listen to what else you have to say."

After the Reno meeting, says Paterson, "Vaughn lowered his profile at future dealer meetings and we brought in some new faces." Harley also replaced its national dealer convention with a series of smaller, town-hall style get-togethers in a dozen different cities where dealers could, comfortably, question Harley senior managers on anything they wanted.

To help patch up the problems, Jim Marcolina, director of marketing development, was assigned to act as an ombudsman between Harley and its dealers. This signaled a major change in Harley's approach to dealer relations from confrontation and dictation to conciliation and two-way communication.

Marcolina immediately surveyed dealers to learn the depth of their problems with Harley. Much of the response was negative, but the survey was a start in convincing dealers that

Harley management wanted to know about the issues that were troubling them. And Harley addressed these issues by making modifications in the controversial Bonus Bucks program. A second survey in 1986 showed a definite improvement in relations with dealers, who now felt that Harley management was really listening to them. Marcolina himself visited dealers personally to listen to their problems—and even attended a Dealers Alliance meeting at which he heard a full panoply of complaints.

Gradually the Dealers Alliance weakened, and today it is primarily a social organization, with under 20 members. Dealers' improved sales and profitability have helped to soften their animosity, although they still complain. "But before they complained about having to take motorcycles they didn't need," says Marcolina. "Now they complain that we're not sending them *enough* bikes."

chapter 10

Hardball

C apital was always what Harley-Davidson needed more of, beginning with 1981, the year of the buyback, which was followed by a 1982 spring when motorcycles had failed to warm up with the weather and U.S. dealers had heavily discounted their Japanese machines.

Harley had ambitious plans for answering the Japanese onslaught, the centerpiece being new, improved products. Fresh models were waiting in the wings, as were state-of-the-art water-cooled engines. But bringing new products on stream takes big bucks, and debt-ridden Harley-Davidson had empty pockets.

Between 1981 and 1986, prospects for obtaining more capital were never bright. From almost the beginning of its relationship with its chief creditor, Citicorp, the company was in a state of "overadvance." It was borrowing money just to keep going—and to make payments on money it had previously borrowed.

Overadvance needs some explaining. Harley-Davidson's total line of credit was $100 million. However, it could only draw on this line according to the extremely conservative lending formulas Citicorp had imposed. And by early 1982, Harley-Davidson was already borrowing more money than the formulas provided; hence, the overadvance (for which Citicorp tacked on a fee of $5 million).

Bankers are understandably nervous about overadvances, because they entail lending a company more cash than the banking formulas say they should. That's risky and can lead to sleepless nights for the lenders. How does the bank get its money out of the deal if there's a downturn? On the other hand, what if the bank cuts off overadvance and the company goes under?

Citicorp's Jack Reilly, who handled the Harley account until 1984, says:

> Overadvance was always our main problem with Harley. When you're a collateral lender, every day that you fund losses you're in worse and worse shape on the loan. But Harley reacted very quickly to that by using just-in-time inventory to pull cash out of the business—so that even though they had significant losses, they were generating positive cash flow. That reduced our exposure and enabled us to go on financing them. Otherwise, I would have had to protect the interests of Citicorp stockholders by recommending drastic alternatives—even liquidation. But since Harley did move so fast and had a solid, long-range plan for turning around, I felt that our best bet was to work with them.

Nevertheless, the option of cutting off any more overadvance to Harley-Davidson was seriously discussed by Citicorp loan officers in late 1982. Because of the deteriorating economy and the declining motorcycle market, the company was suffering heavy losses and had requested a sizable overadvance that would give it $20 million over its agreed-upon credit line.

Considering Harley-Davidson's dire straits, refusing this request might have seemed to be the least risky course of action for Citicorp. In his review of the request, however, one of Jack Reilly's assistants, William Laughlin, argued against a cutoff and cited several reasons for recommending more overadvance for Harley-Davidson (although not as much as it requested):

- Without overadvance, Harley-Davidson would probably be forced to file a Chapter 11 bankruptcy petition. Unless it was able to reorganize successfully or find a purchaser—both highly unlikely outcomes—the company would go under, and Citicorp could take a bath. Also, just to close Harley-Davidson's plants and sell its assets would require a sizable overadvance in and of itself.

- Harley-Davidson's new owners had taken actions to revitalize the company that were "tough-minded, necessary, correct, and made promptly on their own initiative."
- In just a little over a year the company had cut its operating expenses while raising product quality levels: It had reduced its breakeven point 34 percent, from 53,000 units to 35,000. On a turnaround: "The jury is still out, but it is a reasonable bet that they will succeed. Management's performance to date warrants continued confidence."

Harley-Davidson got its overadvance, though less than it wanted, and at a special overadvance fee of $5 million in addition to the prevailing interest rate, then more than 20 percent.

But this was a tenuous thread of life at best. Like the sword of Damocles, a constant threat hung over the heads of Harley-Davidson's new owners: liquidation. At any point it chose, Citicorp could force the company to sell its assets and turn over the proceeds to its lenders. The bank could do this because Harley-Davidson was already in violation of loan covenants requiring it to maintain a minimum tangible net worth and to limit its pretax loss to a certain amount.

So Harley-Davidson headed into 1983 with Citicorp seemingly ready to provide the cash that the beleaguered company needed to stay alive. But the new Harley owners were also very aware that Citicorp kept a detailed plan in its files under the heading "Liquidation Scenario," which it could use to pull the plug at any moment.

Back in the Black

After staggering losses in 1981 and 1982, Harley-Davidson's revitalization efforts began to show up on the bottom line. In 1983, it had its first profitable year since the buyout from AMF. The following year was even better.

Moreover, Harley-Davidson's market share, after being decimated for five years, was on the upswing again. In the super-heavyweight class (850cc's and up), which Harley had owned until the Japanese invasion, its share rose from a low of 23.3 percent in 1983 to 26.9 percent in 1984. Its share of the heavyweight class (over 650cc's) improved from 12.6 percent in 1983 to 15.5 percent in 1984.

With these rising fortunes, things looked much rosier. Small wonder then, that no one at the company ever dreamed they were about to go through the worst survival crisis in Harley-Davidson's 80-year history.

Bankers Doing What Bankers Do

Despite those commercials of caring bankers showering happy loan applicants with bundles of money, sentimentality is not a major ingredient of banking culture. In 1984, Citicorp loan officers were not walking around in Harley T-shirts inscribed "Don't Let the Legend Die."

Not that bankers want to see their clients go out of business. But their reasons have nothing to do with preserving legends. Their worry is that if a client goes under, they won't recoup their loan. A company on the skids can't command much for its assets.

So when Harley was in deep trouble in 1981 and 1982—losing money both years—Citicorp kept it going with overadvance funds. Not to do so would have meant bankruptcy for Harley and a loan loss for Citicorp. In addition, Harley had a supportive senior loan officer in Jack Reilly during those years.

Then Harley had two profitable years in 1983 and 1984. It was catching up with Honda in super-heavyweight market share, improving its quality, reducing its breakeven, and marketing more aggressively. Ironically, that's when Citicorp started to become uneasy. There were four major factors involved:

- Since Harley was now making money and on the upswing, Citicorp figured it could get enough from selling the company's assets to pay off its loan. (As Harley's Rich Teerlink says, "In an LBO, your problems with the bank aren't when you're in difficulties—they're when you start to improve. That's when the bank gets tough.")

- After peering into their crystal balls, Citicorp economists decided that another recession was on its way and that Harley's basically blue-collar customer base would be hit hard.
- Citicorp was worried about the unlimited availability of competitive Japanese bikes once the protective tariff came to its scheduled end in 1988.
- Jack Reilly, Citicorp's supportive senior loan officer, left for another Citicorp division in 1984 and was replaced by Todd Slotkin, who showed very little confidence in Harley's future and who had been against the leveraged buyout deal when it was first proposed in 1981.

Vaughn Beals believes that bank relations took a turn for the worse with this replacement. Jack Reilly, while always looking out for the bank's interests, had been positive toward Harley's chances for recovery, based largely on his confidence in the Milwaukee management team. Todd Slotkin seemed to view Harley from a totally different perspective, one that emphasized the high risk Citicorp was taking in supporting a precariously situated company.

Moreover, there was poor personal chemistry between Vaughn Beals and the new man in charge. Beals's viewpoint was that although Slotkin may have sincerely believed there were solid financial reasons for his position, he also could have had career reasons: When the LBO had first been proposed, he had reacted negatively to it.

Rich Teerlink, who as Harley's chief financial officer at that time (he's now CEO) is credited by Vaughn Beals and many others for extricating Harley from its financial crisis, takes a dispassionate view of Slotkin's position.

> Bankers have a very simple philosophy—they want to be paid back for their loans. This particular banker took a strong position for himself personally and for his bank. He wasn't trying to be a partner with Harley the way Jack Reilly had. Reilly had taken a strong position for the bank, too. The difference was that when he had our account we were very shaky, and he had to support us or we would have gone under and Citicorp would have

taken a bath. When Slotkin took over, we were doing a lot better—and since he lacked confidence in our ability to weather the expected recession, he figured Citicorp should get out of the deal before that happened so its losses wouldn't be any bigger. That made sense, because if you're trying to get out of something you'd better do it while it's moving up.

Besides, says Teerlink, Slotkin certainly wasn't acting on his own. He was acting for senior management, which had said, "We don't want to be in that account." Teerlink sums up the episode this way:

> His was a prudent banker's judgment. The bank didn't see a favorable market for Harley motorcycles. It saw us as existing at the will of the Japanese, and if the Japanese motorcycle companies went after market share—which they tend to do when things get tough— what was going to happen to Harley?

Slotkin's predecessor, Jack Reilly, says, "Slotkin was looking to protect the interests of Citicorp—just as I was—but he had a different perspective." (Slotkin himself did not respond to requests for his own views.)

For whatever reasons, however, Citicorp precipitated a financial crisis for Harley-Davidson that Vaughn Beals likens to "standing on the edge of a cliff with one foot on a banana peel."

Pulling the Plug

In November 1984 Beals and Teerlink had lunch with one of Slotkin's assistants. What they learned killed their appetites. The message was ominous: Citicorp wanted Harley to look for another lender. Harley executives had heard this before, but this time it was backed up by a warning that Citicorp was reluctant to provide any more overadvance beyond early 1985. In other words, Citicorp wanted out.

That news generated shock waves. Cutting off overadvance with such short notice wouldn't just hurt Harley—it was

Harley-Davidson Chairman Vaughn Beals had never even been on a motorcycle when he joined the company in 1975—but he soon became a dedicated enthusiast. The black leathers are not for "image"—they just happen to be the most protective garb for motorcycle riding. (Chapter 4)

Harley-Davidson's legendary V-twin engine (top) was unique until Japanese "lookalikes" like this Yamaha Virago began appearing in the early '80s. (Chapter 6)

As vice president of engineering, former Yale professor Jeff Bleustein (right) built up an engineering department that helped to stem the Japanese tide by designing technologically competitive new products. Now senior vice president of parts and accessories, he's seen here talking to two Harley customers. (Chapter 4)

The first Low Rider model, designed in 1977 by Willie G. Davidson as a popular manifestation of the "Easy Rider" look. This model showed how Willie G. was able to create a new look with special paint and trim and relatively inexpensive modifications, which helped to keep the company going while it worked to get technically improved new products on stream. (Chapter 4)

Harley's vice president of styling, Willie G. Davidson (top), was right on target with his first "factory custom," the 1971 Super Glide. (Today the custom category is 45 percent of the company's volume.) But his innovative 1977 Cafe Racer (center) failed to catch on and was scrubbed after two years. (Chapter 4)

The Wide Glide was an example of how Harley-Davidson based its new designs on modifications being made on standard touring machines by riders. Features included a "Fat Bob" fuel tank, bobbed rear fender, and stepped seat with a "sissy" bar to make sure the passenger didn't get left behind when the throttle was turned on. (Chapter 4)

In the 1960s, Harley-Davidson tried to broaden its market with midrange, Italian-made Aermacchi motorcycles. Here, second-generation founding family members William J. Harley, Walter C. Davidson, and William H. Davidson inspect one of the imports. (Chapter 3)

For obvious reasons, Harley-Davidson's big touring motorcycles—like this Electra Glide Ultra Classic FLHTC—are known as "full dressers." Some models even have built-in stereo systems. The popularity of stripping and customizing Harley tourers led the company to develop new motorcycle models that were customized right at the factory. (Chapter 4)

Harley-Davidson executives and others rumble onto Wall Street for the ceremony that marked the company's listing on the New York Stock Exchange, July 1, 1987. (Chapter 11)

Late in 1986, Harley-Davidson acquired Holiday Rambler Corporation, maker of deluxe motorhomes and other products. (Chapters 11 & 14)

President Ronald Reagan visited Harley-Davidson's final assembly plant in York, Pennsylvania, after the company asked for the removal of protective tariffs he imposed on foreign motorcycle imports. (Reprinted by permission of The York Daily Record) (Chapter 11)

During Reagan's visit, Jerry Knackert, president of IAM Union Local 209, described Harley-Davidson's insourcing program, which brings work into Harley-Davidson's plants that was formerly done by outside suppliers. (Chapters 6 & 12)

After dealer relations hit bottom in the middle eighties, Harley began paying more attention to dealer problems—for example, by holding town-hall-style meetings in which Harley executives (here, left to right, Jim Paterson, Jeff Bleustein, Rich Teerlink, and Vaughn Beals) field questions from dealers. (Chapter 9)

To improve retail sales, scores of Harley dealers have invested in redesigning their stores and utilizing modern merchandising techniques. (Chapter 9)

By repositioning its Sportster model as an entry-level bike and reducing the price to a competitive $3995, Harley won a lot of first-time riders and converts from Japanese machines . . .

. . . and to increase the Sportster's appeal, a full price trade-in was guaranteed to any Sportster owner who moved up to a larger Harley. (Chapter 9)

**THANK GOD
THEY DON'T LEAK OIL ANYMORE.**

With this Carmichael-Lynch ad, featuring Malcolm Forbes's hot air balloon being flown over a crowd, Harley-Davidson made the point that Harley quality had been restored. (Chapter 8)

One of Harley-Davidson's strongest marketing fleet of Harley demo bikes that travels to mot events so that potential customers can get the riding a Harley. (Chapter 8)

Organized activities sponsored by the Harley Owners Group are part of Harley-Davidson's efforts to make motorcycles a way of life, not just a product. One activity is the Ride-In Show, which gives riders a chance to show off their "iron" and win prizes for the Best of Show in various categories. (Chapter 8)

(c)

(d)

(e)

(a)

(b)

Harley's "close to the customer" philosophy in action: (a) CEO Richard Teerlink (center), (b) engineering vice president Mark Tuttle, (c) sales and marketing vice president Jerry Wilke (left), (d) vice president and controller Jim Ziemer (center), and (e) styling vice president Willie G. Davidson (with his wife Nancy) talking motorcycles with Harley customers. Harley executives do this at motorcycle events almost every weekend of the riding season. (Chapters 8 & 13)

Senior vice president of operations Tom Gelb (right) was the driving force behind the radical changes in Harley-Davidson's manufacturing operations. Here he discusses a motorcycle part with Harley employee Dave Gurka. (Chapter 6)

With statistical operator control, Harley employees monitor their own quality and discover problems early on. (Chapters 6 & 12)

As vice president of marketing, Jim Paterson (center) helped Harley-Davidson shift its focus in 1984 from manufacturing and engineering to customer-driven marketing. He's now president of the Harley-Davidson Motorcycle Division. Paterson's wife Jodi (to his left) frequently attends motorcycle rallies and accompanies her husband on motorcycle trips. (Chapter 8)

After losing a large share of police-motorcycle business to its foreign competition, Harley once more dominates this niche. This is an FXRP Pursuit Glide ready for action. (Chapter 11)

Over the years, Harley-Davidson has raised millions of dollars for the Muscular Dystrophy Association. Here, Willie G. Davidson chats with MDA poster child Michael Kronick before the two leave together on the "Love Ride II" fund-raising event—with Michael in the sidecar of Willie's Harley. (Chapter 11)

Thousands of Harley owners rode to Milwaukee from all over the country to join the celebration of Harley-Davidson's 85th anniversary, which raised more than $600,000 for the Muscular Dystrophy Association. (Chapter 11)

Once in Harley Heaven, celebrants listened to rock bands and admired each other's motorcycles. (Chapter 11)

Harley-Davidson employees have contributed many quality-improvement suggestions to help the company's turnaround. Here, a quality circle presents its ideas to CEO Rich Teerlink. From left to right: Janice Biancuzzo, Robin Mather, Linda Dierking, Teerlink, Jim Airoldi, employee involvement administrator, Barb Badini, Kathy Gilbertson, Diane Stenberg, and Ruth Pemble. (Chapter 12)

This is just a sampling of the wide variety of official licensed products that help Harley-Davidson build on its name. Harley-Davidson licenses its name and logo to about 60 companies. (Chapter 13)

a death sentence. Despite its improving situation, it didn't have the cash to keep operating *and* pay off on its huge debt.

"Overadvance was our lifeline at that point," says Beals. "We had no hope in the world of living without it. Telling us we'd get no more overadvance was the same as telling us to hire some lawyers and prepare to file for Chapter 11."

Shaken, Beals and Teerlink appealed a few days later to Citicorp higher management. They got nowhere. It was pointed out that Citicorp had been trying for over a year to get them to secure refinancing, which they hadn't been able to do. Citicorp couldn't extend overadvance forever, they were told. Translation: We want you gone.

The situation looked black. But the LBO team wasn't going to go down easily. They had put too much sweat into saving Harley-Davidson from being wiped out by their competitors to now go under at the hands of their own bank without a struggle.

Their attempt to preserve Harley took two directions. First, they refused to take no as an answer from Citicorp—they kept arguing for their position. At the same time, they redoubled

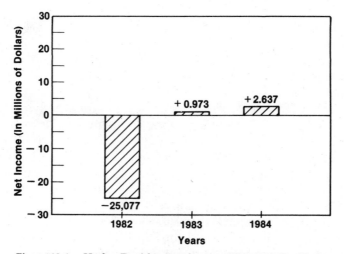

Figure 10-1.   Harley-Davidson net income 1982–1984. For Harley-Davidson and Citicorp, Harley's two profitable years in 1983 and 1984 were significant events, but for vastly different reasons. (Source: Harley-Davidson Motor Co.)

their efforts to seek refinancing from another lender. Recalls Beals:

> We tried to show Citicorp that not only were we doing much better, but that they were very well secured, even in the overadvance position. Their borrowing formulas were extremely conservative. They would lend us only 70 percent of our *manufacturing cost* of a new motorcycle, while other lenders were willing to advance the dealers 100 percent of their *purchase price*. And we ran some numbers to show that Citicorp and its partner banks were lending us only 13 cents for every dollar of retail sales value of our parts and accessories.

Despite Citicorp's desire to get out of the Harley account, however, in March 1985 it extended overadvance privileges for six more months. Only later did Beals and Teerlink realize that this was not the statement of faith in Harley-Davidson that it seemed. It was part of a strategy to *liquidate* the Milwaukee company in November.

Citicorp decided to hold off liquidating Harley immediately for reasons that were outlined in an internal report on the status of the Harley account dated January 25, 1985:

> The best two months of the year to commence a liquidation of Harley-Davidson are the end of April and the end of November. However, the threat of liquidation at this time would produce disastrous results for two reasons:
>
> (1) Management is not "processed" for an orderly liquidation. They believe that the company has "turned the corner" and are still shocked by the banking group's desire to terminate the relationship. The initial reaction to commencing orderly liquidation at this time would be most likely either a walkout (at best) or specific actions to damage the bank's position.
>
> (2) The company is profitable and expects to continue profitable at least through 1985. In addition to the lawsuits that would follow a liquidation in such a scenario, the moral issue could certainly be publicly exploited by management. Vaughn Beals, who often speaks publicly and who has appeared on several

television programs such as the Nightly Business Report, could well mount a public crusade against Citicorp, on behalf of Harley, American jobs, integrity, etc.

In the spring of 1985, all Beals and Teerlink knew was that Citicorp wanted to be rid of them and that a six-month extension of overadvance was not going to help them beyond the summer, when the off-season began and their capital requirements were highest.

As pressure mounted over the summer, Beals and Teerlink chased after other lenders with increasing desperation. But they were in a Catch-22 situation because it was well known that Citicorp was trying to get rid of the Harley account.

From one potential lender after another came the same question: "Why does Citicorp want out?" As Beals remembers these meetings, they'd go this way:

> We'd give our presentation—go through the whole dog and pony show, which took about two hours. We'd show them three years of positive cash flow. Two years of positive earnings. Increasing productivity. Higher market share. Every measure of the business was positive. We'd get through that and the guy would look at you and say, 'Can you run that by again? We must have missed something.' And then would come the crusher: 'Why does Citicorp want out?'

Teerlink recalls that after numerous rebuffs based on that sticky question, he and Beals started to bring one of their other lenders to their presentations. When the inevitable question came up, they'd turn to their banker friend who would explain that it was just internal politics at Citicorp and not at all based on rational considerations.

The only problem with this strategy was that it didn't work. Potential lenders continued to be frightened off by Citicorp's reluctance to stick with Harley-Davidson, and time was running out for the beleaguered company.

Just how little time was left became apparent in September. The bank steadfastly refused to consider overadvance beyond October.

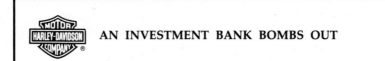

AN INVESTMENT BANK BOMBS OUT

In early 1985, Vaughn Beals and Rich Teerlink spent many hours walking up and down Wall Street talking to investment banks that could help them raise much-needed capital. They narrowed their choice to three firms: Lehman Brothers, Oppenheimer, and Dean Witter Reynolds. After finally selecting Lehman Brothers, they notified the others they were no longer interested in their services.

"Unfortunately," says Beals, "we made a poor selection. Our original contact had been with Lehman Brothers, and someplace in the middle of negotiations they became Shearson Lehman. In the resulting turmoil, I felt we didn't have their full attention. And we were such small potatoes in their world it seemed we only got help when they had some spare time."

When Shearson Lehman did pay attention, they advised Harley-Davidson to sell a side business that had been generating good income, that is, the business of making bomb casings for the Pentagon. Although Harley executives didn't think it could be done, they agreed to try, just to keep their bankers happy.

Ironically, Harley-Davidson ultimately secured refinancing through an investment bank they had originally rejected: Dean Witter Reynolds.

Several weeks later in Los Angeles, hundreds of motorcyclists were revving up their Harley hogs for a ceremonial ride from Los Angeles to New York to help raise $250,000 for the restoration of the Statue of Liberty in time for her 100th birthday the following year. In the vanguard were Vaughn Beals, Willie G. Davidson, and more Harley managers.

It was a joyous occasion. But it was not joy unconfined for the Harley executives, who knew that at the end of their 3000-mile journey they must make one last-ditch attempt to save their company from going under at the hands of the unsupportive Citicorp.

Two weeks later the parade of Harleys rumbled into New York City. After changing from black leather jackets to pinstriped suits, Vaughn Beals and Rich Teerlink met the next morning with Slotkin and his associates across a conference table at Citicorp's offices.

The atmosphere was tense as Beals and Teerlink tried to focus the discussion on their 1986 budget and their overadvance needs for that year—presenting reams of facts and figures that they felt bolstered their case. They might as well have been talking to the wall.

Discouraged, the two Harley executives took a break and wandered off to the men's room. Teerlink suggested that they try to break the impasse with a move that he had discussed with Beals some days before.

"Look," he told Beals, "if they want out so badly, maybe they'll take a write-off on part of the loan. Then we have a better chance of inducing another lender to come in."

Beals doubted that this would be acceptable to the bank. But it was obvious that they were getting nowhere with their present approach—they had no choice but to try a new tack.

Back in the conference room, Teerlink stated that if Citicorp were to take a $5 million write-off it might encourage another lender to refinance Harley so that Citicorp would recoup its loan.

To Beals's and Teerlink's astonishment, Slotkin hardly batted an eyelash, and Beals quickly raised the amount to $10 million. Again, Slotkin was amenable. "We won't say no to anything if it gets us out of the deal."

Citicorp would take a write-off. Beals and Teerlink believed that write-off would give them a more attractive proposition to present to potential lenders.

Wrong. Financially, the write-off was a good selling point. Psychologically, it was not. They quickly found that out when they went back to some lending institutions that had previously rejected them.

According to Beals and Teerlink, the problem was that these lenders all thought of Citicorp people as smart operators, and they said to themselves, "Well, if Citicorp is willing to take a $10 million write-off, Harley *must* be in a mess!"

Seven Days From Chapter 11

The situation in October 1985 was grim. Just how grim was revealed to Harley executives unexpectedly. Through an unrelated court discovery action they learned exactly what Citicorp had in mind for Harley.

Several years before, Harley-Davidson and Citicorp had become embroiled in a lawsuit and counterlawsuit with a third party. As a result of the discovery actions that ensued, Harley was given hundreds of pages of Citicorp memos, status reviews, projections, and strategic plans relating to the Harley-Davidson loan account, covering the years 1981 through September 1985. These documents confirmed that Citicorp had, indeed, been working toward the liquidation of Harley-Davidson—friendly liquidation, if possible, but liquidation nevertheless.

Clearly, the clock was ticking. There was no alternative; they had to prepare for the worst (accounts payable were stretching to six-week levels and creditors were getting testy). Harley executives agreed that unless they could obtain refinancing within a few weeks, they would be forced to file for protection under Chapter 11 by the first week in January 1986. Shortly after the meeting, Harley-Davidson hired bankruptcy counsel to prepare a filing plan.

Harley's only hope for refinancing seemed to be some interest shown by Heller Financial, Inc., a Chicago firm. Heller and Harley had been brought together late in the summer by Steve Deli, managing director of the Chicago office of Dean Witter Reynolds. (Because of his dedicated efforts to keep Harley-Davidson from going under, Deli is on the company's informal roster of "saviors.")

Major events often turn on chance. In this case, says Rich Teerlink, it may have been the fact that Heller's No. 2 man, Bob Koe, was a Harley buff that made the difference. He remembers a dinner at the Chicago Club, where Steve Deli first introduced him to Koe. They talked motorcycles, but Koe also probed hard for weak points in Teerlink's presentation of Harley's case. By the end of dinner, Koe was favorably impressed, and the stage was set for exploring a possible refinancing deal.

But time was extremely short for setting up a complex financial transaction involving many millions, four different banks, and a company that was struggling to make ends meet. By the time Heller and Harley had signed a letter of intent and Heller had done its "due diligence"—that is, investigated Har-

 **HEADS-UP THINKING**

To show Heller Financial's Bob Koe the extent of Harley's manufacturing turnaround, he was invited to visit the York, Pennsylvania, assembly plant. Koe was impressed by Harley's achievement in reducing costs while lifting quality levels. But, reports Steve Deli, the highlight of Koe's day was when he took a new Harley out on the test track behind the plant. However, says Deli, "To maximize the chances that Koe would survive until Heller could consider a refinancing deal, we insisted that he wear a helmet, even though he never wears one when he rides his own bike."

ley's background and financial reliability—it was almost Christmas. Under the proposed deal, Citicorp would be paid off after taking an $8 million write-off on its principal and withdrawing the $5 million overadvance fee, while the other three lender banks would stay in. But the deal had to be closed by year-end or Harley-Davidson was out of business.

December 23, Chicago. The scene was Heller Financial's offices. Despite the letter of intent and Heller's seemingly positive interest in the deal, there was still no commitment. Harley executives—including Beals, Teerlink, and operations vice president Tom Gelb—had gathered to make their final pitch.

The presentation to Bob Koe and Heller chief Norm Blake seemed to go well. Optimistic, the Harley executives retired to the offices of Dean Witter Reynolds to await Norm Blake's decision. But after two hours, it was nail-biting time. After another hour, they were sure that something bad, very bad, had happened.

They were right. A call to Bob Koe confirmed their worst fears. Despite Koe's efforts on Harley's behalf, Norm Blake had blown the deal out of the water, turned it down cold. Again it was that old bugaboo, the Citicorp write-off. Why was the bank so anxious to get rid of Harley-Davidson that it would forgo a large chunk of its loan? In addition, Blake was concerned that

Harley's asset base was not substantial enough to secure a loan and that Harley would never be able to pay off its long-term debt.

Teerlink recalls, "We just sat there. We were devastated. It looked like our last chance had just gone up in smoke." Steve Deli's secretary, Dawn Hardies, recalls that when she looked into the room their faces were so white she thought they had just learned of a death.

But they didn't give up—they had invested too much of their lives in saving Harley-Davidson to throw in the towel now. They decided to go back to Heller that afternoon to try and restructure the deal to make it more acceptable to Norm Blake.

It was only after Bob Koe went to bat for Harley that Norm Blake agreed to even sit down again. With Steve Deli acting as intermediary, the two sides bargained late into the afternoon. In the end, Blake consented to a deal. Moments afterward, Rich Teerlink headed for the door. He was four hours late for a family holiday dinner.

Blake's new terms were harsh: a 90-day demand note and less capital for Harley-Davidson at higher cost. But the Mil-

 DECISIONS, DECISIONS

Right before Christmas of 1985, on the brink of filing for Chapter 11, Harley-Davidson was scheduled to take two-thirds of its entire dealer network—approximately 1000 people—to Hawaii in January.

Dilemma: If Harley filed for Chapter 11, it clearly wouldn't be appropriate to send dozens of corporate personnel to Hawaii with the dealers. On the other hand, the travel expense had been prepaid and the dealers had earned the trip as part of an annual incentive program. It didn't seem right to ask them to cancel their trips.

Decision: Don't cancel. If worse comes to worst, send one or two people to represent Harley-Davidson.

This turned out to be the right decision—and it was a great party, for everybody.

waukee company had no choice. It was either take the less favorable deal or go belly-up.

Despite the new lease on life, the ordeal was not yet over. Under the terms of the agreement with Citicorp, the Heller deal had to be closed and the money from it transferred to Citicorp by the end of the year, meaning the end of the business day on December 31.

It was a cliff-hanger. According to Thomas Rave, vice president of First Wisconsin National Bank of Milwaukee, on Tuesday morning, December 31, Rich Teerlink showed up in his office in jeans and a flannel shirt to sit with him and make sure that the money moved from the various lenders and ultimately to Citibank to pay off Citicorp Industrial Credit.

Because it was the last business day of the year, wire transfer rooms were hectically busy—and Citibank planned to shut down its own wire room at noon to balance out the transactions and close the books on the year. Meanwhile, Citicorp informed Rave and Teerlink that if the money did not reach them, they would terminate the financing package at the close of business that day, which meant that Harley would have to file for protection under Chapter 11 or face liquidation of the business.

On that same Tuesday morning, Walter Einhorn, who had represented Mellon Bank East in Philadelphia in the transaction and had signed the credit agreement documents on behalf of that bank, couldn't find the people with authority to initial the outgoing wire transfers that were necessary to complete the refinancing.

Still sitting in Tom Rave's office, Teerlink got a telephone call from Heller Financing saying the deal would not close in time because Mellon Bank wasn't reaching the right people to sign off on the papers so the money could be transferred. And because it was New Year's Eve, Heller was shutting down early.

Teerlink persuaded Heller to stay open a little longer, and got on the phone to Einhorn to tell him how desperate the situation was. "He chased around until he got the signatures he needed. The money was transferred with just minutes to spare."

Reliving that day, Teerlink gives a sigh. "It was close, so close. But the deal went through, and we were on our way."

Although still heavily in debt and operating under restrictions from its new creditors, Harley-Davidson now had breathing room to pursue strategies that would both free it from these burdens and make it once more the world's leading manufacturer of super-heavyweight motorcycles. Ironically, it never would have been able to accomplish this if Citicorp hadn't forced it out. "Reluctantly, we've got to give Todd Slotkin one of our savior awards," says Teerlink.

chapter 11

Turnaround

W hy not go public?
Steve Deli of Dean Witter Reynolds, who had helped Harley secure the refinancing deal that saved it from extinction, posed that question to Rich Teerlink one spring day in 1986.

"I thought the idea was nuts," Teerlink says. "For one thing, we didn't have the confidence to go public—we didn't think we'd built that good a record yet. And it was sort of nice owning our own company."

Vaughn Beals also had grave misgivings. "There's no question we would have preferred staying private. And we'd still rather be private, for obvious reasons: You have a lot more flexibility in your operations, and your competitors don't know as much about your activities as they do when you're public. Also, we had just refinanced the company with Heller in December, and we thought that we could survive and prosper on our own."

But Deli was undeterred. And listening to his persuasive arguments, Beals and Teerlink began to see the cracks in their thinking. For one thing, their contention that Harley was its own company was not totally true. Technically, Harley-Davidson was its own company, but actually it was controlled by its debt. As Teerlink himself pointed out in an interview with *Motorcycle Product News*:

> We were an asset-based borrower. And when you are, you really don't have the complete right to manage your own business. Your lenders put in a significant number

of covenants as to how you should operate. Those covenants usually come to bear at the worst times. When things are tough is when the covenants start to crunch you and limit your decision-making ability.

Deli hammered away at the positive aspects of going public. He made three major points:

- Harley's turnaround gave it a strong, believable story to take to Wall Street.
- By going public, Harley could raise the kind of capital it needed to develop, manufacture, and market new products—and to do all these things sooner.
- Going public would actually give Harley *more* control over its long-term destiny in that it would no longer be driven by debt or shackled by lender covenants.

"When Deli told us he thought we could raise $65 million from the sale of stock and subordinated debt, we really paid attention," says Beals. "Frankly, had anybody but Steve Deli come in with these numbers we would have thought he was crazy. But since Steve had delivered the goods in the past, we trusted his judgment."

That trust was well-placed. When the results were in, the Harley-Davidson offering in June 1986 had raised $25 million more than Steve Deli had projected: $20 million in stock and $70 million in subordinated debt—on the same or better terms. Harley-Davidson was officially listed on the American Stock Exchange in June 1986 (one year later it moved to the New York Stock Exchange).

Looking back, Teerlink thinks Harley made the right decision. "What gave me particular pleasure," he says, "is that going public allowed the people who had helped us survive—employees, dealers, suppliers, and riders—to own 'a piece of the legend.' " Owning a piece of the legend has provided more than a sentimental reward for Harley fans. The stock, which initially opened at $11, was hovering around $30 at this writing. The company has received more than one letter from Harley enthusiasts who apologetically explained that after investing

WALL STREET RALLY, HARLEY-STYLE

When companies go on the New York Stock Exchange, the event is usually celebrated by a dignified luncheon. Not so when Harley-Davidson was listed on the NYSE in the summer of 1987. A Harley Heritage Softail motorcycle was displayed above the floor of the Exchange. The Harley flag flew outside. And a big motorcycle parade led by Harley executives rumbled down to Wall Street from 59th Street, escorted by New York City police officers also on Harleys. Along the way, they were joined by other Harley riders who happened along, some wearing far-out riding gear.

Several hundred bemused bystanders watched as the riders in the Harley contingent reached the Exchange, shut off their engines, and were officially welcomed to the Exchange by its president, John Phelan—the first time ever that this ceremony had been conducted on the sidewalk.

Only then did everyone troop into the Exchange for the traditional luncheon.

they later sold their stock at a profit and used the proceeds to buy a new motorcycle.

Citicorp also chose to relinquish *its* final piece of the legend by cashing in its 430,000 Harley-Davidson warrants, thereby reducing its total Harley-Davidson loss by $6 million.

Harley-Davidson's successful offering left it in an unaccustomed position with a pleasant problem to solve: Because the offering had done so much better than expected, the company would have a $50 million cash balance by the end of 1986. What to do with it?

Harley's investors and lenders hadn't provided it with excess cash so that Harley could become a bank, so management tried to figure out what to do with it that would be productive and profitable for the company. Steve Deli suggested a number of alternatives. The one that appealed most to Harley management was diversification.

"We had a strong need to diversify our revenue base," Beals says. "The motorcycle market was mature, and it had been eroding for two or three years as the boom generated by the Japanese continued to subside and consumers were presented with more leisure-time options. Although we were gaining share in the market, we knew that couldn't go on forever. We felt that by broadening the company's base we could build some stability to get us through future downturns."

The search for a logical acquisition began. After considering many industries, management narrowed the choice to two businesses: recreational vehicles and branded automotive aftermarket parts and accessories.

For three weeks Harley management considered possible candidates in these two fields. Then one day Rich Teerlink's morning mail included a large envelope from Steve Deli. Inside was a selling memorandum for Holiday Rambler, a private Indiana company that made deluxe recreational vehicles.

"I let it sit on my desk for quite a while," Teerlink remembers. "I kept telling myself, it's too big for us, much too big. We had planned on spending something around $50 million— and this was more than $150 million."

Like Teerlink, Beals didn't get too excited about Holiday Rambler. They were both unfamiliar with the recreational vehicle industry and lacked a perspective on Holiday Rambler's position in it. More homework was needed. But after several polite reminders, Steve Deli finally got their attention by pointing out that the first principle of buying a company is that you have to find one for sale. "This one's for sale!" Deli told them. "At least go and look at it."

After that, they agreed that Teerlink should fly out to Indiana to visit the motor-home maker. He was favorably impressed by what he saw:

- An exceptionally efficient manufacturing system that turned inventory 20 times
- A highly motivated production work force that was paid through an unusual group-incentive system
- A superior quality level that had made Holiday Rambler the industry leader in high-end recreational vehicles for many years

Teerlink returned to Milwaukee to tell Beals that it was an exciting prospect but that they needed more data.

A week later, Beals and Teerlink took off for Indiana to talk to Holiday Rambler founder and CEO Richard Klingler. It was a case of instant rapport. After three hours of discussion and number-crunching (which revealed that Holiday Rambler had the highest margins in the recreational vehicle industry), Beals said, "We're interested."

"Well, if you're really serious, we need a letter of intent by Friday," Klingler replied.

"That was a shock," says Beals, "considering that this was Wednesday. I explained to Klingler that we were a newly public company and had just had our first board meeting in July. We'd have a tough time getting the board to authorize us to buy a company as big as we were on such short notice."

But it was clear that this is what would have to be done if Harley wanted the deal because there were other bidders actively negotiating. A few quick phone calls rounded up two of Harley's three directors, Michael Kami and Richard Hermon-Taylor, and after a seven-hour meeting in New York on a Friday night the board agreed to proceed on the purchase. Beals and Teerlink were authorized to spend up to $155 million on the deal, provided that the parent didn't have to guarantee the debt.

Tough face-to-face negotiations with Klingler and his advisors followed the next day in Florida, continuing into Sunday morning. At midday, the agreement was sealed with handshakes and a simple letter of intent. "Klingler's parting comment," says Beals, "was that since we were paying $155 million for his company, he hoped we'd throw a new Harley into the deal. Since we were glad to get him off the Japanese brand he was riding, we readily agreed."

Besides being a well-run company, Holiday Rambler was also a perfect fit for Harley-Davidson. It seemed to be a marriage made in Hog Heaven. "We're both really in the same business," Beals says, "making big toys for big boys." Like Harley, Holiday Rambler is a niche marketer, selling premium-priced products to a committed group of enthusiasts whose lifestyles are heavily influenced by their recreational activities. What made it an even more logical extension for the motorcycle company was the fact that more than two-thirds of Holiday Rambler customers are over 55, an age at which many of Harley's customers stop buying motorcycles and start looking for less rugged forms of recreation.

Throwing Away the Crutches

On March 17, 1987, Harley-Davidson announced that it no longer needed special tariffs to compete with the Japanese motorcycle giants. Harley's press release said:

> We're taking this action now because we believe we're
> sending a strong message out to the international
> industrial community: U.S. workers, given a respite
> from predatory import practices, can become competitive
> in world markets. But U.S. industry must also be
> aggressive and take the initiative to regain
> competitiveness.

To be sure, this was a largely symbolic gesture, because the tariffs, which had started in 1983, were scheduled to end in 1988—and they hadn't been all that effective anyway. Some observers called it simply a clever public relations move. Michael Oneal, in *Continental Magazine*, described it as "one of corporate America's finer PR coups." And Oneal quotes American Honda's George G. Grauwels as saying, "Harley helped Harley. Calling for removal of the tariff was a publicity stunt. What did it have to lose?"

Harley management readily agrees that the company received a lot of favorable publicity from its petition to the International Trade Commission. But it insists that its motives went far beyond sheer publicity.

First, it says, Harley-Davidson was concerned about the growing sentiment in Washington for protectionism. It was afraid that the country would move toward major import duties, which in its opinion could be fatal to world trade. Next, Harley-Davidson management believed that the company represented one of the few successes that the Reagan administration had experienced in using existing trade laws. And it hoped that by demonstrating that Section 201 (which helps industries hurt by unfair foreign competition) could actually benefit U.S. industry it could help to head off more protectionist legislation.

At the same time, Harley's petition for early tariff termination was obviously an excellent way of trumpeting Harley's recovery and announcing that it had achieved some major objectives: to fully recover its market share, to get new products on stream, to return to profitability, and to recapitalize the company. Originally, Harley had hoped it would get these things done in five years, which was ambitious enough—but it was able to accomplish them in four.

The publicity barrage that followed Harley's request for termination of the tariffs was climaxed in May by President Reagan's ceremonial visit to the company's assembly plant in York, Pennsylvania. As soon as the presidential helicopter landed on the test track behind the plant, it was obvious that this was to be a festive occasion—a celebration of the remarkable comeback of an American company that had narrowly escaped being dispatched to the junkyard by Japanese competition.

After touring the assembly plant, President Reagan started up the engine of a newly built 30th anniversary edition Sportster (but not before asking his hosts, "This thing won't take off on me, will it?"). He then delivered a brief congratulatory talk to a crowd of enthusiastic Harley employees, many of them waving small American flags. In his opening remarks, he summed up Harley's accomplishments of the past four years:

> You asked us to give you breathing room so you could
> finish getting into shape to meet unexpectedly strong
> foreign competition. It was like giving a boxer a few
> extra weeks of training before a fight. We looked at you
> carefully. We asked, "Is Harley-Davidson really serious
> about getting into shape?" And the answer came back
> a resounding yes. Harley was hard at work with new
> products and finding better ways to make better bikes.
> And Harley's shape-up was not relying just on top
> management. *Everyone from the board room to the factory
> floor was involved.* So when I was told that you wanted a
> little more time to train, I said, yes, kick on the engine,
> Harley, and turn on your thunder.

And that's just what you did. You cut the hours of work needed to make a motorcycle by one-third. You cut inventory by two-thirds. You tripled the number of defect-free machines you shipped. And with productivity up, you kept price increases small, and on some bikes, even lowered prices. You expanded your product line from three models, 10 years ago, to 24 today, and once again became a leader in developing new motorcycle technology. . . . You're the only major motorcycle manufacturer in the world to have increased production last year.

Perhaps Reagan's most telling comment was that everyone from the board room to the factory floor was involved in Harley's resurgence. This is a theme that is stressed over and over again by Harley management. Operations vice president Tom Gelb says, "This is a total team effort with every employee at Harley-Davidson contributing to our turnaround. Our challenge is to make continuous improvements in quality and productivity the driving force in each of our daily jobs."

Rich Teerlink adds that every functional area in the company deserves credit for the turnaround:

I sometimes think we overemphasize the manufacturing area because it's easier to talk about. But our marketing people, our engineering people, our financial people have all made a tremendous contribution—as well as all the people in the other functions. And we have to remember always that manufacturing superiority won't make us successful by itself. Success comes when every function in the organization focuses on the same goal: meeting customer needs.

How Sweet It Is

The remainder of 1987 showed clearly that the battle for survival had been won and Harley-Davidson was now enjoying the fruits of its remarkable turnaround. Highlights included:

- A successful $18.7 million stock offering
- An equally successful $70 million subordinated note offering by subsidiary Holiday Rambler

• A 40 percent market share in the super-heavyweight motorcycle class, 11 points ahead of its closest rival, Honda, and 17 points above its 1983 low of 23 percent

• Record net income of $17.7 million (including Holiday Rambler), on sales of $685.4 million

The good news continued in 1988. Harley-Davidson continued to sell every motorcycle it could make. Net income was up again, to $27.2 million (before extraordinary items) on sales of $757.4 million. Harley's market share in the super-heavyweight class surged to 46.5 percent, almost double the 24.1 percent share of its closest competitor, Honda—a virtual reversal of their relative market positions just five years earlier (see Figure 11-1).

The company received a $9.8 million Defense Department contract to make 500-pound metal practice bomb casings and also became the first defense contractor to be certified under the U.S. Army's Contractor Performance Certification Program, which recognizes contractors that have reduced the government's procurement costs through a consistent commitment to the quality of the delivered product. For the fourth time in five years, Harley-Davidson won a major contract from the California Highway Patrol for police motorcycles—a sweet victory indeed, since Harley had lost this contract to Japanese makes

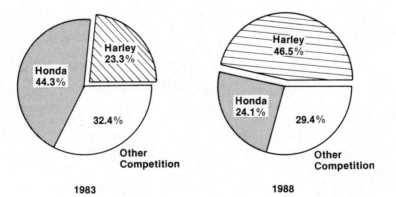

Figure 11-1. Harley-Davidson's share of the U.S. 851+cc market 1983 versus 1988. Other competition includes BMW, Kawasaki, Suzuki, and Yamaha. By 1988, Harley's manufacturing and marketing revitalization program was paying off solidly in market share. (Source: R. L. Polk & Co.)

in the early eighties. Another satisfying development was the surge in exports, highlighted by a 56 percent increase in shipments to Japan, which, ironically enough, became Harley's largest foreign market outside of North America.

On the labor front, the company signed a precedent-setting labor contract that commits both the union and company management to develop a joint vision of their future. Says Vaughn Beals: "Although our labor unions have been solidly in our corner during our tough recovery process, we are still looking for ways to improve relationships. After signing this contract, a group of 80 union and company leaders developed a joint vision, and we are now involving all our employees in identifying and clearing away the barriers to obtaining an even brighter future."

Later in 1988, Harley-Davidson and its four unions received the first Union Label award ever given out by the AFL-CIO, in recognition of "the foresight and cooperation shown by unions and management in helping to revitalize the company." The four unions that shared the award were Allied Industrial Workers (AIW) Local 209, representing production and maintenance workers at the Milwaukee plant; AIW Local 460, from the Tomahawk, Wisconsin plant; Machinists and Aerospace Workers (IAM) Lodge 175, representing the York plant; and IAM Lodge 78, representing tool-and-die workers at the Milwaukee plant.

Perhaps the emotional high point of 1988 for Harley-Davidson was the rousing celebration of its 85th anniversary.

Harley-Davidson's Birthday Bash

They converged on Milwaukee by the thousands on their Harley hogs, rumbling along I-94 as waving spectators lined the overpasses and side roads to cheer them on. They responded with V-for-victory and thumbs-up signs.

Eighty-five-year-old Harley-Davidson was throwing a birthday party for itself in the summer of 1988, and everyone was invited—even those who didn't ride Harleys. All they had to do was contribute $10 to Harley-Davidson's favorite philanthropic organization, the Muscular Dystrophy Association (MDA). More than 40,000 people accepted the invitation.

Organized groups of motorcyclists rode into Milwaukee along 10 separate routes with starting points ranging from San Francisco to Orlando, Florida, to Augusta, Maine. Each group was led by a Harley-Davidson executive, including Vaughn Beals, Rich Teerlink, Jeff Bleustein, Jim Paterson, and Willie G. Davidson. At stops along the way, Harley memorabilia were auctioned off for the benefit of MDA. In LaSalle, Illinois, a biker wearing leather pants and a leather vest with no shirt bid $450 for a Harley-Davidson 85th Anniversary banner signed by Harley executives—and then returned it to be auctioned again, "for Jerry's kids." Chairman Vaughn Beals rode into Milwaukee with his pants held up by a makeshift rope belt because the night before he had auctioned off his pewter commemorative belt buckle for $1000 to benefit MDA. (In all, more than half a million dollars was raised for MDA by the weekend event.)

Thousands of Harleys poured into Milwaukee on June 18, the air shaking with the thunder of massed V-twin engines. Some riders had their dogs perched on the back, others their children, and American flags flew from many bikes. Clothing ranged from minimal to a staggering variety of Harley T-shirts (see box) to black leather vests with every inch covered by Harley buttons, emblems, and other mementos. Riders were of all ages, from young gas-pump jockeys to octogenarians. Every kind of Harley customer was represented, including a sprinkling of Sinners and Saracens. They came from every walk of life and every occupation. The only thing many of them had in common was that they loved to ride Harleys and they had come home to Harley heaven.

When they had all arrived in Milwaukee, the parking lots at the Summerfest grounds on the edge of Lake Michigan were a vast ocean of gleaming chrome and flamboyant colors. (Amazingly, no one seemed to have any trouble finding his or her own bike when the festivities ended long after midnight.)

Off their bikes, the celebrants spent the day participating in organized activities and some that were not so organized. During the day Harley-Davidson executives, including Vaughn Beals and Rich Teerlink, submitted themselves to the celebrity

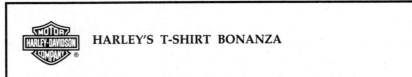

HARLEY'S T-SHIRT BONANZA

"It's wonderful how many black T-shirts a Harley enthusiast needs to be well-dressed!" Wonderful, as Jeff Bleustein says, because the Harley T-shirt is an incredible merchandising phenomenon that is unrivaled by any other U.S. company and brings millions of dollars to Harley and its dealers.

Even in this age of T-shirt mania, there's nothing quite like the Harley T-shirt. You'll look in vain for more than one or two varieties of Yamaha or Honda T-shirts, but the variety of Harley T-shirts is positively awesome. Emblazoned with screaming eagles, roaring bikes, and the Harley bar-and-shield logo, the shirts carry a seemingly endless assortment of messages:

- Patriotic: "Harley-Davidson—The Last Great American"
- Boastful: "It's hard to be humble when you're riding the best."
- Poetic: "They shall mount up with wings as eagles. —Isaiah."
- Long-Winded: "I would rather push my Harley to Mole Lake, Wis. and back than ride a Hondasaki to the Great Northern Bluegrass Festival."

The beauty of it is that for Harley buffs, one T-shirt is not enough. Far from it. If they see a shirt they don't own already, they have to have it—at around $12 a pop. Some riders on long tours stop in every local Harley shop along the way to purchase a T-shirt with the dealer's name and city inscribed on the back.

Harley used to sell the T-shirts itself, but it only managed four or five designs a year. Now, with a full-fledged licensing program, there are half a dozen licensees making about 85 designs a year. And the shirts are worn not just by riders but by a wide variety of nonriders—or "wanna-be's" as they're known around Harley—who are attracted by the Harley name and graphics. The result: sales of 2.5 million Harley T-shirts a year.

dunk tank, where they were unceremoniously dumped into the water by on-target baseball throwers. At one pavilion, classic Harleys were displayed, inspiring riders to talk about their dedicated searches for authentic parts (even for parts as small as a bolt) that would make their own classic bikes complete.

Music resounded throughout the grounds, starting with the Booze Brothers Revue and ending with the Charlie Daniels Band playing at the final ceremonies in the Amphitheater. There the celebration reached its climax as 24,000 homecomers watched a videotape of their ride to Milwaukee projected onto two giant screens. A continuous roar from the crowd was punctuated by shouts of recognition as riders saw their own groups on the screens. Thousands of Harley owners rose to their feet, clenched fists aloft, in a clamorous demonstration of product loyalty probably unrivaled anywhere in the world.

They were celebrating the rebirth of a legend.

A Vision of Excellence

Today, Harley-Davidson is on a roll. Demand for its motorcycles is outrunning supply. But complacency is not part of Harley's culture—and its people are too busy thinking about the challenges ahead to spend time patting themselves on the back. Remarkable as their resurgence has been, they become uneasy when it receives too much hype. They are operating with a vision of where they want to be—and they're not there yet.

This is not to say they are hiding their light under a bushel. Justifiably, the company's annual reports point with pride to the striking improvements in quality, efficiency, and profitability that have been achieved by the whole Harley-Davidson team. But when discussing the company's present and future, Harley-Davidson executives say that its very success in turning around can create problems that in some ways are harder to deal with than those it faced during its survival crisis. They recognize the cold reality that a philosophy of continuous improvement becomes more difficult to implement—not less—once the dramatic initial gains have been made.

Rather than dwelling on what they call their "islands of success," they are zeroing in on the new challenges that an ever-changing environment presents. They are intent on avoiding a trap into which many U.S. companies have fallen, that is, letting down after a first big burst of accomplishment. "A letdown is understandable," says senior vice president Tom

Gelb. "Once you've gotten quick results with the easy stuff, you tend to relax. But that's just when you should work harder, because then improvement becomes more difficult to achieve. Perhaps it's not as exciting and the results aren't as dramatic, but continuous improvement is the only way we're going to keep our competitive edge."

Mindful of the crises that have hit the company throughout its long history, Harley-Davidson is now pursuing a dual strategy:

- Avoiding crises of its own making, such as the survival crisis from which it has just emerged, by committing itself to continuous improvement in each and every aspect of the company
- Assessing major external risks that could cause a rerun of earlier history—and being prepared to adjust to external events quickly and survive their impact

Continuous improvement means continuous critical analysis. Harley-Davidson's analysis covers the whole spectrum of its operations: manufacturing, product development, marketing, human resources, finance, and administration. The company has made great progress in most of these areas, but management believes that Harley has just scratched the surface and that the techniques it has already implemented in these areas must be extended throughout the organization. The company is confident it can do that, because it is continually discovering new opportunities and identifying areas in which it can make major improvements.

Harley-Davidson is driven by a constant vision of what an excellent company should be: One that is never satisfied with the status quo but is always searching for ways to do things better.

As Jeff Bleustein puts it, "The day we think we've arrived is the day we should all be replaced by managers of greater vision."

2

How Your Company Can Do What Harley-Davidson Is Doing

Strategies for Improving Processes and Involving People Through the Productivity Triad

Thus far, management teams from more than 650 companies have attended Harley-Davidson training seminars to learn its manufacturing strategies and techniques for overcoming massive Japanese competition and becoming a world-class competitor. Both large, complex manufacturing plants and smaller operations can achieve superior quality and productivity by applying Harley-Davidson's approaches.

Four Basic "World-Class" Manufacturing Strategies

1. Fix the Systems First

When an organization first becomes enamored of computers, it usually thinks it can fix all its systems problems by buying a computer. The reality is that if the company doesn't have a good manual system, it isn't ready for computers.

Initially, Harley-Davidson's manufacturing plants were laid out with all similar machines grouped together—lathes in one place, grinding equipment in another, and so on. Operators would turn a piece and then put it on a forklift and haul it over to the grinding department. Other operators would grind it, put it back on the forklift, and haul it over to still another department for yet another operation. Harley-Davidson used this system because it did not believe that machines dedicated to one part were feasible for the company's low-volume production.

If Harley had introduced automation into this system, it would have had numerically controlled turning equipment, automatic grinders, and other state-of-the-art machines. But it would still have been hauling parts around the factory from place to place and using a batch process rather than a continuous flow process.

It's surprising how many American companies take this approach. They try to leapfrog the pain and suffering of straightening out their manufacturing processes by throwing millions of dollars into Star Wars technology. But automating a process that is inefficient to begin with simply gives you an inefficient automated process. Indeed, Harley-Davidson's senior managers used to say that the only benefit of poverty was that they *couldn't* invest in automated equipment to increase productivity.

Harley-Davidson was forced into a different strategy: It had to focus attention on the manufacturing *process*. It recognized that it was wasteful and uneconomic to move one part all over the plant for different operations.

With the just-in-time (JIT) system, Harley was able to group parts together into families that required similar processes. Then it arranged machines into work cells, so it could perform all the necessary operations in one location. In many cases, one worker manufactures the whole part from stem to stern, which can be personally far more satisfying to an employee because of the feeling of "ownership" he or she can derive from being solely responsible for the quality of the part. Moreover, stem-to-stern responsibility makes it easier to determine where production problems and training needs lie. Union leadership and membership at Harley fully identified with these concepts and facilitated their early implementation.

2. Make Continuous Improvement a Way of Life

This is the heart of the Japanese process. The objective is to make each piece identical, rather than the traditional U.S. objective of making each piece to specification.

Here's an example: If the problem is to produce shafts of 1.000 inches in diameter with a tolerance of plus or minus .010 inches, a U.S. manufacturer would be happy to make shafts consistently between .990 and 1.010 inches—in other words, to specifications. It is considered a job well done if 100 percent of the products fit within this range.

By contrast, the Japanese objective is to make every shaft precisely 1.000 inches—and then go for the next objective of 1.0000!

Think about what making everything identical really means. Engineers usually know exactly what dimension they want, and they specify tolerances only to acknowledge manufacturing's inability to make all parts the same. But once manufacturing can make them all the same, then the engineers can design more closely.

One illustration of this is the apparently flimsy passenger-car window crank mechanism, which, upon closer inspection, we find works just fine because of the precision of its manufactured components.

Continuous improvement is one of the most difficult of all manufacturing strategies to implement. The continuous improvement of work processes means that you are always aiming for perfection, even though you never achieve it. The goal of continuous improvement is to go beyond meeting manufacturing tolerances and eliminate variability totally. This, in turn, enables engineering to design closer to the ideal. The ultimate result: continuous improvement of product quality.

Particularly in its early stages, *continuous improvement* can seem like a synonym for *continuous frustration*. According to one senior manager: "Every time we solved one problem and tightened up the system, we created two more problems. You never know what a lousy manufacturing operation you're running until you start to change it. And after you think you've improved it 200 percent, you realize you haven't scratched the surface. Your only consolation is that you know you're going in the right direction, and that eventually you will get there and be more competitive in the marketplace."

3.   Revitalize Operations (While Generating Cash) Without Spending Big Bucks

After Harley-Davidson left AMF, one of its advantages was that it couldn't afford to *invest* its way to productivity. When it had been a part of AMF, that's what it had been trying to do; it had been convinced that about 85 percent of its machinery was not capable of producing quality products.

When Harley was planning the tooling for its NOVA engine project, for example, it had considered investing around $80 million in sophisticated equipment to achieve the high quality it wanted at low unit costs. To evaluate the equipment, AMF spent $4 million for Detroit-type transfer machines to tool a new transmission. The test revealed that while the equipment produced good quality at fairly good costs, it was so inflexible that if Harley were to make a design mistake or a marketing mistake, it would take major money to change the tooling. Harley didn't invest further in that type of equipment.

Once it left AMF, Harley just plain couldn't afford major capital investments in new machinery. Therefore, it went about fixing the systems. Unable to spend its way to higher quality and productivity, it was forced to seek alternative solutions— which turned out to be not only cheaper but also *better*.

For example, to everyone's surprise, Harley discovered through applying statistical process control methods that most of its existing machinery and equipment actually *was* capable of producing quality parts and that it was the *processes* that were not capable. Harley simply was not paying enough attention to detail in these processes, as well as in its tooling and machinery. Fortunately, these problems could be identified and corrected at relatively little cost. (The upcoming section about the Productivity Triad will tell you what Harley had to do to get the most out of its equipment.)

4.   Achieve Parity With Your Toughest Competitor in Quality, Cost, and Productivity

Harley knew it had to offer the same level of quality and reliability as the Japanese did; that is, each part in the motorcycle had to do the job it was designed to do. And that it couldn't confuse quality with features: Using a metal fender instead of a plastic fender is not an improvement in quality—it is an additional feature.

Harley had to make sure that the only difference in cost between its products and those of its competitors was in features and benefits. Clearly, you can't supply steel fenders at the same cost as fenders made of injection-molded plastic. And you can't use thicker aluminum cylinder castings (to permit reboring) for the same price your competitors spend on thin-wall castings.

There has to be cost *parity*, meaning that if Harley and a competitor both manufacture precisely the same motorcycle with the same materials and the same design, it will cost exactly the same.

And, as Harley learned, this has to be *real* cost parity based on actual productivity, rather than parity based on outside factors, such as a favorable difference in the exchange rate that might force competitors to charge higher prices. Originally, Harley had stated its objective simply as trying to achieve "parity in quality and cost." As the foreign exchange rate moved in Harley's favor, it was, indeed, achieving cost parity, but the parity was obviously one that could vanish if the exchange rate moved the other way. Harley then raised its goals and restated the objective. Harley now says that it is trying to achieve "*productivity* parity."

In the 1970s and early 1980s, Harley was not delivering the same reliability and quality its competitors were delivering. Today its quality is rapidly approaching that of its competitors; in fact, the motorcycle press is already according Harley-Davidson equivalent quality and reliability.

As of this writing, Harley continues to achieve cost parity as a result of the exchange rate. While its productivity parity has improved, it is still not there yet—but it is gaining.

Tactics and Techniques: The Awesome Power of the Productivity Triad

The components of the Productivity Triad—just-in-time inventory (JIT), employee involvement (EI), and statistical operator control

(SOC)—are not new. What's new to most U.S. companies is the concept of using all three in an integrated approach to improve quality and productivity. Harley-Davidson learned the hard way that JIT, EI, and SOC produce the best results when they are used together. Just why they do we will try to explain in this section.

Harley-Davidson's experience can make it easier for you to get the most from these powerful tools and, in the process, eliminate squadrons of planners, inspectors, materials handlers, accountants, and administrative people.

Timing

The time to get going on the Productivity Triad is *before* the crunch of competition—foreign or domestic—produces panic. These are not changes that can be accomplished overnight. To do it right takes years.

If you wait until you really have a competitive problem before you begin thinking about the Productivity Triad, it will most likely be too late for survival. Under mounting pressure from the Japanese motorcycle giants, Harley-Davidson didn't have the time to make the changes the way it now knows they should have been made—and as a result it almost blew the whole game. It was saved only by the extraordinary brand loyalty of Harley riders. Although most consumer durables enjoy some degree of brand loyalty, few match Harley-Davidson's. For years Harley riders suffered poor quality and still came back to buy a Harley.

Manufacturers of industrial products don't have this luxury, and they are particularly vulnerable to Japanese incursions. Industrial purchasers usually buy "by the numbers." They give product loyalty transiently; when the numbers show they are suffering a cost disadvantage, they quickly switch to the competition. So for manufacturers of industrial products, it is not too strong a statement to say that those who don't get started on the Productivity Triad until they're attacked won't survive.

Coordinating the Components

If there is one message that Harley-Davidson tries to get across to companies considering the Productivity Triad it is this: Do all three components together.

This approach can run into resistance, however. For example, Harley supervisors and managers started to get uptight when the management tried to introduce SOC. They had lived through the start-up of quality circles in 1978–81 and JIT from 1981–1983, and they knew the company had a long way to go in both. Their plea was not to start any more new programs until they had digested the first two. But Harley concluded that without SOC it would never be able to finish the other programs properly. All three concepts had to be embraced simultaneously.

Union Cooperation

To many unions, attempts to increase productivity represent a threat to job security, which is why companies who embark on the Productivity Triad and ignore their unions do so at their own peril. In the early stages of mounting a quality-improvement program, one *Fortune* 500 company produced a 21-page plan that didn't mention unions until page 18, and then merely said: "The labor union's involvement and active commitment greatly enhance quality-improvement functions."

But it is not a matter of "enhancement." It's a matter of success or failure. The full participation of your hourly employees and their elected representatives is critical to success.

Management Commitment

Harley-Davidson's CEO and Chairman both say that their criterion for explaining the Productivity Triad to other companies is whether or not the management really has the will to change. If the request for help with the Productivity Triad does not come from top management, they turn it down, because without top-management support, change will not occur.

Productivity Triad Component 1: Just-In-Time Inventory (JIT)

Sure you're tired of reading about JIT. Maybe you've tried it and it doesn't work. There are a lot of reasons why the system might not work, and Harley-Davidson's management knows all of them. But the company surmounted dozens of mistakes and obstacles to make it work and now swears by it. What follows are some of its results and some of the things it learned during the process.

When JIT Works, It Really Works. Harley's figures tell a story of impressive improvement since 1981:

- Inventory turns up from 5 to 20
- Inventory levels down 75 percent
- Percentage of motorcycles coming off the line complete up from 76 percent to 99 percent
- Scrap and rework reduced by 68 percent
- Productivity up by 50 percent
- Space requirements down by 25 percent

JIT Can Throw Off Tremendous Amounts of Cash. Initially, Harley-Davidson's senior managers say, they started JIT for only one reason, that is, to reduce Harley's investment in work-in-process inventory, thereby releasing cash to repay its buyout debt. Success in this was what kept the company from going under during the first few years.

Table 12-1. Improving Inventory Turns: The Financial Impact of Three Inventory Turns

	Base: Three Inventory Turns
Revenue	$100.0
Cost of sales	75.0
Gross profit	25.0
Selling, general and administration	10.0
Inventory carrying costs (at 20%)	5.0
Return on invested cash (at 10%)	0.0
Income before tax	10.0
Net income after tax	5.0
Raw material and work-in-process inventory	25.0

What is the key to using JIT as a source of cash? Increased inventory turns. To illustrate how this works financially, take a simplified example involving a typical U.S. company. (See Tables 12-1, 12-2, and 12-3.)

Assuming three turns of raw material and work-in-process inventory, this company requires $25 of inventory per $100 of sales. But if it achieves 15 inventory turns, it has cut its inventory capital requirements from $25 to $5. If it costs 20 cents to finance, store, and handle each dollar of inventory, the company has saved $4 and improved pretax income by $4. Thus, increasing turns from 3 to 15 improves profitability by 40 percent and generates $20 of cash for every $100 of revenue. (This assumes that cash is invested at 10 percent.)

But that's not all. JIT also increases productivity—according to one researcher, by as much as 38 percent for every doubling of inventory turns. Even applying that 38 percent figure more conservatively to increasing inventory turns by a factor of 5, as in the simplified example, gives you a company operating with 80 percent less inventory *and* a profit margin that has more than doubled. That's powerful stuff.

Table 12-2. Improving Inventory Turns: The Financial Impact of Fifteen Inventory Turns Versus Three Inventory Turns

	Base: Three Inventory Turns	Fifteen Inventory Turns
Revenue	$100.0	$100.0
Cost of sales	75.0	75.0
Gross profit	25.0	25.0
Selling, general and administration	10.0	10.0
Inventory carrying costs (at 20%)	5.0	1.0
Return on invested cash (at 10%)	0.0	2.0
Income before tax	10.0	16.0
Net income after tax	5.0	8.0
Raw material and work-in-process inventory	25.0	5.0
Cash throw-off		$ 20.0

Table 12-3.   Improving Inventory Turns: The Financial Impact of Fifteen Inventory Turns Plus Thirty-Eight Percent Productivity Increase Versus Three Inventory Turns

	Base: Three Inventory Turns	Fifteen Inventory Turns	Fifteen Inventory Turns + 38% Productivity Increase
Revenue	$100.0	$100.0	$100.0
Cost of sales	75.0	75.0	65.5*
Gross profit	25.0	25.0	34.5
Selling, general and administration	10.0	10.0	10.0
Inventory carrying costs (at 20%)	5.0	1.0	0.9
Return on invested cash (at 10%)	0.0	2.0	2.1
Income before tax	10.0	16.0	25.7
Net income after tax	5.0	8.0	12.8
Raw material and work-in-process inventory	25.0	5.0	4.4
Cash throw-off		20.0	20.6

*Labor costs = one-third cost of sales ($25).

JIT Is Even More Important as a Quality Program Than as a Cash Generator.   Although Harley was initially motivated by its need for cash, it later realized that JIT was the driving force of its quality-improvement program. Very simply, as you operate with lower and lower inventories, it becomes essential that *all* your inventory is usable. If you're only going to get a few parts, they all have to be good ones.

Look at the implications. In a traditional just-in-case system, when you move a week's supply of inventory to the next work station and the operator finds it's bad, you now have a week's supply of problems. Maybe you can sort out the good ones; maybe you can rework some of the bad ones. But maybe you're forced to use some bad ones to keep the line going. By contrast, at the extreme of a pure flow process (as opposed to a batch process) with the JIT system, the probability of having to use bad parts in production is lower, scrap is lower, and rework is lower. Hence, product quality and productivity go up, and the cost of scrap and rework goes down. In short, the reduction of inventory becomes a powerful tool that facilitates improvements in both quality and productivity.

JIT Reveals Many Problems That Have Been Completely Hidden by Traditional Inventory Levels. This ability to reveal hidden problems is probably the most important benefit of the JIT system. Harley formerly used a complex, computerized Material Requirements Planning system that was based on maintaining safety stock, that is, extra stock kept on hand in case something happens. It seemed to make sense, because if a process generated bad parts, a machine broke down, or a supplier didn't deliver on time or delivered defective parts you could still continue to run your assembly line.

But this just-in-case system covered up problems rather than solving them—it was a little like sweeping dirt under the rug. Suppliers continued to deliver substandard parts, machines continued to break down, systems continued to be inefficient. Instead of addressing these problems, the procedure was to put more and more safety stock in the stockroom.

Harley's senior vice president of operations, Tom Gelb, uses the analogy of a lake. As you reduce the water level you expose hidden rocks; as you reduce inventory levels, you expose hidden problems. And with JIT, these are problems you can't live with any more, as you could when you had a security blanket of bulging stockrooms. As each problem is exposed, you are forced to identify its cause, fix it, and move on to the next problem that is revealed. It is a frustrating process, but it leads to a vastly improved manufacturing system. In this way, *JIT is the engine* that drives the quality-improvement program.

There are five essential elements of a JIT program: setup reduction, focus flow processing, containerization, parts control, and operator preventive maintenance.

1. Setup Reduction

This is the key to successful JIT that U.S. manufacturing engineers have overlooked for decades: Reducing machine-tool setup times so that parts can be made in smaller quantities with quick changeovers.

JIT won't work with traditional setup methods, because using these methods to adjust a machine to run a different part takes too much time to make short runs feasible. When you examine the real costs of a traditional setup sequence the results are shocking: Set up, run sample, inspect, adjust, run sample, inspect, adjust, and so on until an acceptable part is made. Along the way, you generate scrap, cause rework, and create many opportunities for nonproductive time. For example, too much time is usually spent looking for and gathering tooling while the machine is stopped for a setup. The total scope of setup time is measured from the time the last part is made on the prior run to the time the first acceptable new part is made. This can sometimes be days—that's why long batch runs are obligatory once a setup has been made.

Harley's problem was that, like most other U.S. manufacturers, it had always considered lengthy setup time to be a given, and instead of trying to reduce it everyone argued over which economic-order-quantity formula to use in deciding how many parts to run.

But to make JIT work, the objective has to be to reduce and simplify setup so the first part after the setup is perfect 100 percent of the time. The benefits are reduced setup time, scrap, rework, and inspection time, plus reduced inventory and invested capital.

Harley-Davidson people say that, from their experience, there are six basic rules for achieving remarkable reductions in setup times:

• *Move main-line setup steps to off-line preparation.* Searching for fixtures, waiting for equipment, and setting tooling are all elements of setup that should not use up main-line time. Instead, they should be handled off-line while the machine is still running the previous job.

• *Eliminate unnecessary movement.* Eliminating walking, reducing manual effort, providing written setup procedures, and having setup teams are ways of reducing unnecessary movement. Harley had success applying this concept to a punch press, for example. Formerly, the dies were stored in another building and had to be retrieved each time the job was changed. Now all the dies are stored at the press itself, on a table with roller bearings that permit the heavy dies to be rolled around easily. Doing this reduced setup time from 1 hour to 10 minutes and eliminated a forklift.

• *Eliminate nuts and bolts.* Instead, design C washers or slotted holes into the machines so that nuts and bolts do not have to be removed when doing setups.

• *Eliminate machine-based adjustment.* This can be accomplished through preset tooling, spacers, or guide blocks, to name a few possibilities. The goal should be to design and build the fixture so that it can be changed without adjusting the table position.

• *Standardize dies, tooling, fixtures, part design, and part specifications.* Design engineers must be involved in this step. Before new parts, tooling, or fixtures come off the drawing board, the designers must examine what is currently being used and try to design new items that will reduce setup times.

• *Use block gauges and templates for adjustments.* A boring machine makes a good example, because between two jobs the stops must be moved. You can ensure a fast setup for the next job on a boring machine by using a notched template to show the proper location for the stop.

Reducing setup time is a major undertaking. It should be accomplished in three phases:

• *Phase 1.* The "best" solutions are not sought in this phase. Instead, employees and their supervisor get together and ask, "Just what are the little things we can do to start bringing the time down?" Very little cost is involved here. The solutions can be achieved in a short time and show about a 20 to 30 percent reduction in setup time.

• *Phase 2.* In this phase some cost is involved in making minor modifications of tools, dies, fixtures, machines, and procedures. This is also a short-term phase, and it will produce benefits of 30 to 50 percent reduction in setup time. The first and second phases are often done together.

• *Phase 3.*   In this phase you can expect to reduce setup time between 10 and 40 percent. This phase can take years, and large capital expenditures may be required for design change and standardization of dies, tools, and parts.

Harley's efforts to reduce setup time have paid off well. It averaged a 75 percent reduction in setup time for the machines in its plants—and that average includes some machines on which it could not reduce the time. Just a few examples of the reductions it did achieve: 24 hours reduced to 4, 31 minutes to 6, 15 minutes to 0, 52 minutes to 0, 2 hours to 3 minutes. Let's look at this last reduction—two hours to *three minutes*—in more detail.

Harley manufactures two crankpins that are very similar in shape. The only difference had been the angle of an oil hole: one angle was 45°, the other 48° (see Figure 12-1). Because of this angle difference, there were four fixtures per part, each with its own hydraulic unit for clamping. It was a very time-consuming arrangement (see Figure 12-2). The problem was given to the Design Engineering Department, which concluded that the angle of the oil holes could be made the same (see Figure 12-3). Next came the Tool Design Department, which developed a design that made it possible to use the same four fixtures for both parts. Now in changing the setup, the operator only has to add or take away four spacers that position the part properly. Time for doing this: three minutes (see Figure 12-4).

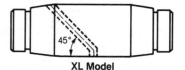

XL Model

FL Model

Figure 12-1.   Crankpin before design change.

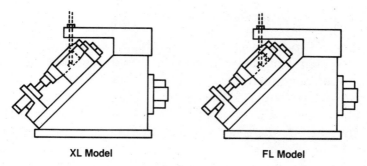

XL Model   FL Model

114 Minutes

Figure 12-2.   Crankpin fixtures before design change.

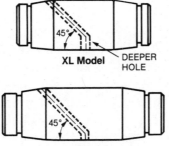

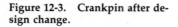

Figure 12-3.   Crankpin after design change.

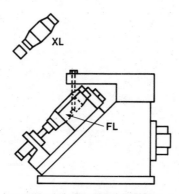

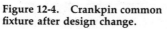

Figure 12-4.   Crankpin common
fixture after design change.

2. Focus Flow Processing

Reducing setup times makes it possible to change over a production system from batch processing to flow processing—with tremendous benefits in terms of quality, productivity, and cost. Before the changeover, Harley's production system was a huge, mazelike operation in which parts were tooled in large batches and moved from one machine to another all over the plant (see Figure 12-5).

Now parts are grouped into families that require similar machining operations and produced in a "cell" or "U-line" that includes all the necessary machines (see Figure 12-6). One U-line may include two horizontal-spindle-machining centers, a drill press, and a broaching machine (see Figure 12-7). There can be one person on the line, or two, three, or four, depending on production volumes.

Now that Harley can run all the parts it needs every day—that is, "just in time"—it has been able to cut inventories by at least 75 percent. In fact, both main plants are operating without stockrooms—all the material is on the floor.

There's a big difference between the old system and the new system. When Harley ran parts in batches of 1000 pieces, it experienced one bottleneck after another. One part might require 10 different operations, and most of the time it was queued up trying to get into a particular machine. The whole

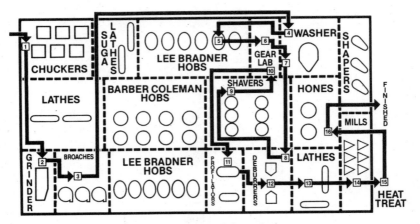

Figure 12-5. Typical flow—before.

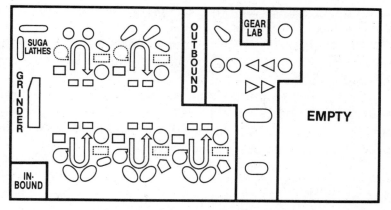

Figure 12-6. Gear and sprocket department—after.

process could take anywhere from six weeks to four months. But by grouping the machines into cells, the bulk of the operations on a part can be done in minutes. It reduces lead time, it reduces inventory, and, most important, *it reduces defects and improves quality.* Also, one employee now performs *all* the operations on one part. Defects are discovered very quickly, before many pieces have been run, which is far superior to running a batch of 1000 pieces through seven operations and then discovering a problem.

One example of how flow processing reduces *throughput time* is the line for making motorcycle frames. When the frame-

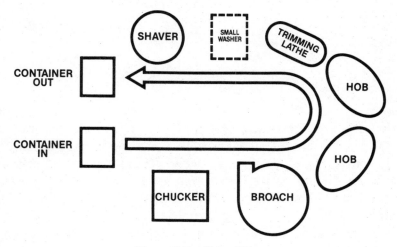

Figure 12-7. U-form lines.

building was scattered all over the plant, making a frame took 72 days and many miles of travel. Now it takes under three hours and about 200 yards, all in a straight line starting with a computer-controlled tube-bender and ending with a frame-painting facility.

Four other benefits come out of flow processing: (1) it reduces scrap and rework, (2) it enables quick reaction to engineering design changes and market demands, (3) it saves floor space, and (4) it increases productivity.

3. Containerization

The inventory system Harley once used was a "push system" in which a computer determines part quantities and issues orders to production and purchasing. In contrast, JIT is a "pull system"—that is, the final assembly line *pulls* parts as they are needed from subassembly areas, which, in turn, pull parts from component departments.

In the pull system, Harley uses containers on the final assembly line. When the empty container is returned to the sourcing department, that's the signal to produce another container load. To avoid the use of forklifts, Harley tries to make the containers movable by hand. And to eliminate transfer of parts from one container to another—which can result in damage—it tries to have purchased parts delivered in the container that will be used on the production line. The containerization system is childishly simple. It doesn't take computers, and it doesn't make mistakes.

4. Parts Control

Too many companies embarking on JIT programs get hung up on what kind of a control system to use. The answer is simple: What's important is that as parts are consumed on the assembly line, some kind of signal goes back to the departments or suppliers producing those components and tells them to make some more. This system is known in Japan as *kanban*, which simply means "signal." The signal can be an empty container, a red ball, a light, or—to get a little more sophisticated—a bar-coded card.

5. Operator-Involved Preventive Maintenance

One reason some JIT systems fail is that they lack a strong preventive maintenance program. With JIT, you have to troubleshoot maintenance problems *before* they occur. JIT is constantly threatened unless unexpected delays in the production process are eliminated. Unplanned downtime is one of the biggest culprits. Harley combats downtime by trying to involve machine operators in a preventive maintenance program in which the operator is responsible for periodic lubrication, daily cleanliness, and special checks. The operator is required to note any abnormalities in the machine or tooling functions.

Harley has developed a preventive maintenance lubrication schedule for each manufacturing machine in the plant and equipped each machine with a checklist for identifying the maintenance work to be performed by the operator.

This operator-involved preventive maintenance program has helped reduce machine downtime significantly. To reduce it even further, one EI team is currently implementing a full-fledged preventive maintenance program utilizing skilled trades, planned inspections, and machine parts replacement.

To Make JIT Work, You Must Stabilize Your Production Schedule. Harley-Davidson lives by the rule that the next 30 days' schedule is sacrosanct; it cannot be changed. They can change the second 30-day schedule by 10 percent plus or minus and the third 30 days by 20 percent plus or minus. Unless schedule stability is supported and enforced, JIT will not yield its full potential. Why? Because you will only confuse and irritate your employees and your suppliers by suddenly changing the production goals you've already asked them to achieve. They should be able to plan ahead for 30 days knowing you won't switch goals on them.

JIT Should Be Introduced Incrementally—With Full Employee Participation in the Planning and Implementation. When Harley-Davidson decided to introduce JIT at its York assembly plant, it gathered together a dozen employees from all levels—salaried, hourly, bargaining unit—including a production control person, a quality engineer, a milling machine operator, a production helper, and a materials handler. The plant manager explained the basic concept and how this thing could work and then said, "Let's all start from scratch and decide how we're going to do this." At first those gathered were dubious, but once their questions were answered they were saying, hey, wait a minute, maybe this thing *will* work.

The group met twice a week to work out the system. The next step was to try it. The group decided to take the toughest part in the plant and put the system in for that part. It chose a jackshaft, a component of the starting mechanism. To convert production of this part to JIT was a real challenge because the part was processed all over the shop. But the system worked, so the group tried it on five more parts, meeting every weekend to report on what kinds of problems were coming up and how they could be solved. The final step was to put all the parts on the system. The 12 employees in the group implemented the whole thing without a hitch.

The lesson here is: Don't dump a JIT program on somebody's lap and say, "Here it is; you've got two months to install it." Get employees involved and start *slowly*. Harley-Davidson's incremental approach worked well, because building on a series of small successes made it easier to obtain the bigger successes. The key is to try it and make it work in one area. If there are problems, correct them before going on—this approach makes it easier to convert the next area. Harley's experience was that it became progressively easier and easier to convert areas to JIT because employees were solving a bunch of little problems along the way. If Harley had gone across the board in the beginning, it would have encountered the same problems, but solving them would have meant changing a huge system, not just one part of it. That would have disrupted operations in the whole plant.

Above All, JIT Requires Management Commitment.   A JIT system is not complicated—or costly. But it does demand a great deal of management patience and commitment, because no matter how well it is introduced, all those problems hidden under the inventory rug must be identified and solved, and that can be painful. And because in the beginning JIT seems to create problems rather than solve them, its benefits may not be immediately apparent. Without strong management commitment, a JIT system can easily backslide to more familiar, comfortable inventory methods.

Productivity Triad Component 2: Employee Involvement (EI)

Harley's turnaround has been widely covered by the media in terms of its financial recovery and manufacturing improvements, but the largely unreported story is the Harley vision of establishing and expanding employee involvement in the program for continuously improving quality. This vision is far from being fulfilled, but it is well on the way. One thing is certain: Without the involvement of all Harley employees, the company might not even have survived.

You Say People Are Your Most Valuable Resource, but Do You Really Act That Way?

We hear a lot about "teamwork" and "employee involvement" these days, but they are often simply buzz words rather than true goals. This is too bad, because without management's total commitment to these concepts, manufacturing systems like JIT and SOC will not work well. Introducing the Productivity Triad means change—radical, intense change. Such change cannot take place successfully unless top management lets go of some of its old habits and attitudes concerning employees, both managerial and nonmanagerial.

Distilled from Harley-Davidson's experience, what follows are guidelines for creating the kind of work climate that is essential to a successful conversion to the Productivity Triad.

Don't Overload Your Organization With Multi-Directional Programs

Too often, companies trying to improve their manufacturing systems throw in a whole bunch of programs with no apparent interconnection—a work-methods improvement program, a quality improvement program, an inventory reduction program, a cost reduction program, and on and on. That can lead to disaster, because your employees become confused, threatened, and resentful.

Thus, it is far better to focus on a single, simple, understandable goal—an umbrella under which all of your improvement programs can be linked together. In Harley-Davidson's case, the goal was "quality." For another company, it might be "competitiveness."

Once you determine what your focus will be, stay with it. At Harley-Davidson, they say that if something doesn't relate to improving quality, they aren't going to do it. This is a focus that everybody in the company can understand and relate to. And the quality goal can be applied to just about any aspect of the organization's operations, not just the end product. For example, quality affects morale because poor quality tends to create rework and people get upset over having to do a job over again. Quality affects productivity because it eliminates scrap and rework. Quality reduces costs because doing something right the first time is cheaper than doing it over. So instead of telling your employees they must increase productivity or reduce costs, for example, you make quality your stated goal. This goal is not only less threatening to people, but it also appeals to their pride in turning out a better product—and it works.

Focusing on cost reduction is a mistake many companies make. Yes, cost reduction is an important goal for a company that wants to stay competitive. But cost reduction can't be the *driver.* Any company can cut costs tomorrow, but the most important question is "How does it affect quality?"

Harley-Davidson's goal was to lower costs while maintaining or improving quality. A tough assignment, and sometimes mistakes were made. Example: Engineering introduced a rubber intake manifold into the 1988 Sportster engine. Rubber, it was thought, would be both a cheaper and better-performing material than the aluminum normally used.

However, what engineering failed to consider was that some states allow methanol to be mixed with gasoline—and methanol attacks rubber. Customer complaints flooded in from these states, and Sportster manifolds are once again made of more costly aluminum.

Harley-Davidson believes that there are certain things it

NINE "MUSTS" FOR SUCCESSFUL EMPLOYEE INVOLVEMENT

1. Management, through its words and actions, must demonstrate that continuous improvement of quality and efficiency is a way of life, not just another "program."
2. Management must be firmly committed to the people-building philosophy—that is, the belief that employees are thinking, rational human beings and therefore should be encouraged to develop and grow.
3. All management must be totally committed to the EI program and by demonstrating that commitment foster a mutual trust between employees and management.
4. Employees must be thoroughly trained in specific problem-solving and quality-control techniques.
5. Managers must encourage participation from everyone.
6. Employees must be given responsibility and authority for production, quality, preventive maintenance, and other aspects of their jobs.
7. Individual employees must help each other develop and grow.
8. Employees must attack problems, not each other—that is, there must be no finger-pointing when things go wrong.
9. Creativity must continuously be encouraged through a free, nonthreatening atmosphere.

Adapted from *The Harley-Davidson Employee Involvement Manual*, 1983

should do because they are the right things to do, even if they don't make a lot of sense from a cost-reduction point of view. Take the rearrangement of a machining department to improve the flow process. It may not seem cost-efficient to spend $10,000 to move seven pieces of equipment around, and it might have a 10-year payback. But it increases quality and productivity and helps fosters a climate of continuous improvement.

Harley people are leery of financial justifications, which, they say, often miss the most important element—the "unquantifiables." If an investment improves quality, Harley-Davidson is willing to make it without financial justification.

Don't Put Local Plant Management in a Straitjacket

Many companies with multiple facilities forget that each facility has its own personality. For corporate management to deluge all their facilities with rigid rules, regulations, and directives is a sure way to kill employee participation in the improvement process. Just because an idea sounds good in the boardroom or the president's office doesn't mean it will work well in every location.

Harley-Davidson's senior management told its plant managements the direction it wanted them to go in. It gave them the principles and the concepts, and then said: *We're going to let you alone to implement them in the best way. The basic principles are important, but we don't care whether your JIT system looks exactly like this one over here or that one over there, as long as it works for you.*

As one manager in the York plant said, "I wasn't handed the company song sheet and forced to sing something I didn't agree with and to which I hadn't been allowed to contribute. We got the guiding principles, but after that we were on our own as to what we wanted to do and how we wanted to do it. We were free to create what we felt was necessary for our particular circumstances."

Don't Try to Impose EI Techniques on a Culture That Will Not Support Them

Quality circles. Brainstorming. Task forces. Teamwork training. They're all useful EI formats. But they are *only* formats. Unless these programs are provided in a nurturing organizational climate, their benefits will soon be snuffed out by the existing bureaucratic, authoritarian structure and mind-sets. Trying to change human behavior in an unsympathetic environment is an exercise in futility.

That's why EI efforts at Harley were badly flawed in the beginning. When Harley took a first stab at EI by starting quality circles, they didn't work because they were introduced into an environment that was not conducive to employee participation. Senior management did not fully understand that to fulfill the potential of this concept required a drastic change in its own management style and mind-set. It took a while for it to come to that understanding.

Most people believe that Harley changed because it was a matter of survival. The choice was to change or to die. Unless everybody got involved in trying to solve Harley's tremendous problems they would all go down the tubes together. Management made a strong commitment to that, and people responded, as they always will when they believe management is really serious.

Most important, perhaps, Harley has dropped the concept of white-collars *thinking* and blue-collars *doing*, a notion that has plagued American business but is anathema in Japan. The goal now is to have everybody thinking *and* doing. The color of their collars is irrelevant.

At Harley, the conviction is that formal techniques are not as important as establishing the right climate—a nonthreatening climate. Usually this means a change in management's attitude and its value system. Then the change must be demonstrated to the employees as a reality and not a put-on.

Here's an example that seems very simple and yet conveyed something very important to Harley employees. Management decided to enclose the painting facility at the York plant to keep it cleaner and provide better lighting. Employees at the facility contributed to the design of the enclosure themselves and asked if they could choose the color of the walls. Standard procedure would have been to say, "Sorry, but our color scheme is blue-and-gray, and that's what these walls are going to be." Instead, the plant manager said, "Sure, go ahead and choose your color."

It was perhaps a small thing to management. But not imposing a color scheme from the top gave employees a greater sense of "ownership" in their workplace. Without such a climate of shared control, structured EI programs won't accomplish much.

Harley-Davidson does have quality circles (see box). However, they are not called quality circles throughout the company. As part of the EI process, employees were asked if they wished to use that term or some other term. In the Milwaukee engine plant, employees opted for "quality circles," while the

York assembly plant employees decided to call them "employee involvement groups." For the sake of consistency and because the term *quality circles* has sometimes been abused, we will, hereafter, refer to *employee involvement groups* or EIGs. (Some companies have used so-called quality circles as window dressing to show they were listening to their employees, when actually they were placating and patronizing them.)

 HOW HARLEY EI GROUPS WORK TODAY

Today, Harley's EI groups are only one element in the company's overall EI program—but they are still an important one. All employees receive formal training in problem solving at the company's expense; however, participation in EI groups is voluntary. Typically, groups are made up of employees who share similar tasks and want to work together to solve mutual problems. Each group meets, again at company expense, for one hour a week to solve problems, often with the help of a trained group facilitator.

When there is a special production problem or project, specific workers may be asked to form a project team. This team exists only until the project is completed or the problem solved.

This approach is working well. In the engine plant, for example, employees have formed ESP (Employee Solving Problem) groups. Made up of volunteers, sometimes from different areas of the plant, these groups work on solutions to a major problem. Groups in the maintenance areas have been particularly successful in resolving problems and at the same time learning to work together better.

The company does not tally cost savings generated by its EI groups, because it does not want to shift the emphasis from quality improvement to cost reduction.

EIG participants have made valuable contributions to improving Harley's production processes. But these groups are not Harley's EI program. They are simply a discussion format—a way of working together on a problem—that are available for people who want to work in that format.

Make Listening to Your Employees a Reality, Not Just a Gesture

If you ask Harley-Davidson employees how things are different from 10 years ago, many of them will say, "Management listens to us now." But that's not all they're saying. What they really mean is that management listens to what they say and *does* something about it. What they're saying is that real listening doesn't consist of just looking attentive and nodding your head occasionally. Plenty of managers do that, but when the discussion is over, that's the end of it—nothing ever happens.

Employees must know that what they say will be heard and taken seriously, not dismissed out of hand. If they don't feel that, communication will dry up. York plant manager Bob Miller puts it this way:

> It's when people stop talking that I get worried. I want people to talk about the things that are bothering them. I want them to come to me and say something has to be changed because it's messing up the plant. It tells me that they're concerned, that they don't like what's going on and they want something better. That's what I want to hear. I might not agree all the time, but that's fine. I can't do anything about it if I don't hear about it.

Randy Horning, senior manufacturing engineer at the York plant, summarizes three behaviors he believes that managers must demonstrate to make EI successful:

1. We must actively solicit input from employees on projects that affect them.
2. We must encourage employees to present problem-solving or continuous-improvement ideas individually and through groups.
3. If these approaches result in employee input, then action must be taken. This is not to say that all ideas should be implemented but that each idea deserves a response.

Successful EI, Horning believes, can be measured only by each employee's perception of how well these three behaviors are displayed by managers.

Facilitate Constant, Open, Up-and-Down Communication

Opening communication lines is a major key to achieving teamwork and employee participation. Many companies make it so difficult for their employees to communicate with management that they are discouraged from even trying—which means problems don't come to management's attention until they have already cost plenty of money.

Harley-Davidson's organizational structure was once pretty typical in that it was heavily loaded with bureaucratic levels of management. Managers sitting behind closed doors. Engineers far away from the plant floor. Communication closed down in both directions.

The EI program changed all that. The organization has been flattened to reduce management layers. Managers are far more accessible to all employees. Engineers are now located right in the plant, within walking distance of machine operators.

These changes foster constant problem-solving interaction between management and workers. An engineer working on setup time reduction only has to walk a few feet to consult an operator and ask, "What kind of a fixture do you see that would reduce the setup time on this machine?" It is this daily involvement in making the company better that is essential to true teamwork.

Harley tries to keep its channels of communication as informal as possible, from top to bottom. Bob Miller says:

> People know they can come to me any time without fear of reprisal. I've had employees call me in my office and say, "We want to see you down here right away." I go down and try to resolve the issue through the individual manager responsible for that area. I've had employees call our CEO when they haven't been satisfied with my response to them. That's okay, too, because if they feel that strongly about it maybe I missed something, maybe I should take another look at it.

 **GETTING MANAGEMENT INVOLVED IN CHANGE**

Harley-Davidson recognized that management change was a key ingredient in successful employee involvement. Initially at the York plant, and later in Milwaukee, "team building" efforts were initiated with middle-level manufacturing management, starting with peer groups and later expanding throughout the functional organizations. This concept includes a variety of training in team-building skills, a personality evaluation test, and an agreement to a "psychological contract." The contract reads:

- Spirit of inquiry—a willingness to accept the other person's point of view as legitimate and to explore it with the person.
- Openness; candidness.
- Feedback—confrontation valued and practiced.
- Pushback—acceptable to say no.
- Confidentiality.
- Finally, have some fun.

Extensive team-building has taken place at all levels of the company, including team-building for union leaders, negotiation committees, and stewards. Over 700 employees in almost all divisions of the company have been involved in the team-building process.

Building teamwork is not just a matter of telling people you want them to work together to solve problems. Teamwork must be *designed* into the organization through changes that make communication easier and through a relaxation of traditional barriers that cut employees off from management.

Reach an Up-Front Agreement on Expectations from the EI Program

Whenever you start a program of change, employees develop certain expectations which may be unrealistic. If you start an EI program, an employee may say, "Okay, great, we have employee involvement, so I get to be involved in every decision the company makes." Then, if that doesn't happen, disillusionment sets in.

For this reason it's vital to create realistic expectations up front so that employees don't have one set of expectations and management a completely different set. This can be done through an open discussion of questions like: Where do we expect to be? When do we expect to be there? How will we measure success?

Don't Let Mistakes Kill People's Willingness to Change

In a period of intensive change, you're bound to make mistakes. For example, Harley management wanted to protect parts from the weather when they went from one building to another, so it put in an enclosed walkway—but it was in the wrong place, so nobody used it.

How you handle such mistakes can have a big impact on the way people feel about the overall improvement process. Mistakes in one area make it easy to say the whole improvement program is a mistake.

Harley management tries to take a positive approach to mistakes by saying that what it was trying to do was sound, even though the execution was faulty. *Okay, we tried this and it didn't work. But it's not a failure because now we know what not to do next time. We learned from that and we won't do it that way again.*

Deal Forthrightly With the Problem of Employment Security

The issue of employment security is a continuing problem and can be a major stumbling block to achieving EI. At first, production improvement ideas at Harley-Davidson rolled in at a good pace, but suddenly they began to dry up.

It wasn't hard to figure out why.

Nor were employees reluctant to say why.

What one employee said was: "What do you expect of us? The last improvement project we worked on eliminated one employee, and one of the other projects eliminated two people. How can you expect us to come up with improvements when our friends may lose their jobs?"

Once these problems were aired, however, they were addressed seriously by both union and management. As a result, the union contract for 1983 provided for an active insourcing program designed to bring work into Harley-Davidson plants that had formerly been done by outside suppliers.

"Insourcing is another way that Harley-Davidson is different from most U.S. manufacturers," says Jerry Knackert, head of Allied Industrial Workers Local 209, which represents production and maintenance workers at the Milwaukee plant. "Most U.S. companies are outsourcing work—many to their competition in the Far East. This practice is reducing the U.S. manufacturing base and creating unemployment here."

Harley-Davidson, says Knackert, is doing the opposite: increasing its manufacturing base and creating jobs. But it can only do this because it reduced costs sufficiently through manufacturing improvements to permit it to make parts in its plants that were previously purchased from outside.

This joint union-management effort has brought in 60 jobs, improved quality, and reduced costs by over $2 million. Employment security has been increased, and Harley-Davidson has been able to utilize the plant space it freed up through successful inventory reduction.

Says John Campbell, vice president of human resources, "Harley's unions played a major role in helping to justify insourcing in terms of dollars and cents and quality. Many corporate managers fail to recognize the expertise that many union leaders have in helping to determine the merits of insourcing and bringing new work into their companies."

Harley-Davidson and its employees—union and non-union—certainly have not solved all the problems of employment security that can arise when work processes are improved. Nor will they. New problems will arise as new improvements take place. But what's key is that they both acknowledge that these problems exist and agree that they will work together to deal with them. In particular, management doesn't try to sweep it all under the rug.

Don't Let Management "Solutions" Become the Problem

Harley-Davidson CEO Rich Teerlink pinpoints what he thinks is another major obstacle to real EI when he says that managements have to recognize that it is not their job to hand down solutions to every problem. Management's obligation is to *communicate* the problem. The employees will solve it if management lets them. That may be tough for American managers to accept, but it's the only way to get real participation and commitment from employees.

Teerlink gives an example of what *not* to do: "We were trying to get our bargaining unit involved in solving a problem. But we screwed up. We didn't come to them with the problem and say, 'What are the alternatives?' Instead, we said, 'This is the problem and here is our solution.' And their reaction was 'What the hell are you guys trying to do to us?' "

The lesson here is that when management comes to labor with solutions, labor will feel obligated to nitpick those solutions. That's understandable. If someone presents you with a solution you haven't had any part in working out, there's a natural tendency to find fault with it. When management and labor develop solutions together, they both have a stake in making those solutions work.

Reach Out for a Team Relationship With Your Union

True EI calls for a completely new relationship between management and labor. Management must create an environment that communicates the message: "We're a team, and we're working for one another's common good to solve the problems in our company."

Traditionally, management would say, okay, there's a problem, so we'll solve it by doing this and this and this. Harley-Davidson management no longer takes that approach, according to Teerlink.

> What we say now is, okay, let's talk openly about the issue. Let's put together a joint study group—labor and management—to survey and research what's going on today. We have them come back with various alternatives that they've developed a consensus on and bring those alternatives up to our Labor-Management Council. Joint labor-management research into sticky

issues is an important key to resolving them. It means
we both negotiate from a common database. It's not
going to be the union using its research and the
company using its research and then trying to argue one
another down, because we each have research that
makes our position look good.

Teerlink says that total EI cannot exist until management
and labor can agree that they have a mutual goal: the long-term
success of the company. Says Teerlink:

That means management and labor have to sit down and
talk about our future. Not about today—because then
you just start talking about where we differ. But if we
talk about our future and our goals we'll be able to say,
"Hell, we agree on 80 percent of that; now let's work on
the 20 percent where we differ."

Then we have to sit back and ask, "What do we
think are the critical factors of success? What steps do
we have to take to get where we want to be?"

The concept of participative management is
totally incompatible with traditional, periodic union
negotiations. It makes no sense to be partners on a day-
to-day basis and then use an adversarial process at the
bargaining table. That's why the essence of our new
company-union "joint process" is to change the
company-union negotiation methods to a participative
management style.

In this joint process, joint union-management study groups
identify issues or problems and then research all possible solutions. From a common understanding of a full range of alternatives, the union and company can then approach problem
solving with a maximum of enlightenment and a minimum of
friction. Efforts in that direction have made progress, but everyone agrees that there's still a long way to go. On the plus side,
there is greater acceptance of the "partnership" concept by both
management and the unions. Harry Smith, former head of Machinists Lodge 175, which represents York plant employees,
says, "I'm a firm believer that relations between management
and labor have to change if we're going to beat our foreign

AND NOW FOR SOMETHING COMPLETELY DIFFERENT

Although Harley-Davidson is a niche marketer, it doesn't believe in keeping employees in niches—and it has had some striking functional crossovers. The most prominent examples: Jim Paterson switched from controller to vice president of marketing and is now president of the motorcycle division, while Jeff Bleustein started with Harley as vice president of engineering and is now senior vice president of parts and accessories. And Ron Hutchinson switched from process engineering and program management to quality assurance.

Or take "Head Hog" Mark Cunningham. Cunningham joined Harley-Davidson in 1979 as manager of production and inventory control in Milwaukee, after four years at Allis Chalmers and nine years at U.S. Steel, where he started as an hourly laborer. Over the next eight years, Cunningham made his way upward as manager of manufacturing administration, director of manufacturing operations, manufacturing area manager, and manager of compensation and benefits.

When the job of managing the Harley Owners Group came open in 1988, Cunningham applied, even though he had no marketing experience. "I knew how the inside of the company worked. What always intrigued me were the product and the customer. This was a chance to learn about both."

He got the "Head Hog" job and he's doing great.

Cross-functional moves, which at Harley-Davidson are made at all levels, not just managerial levels, have advantages for both the company and its employees. Employees know that if they want to move on to something different, they're not caught in a dead end. And the company benefits by getting people who bring a fresh perspective to their jobs. If someone is always promoted in the same department, there's a tendency for that person to get stale and rigid, while many jobs today really require flexibility and innovation.

competition. And we've made a lot of progress in that direction. We came down from 95 arbitration cases to practically none. That came from working hard and keeping good faith on what we negotiated."

But acceptance of a team relationship is still not total on either side. As Bob Miller at York says, "Some of our managers have accused me of taking sides with the union. My answer is to say, sure, I take their side if they're right, and I'm sure the union president gets accused of taking the company's side. But if we're not working together, we're dead. They're a vital part of this organization, and I can't ignore them. I want them to be involved. I want them to represent our people."

That's a hard concept for some managers to accept, because it goes against the grain of everything they've always believed.

On the other side, not all rank-and-file employees are convinced that their union should be getting cozy with management. They are afraid that unless the union fights management aggressively on every issue, the employees will lose out.

Milt Kornburger, a machine repairer at the Capitol Drive plant, reports: "The problem-solving groups, chartered by the jointly led process, are coming out of their infancy. They are beginning to 'crawl' around and get into things. But traditional union people and salaried and management people are having difficulties accepting decisions made by group consensus. Because of this resistance, problem-solving groups are not finding it easy to get their decisions implemented."

Both sides agree that changing these attitudes is a slow, sometimes painful process. To say things are always going to be great, that everybody's going to love each other and be nice to each other is, both say, not realistic. There are going to be ups and downs.

But both sides also agree that a team relationship will ultimately work. Progress so far has been encouraging, and both sides are committed to making it even better. The alternative—for Harley-Davidson or any U.S. manufacturer—is to be seriously weakened as a worldwide competitor.

The Road Ahead

It has sometimes been bumpy going for Harley's EI program. Many employees have lived through three radically different management environments: a family-run business with a paternalistic style, a conglomerate with traditional management style, and now a publicly owned company with an employee participation approach. So it's not surprising that some employees have been skeptical about management's sincerity and have questioned whether its programs will be ultimately beneficial.

That said, most Harley-Davidson employees appear to feel that their work life has improved over what it was under previous management styles. Most seem to enjoy the added responsibility they now have for quality and efficiency and welcome the opportunity to participate in solving problems, rather than having solutions imposed from above. The net result seems to be a high level of pride in what they are producing—and a concern for achieving the best possible quality.

Productivity Triad Component 3: Statistical Operator Control (SOC)

At many employee work stations in Harley-Davidson's Milwaukee engine plant is what looks like a yellow music stand. But rather than a musical score, the stand holds "control charts." After completing each manufacturing process, operators record data which they then analyze to determine the range of variation in the process being measured. This is SOC, the third leg of the Productivity Triad.

It took Harley-Davidson a while to realize that SOC was the missing ingredient in its manufacturing "revolution." JIT and EI were in place. But because JIT requires such high levels of quality, Harley found that giving employees more responsibility for quality is meaningless unless they are also given the statistical tools they need to reach those quality levels.

How SOC Interacts With JIT and EI

SOC plays an important role in the Productivity Triad, and it must go in tandem with JIT. When you install JIT, you must get quality under control because as you reduce inventory, lead times, and process times you minimize your ability to react to a quality problem. In the old days, when Harley had 20 weeks of process time to make a batch of a particular gear and a quality problem developed somewhere in that process, the procedure was to stop everything and fix it. Maybe a week would be lost, but it was still possible to "expedite" gear production and get

   **EI SUCCESS STORIES**

Both individually and in groups, Harley-Davidson employees have been responsible for many significant improvements in the company's operations. Here is just a sampling:

- A quality circle at the York plant polishing department worked on the problem of reducing scratches and nicks that created rework costs on lamp brackets, saddlebag supports, fork brackets, and horn covers. This group came up with ideas that achieved a net savings of more than $89,000—and, more important, cured a chronic quality problem.

- Machine operator Philipe Cruz suggested a process change for a rectangular frame support tube he runs on his machine. As a result of the change, production on his operation for that part increased 30 percent and production on the preceding operation increased 40 percent.

- Rome Stifler, a setup employee in the machining area, suggested a new cutting-tool design for longer tool life. The change not only improved tool life by 20 percent but also reduced the tool's cost by 60 percent.

- Toolmaker Ken Painter designed and built special boring machinery from surplus equipment, and improved vital machining operations on brake levers.

- In the Milwaukee Capitol Drive plant, daily employee meetings use SOC methods to solve production problems. In addition to solving many of these problems, the meetings have led to an increase in the use of SOC on a regular basis from 45 percent to 98 percent.

- At the Tomahawk, Wisconsin, plant (where fiber glass and Lexan® accessories are made), a quality circle designed a jig fixture that eliminated the problem of spray paint getting on the inside of saddlebags when the outside was being painted. As one of those who participated, Al Dean (who happens to be president of the union local), says, "That problem really upset me because I know how I would feel if I bought a $10,000 bike that looked beautiful on the outside and had a bunch of overspray paint on the inside of the saddlebags."

the gears to the line on time. Now, with a shorter setup time and families of parts put together in a flow-processing mode, the longest gear lead time is *five days*. If Harley has a quality problem, it can't fool around with it very long or there'll be no parts on the lines. SOC allows operators to know *before* they make bad parts that a process is out of control.

Here's an example from a machine operator at the York plant: "Let's say my permitted design tolerances are plus-or-minus .0010 inches and I've normally been producing within a band of plus-or-minus .0002 inches. When I chart the average and see it trending upward to plus-or-minus .0005 inches, I start to pay attention and look for causes. As soon as I see the trend I can start to analyze the problem and hopefully find out what has deteriorated. Then I can try to fix it before it exceeds acceptable tolerances."

SOC is an equally important adjunct to EI. Harley made several false starts in trying to get employees involved in improving quality. It first had a program *called* operator control, but this program consisted primarily of just telling the operators that they had the responsibility for quality. What Harley did not do was provide them with the tools or methods for understanding what was happening to quality in their particular process. It was sort of like putting the engineer way back in the caboose of the train and making that engineer responsible for where the train goes.

When senior management realized its mistake, it introduced SOC. SOC provides a very simple way of letting employees lead the revolution in quality improvement on the shop floor. SOC turned out to be one of the keys to Harley's successful turnaround: When employees got the tools plus a management that would listen to them, they immediately grabbed the opportunity to improve quality. After all, they had been telling management for 10 or 20 years that things were all screwed up and nobody ever listened to them. Now they finally had some techniques they could use to identify, document, and prove beyond a shadow of a doubt that things *were* in fact screwed up.

Some plant employees feel that this is the most important benefit of SOC. One put it this way: "I might be able to achieve the same quality without SOC. But I need the record. When I go to the supervisor and say I'm having a problem with the job, the first thing the supervisor says is, where's the chart, show me on the chart."

How SOC Works

Basically, SOC involves using simple statistical techniques and control charts to monitor the variation in a work process. The techniques include $\overline{X}$ and R charts, histograms, capability studies, and other statistical methods. Although these are the same methods used by traditional quality systems there is a major difference. Rather than engineers and specialists checking quality after the fact, plant operators themselves control the quality as they are making the product.

With statistical methods, the operator can answer two crucial questions about the process *as it is going on*:

- Is the process in control? That is, is it operating in a stable, predictable range of variation?
- Is the process capable? That is, is it able, consistently, to remain within the desired specifications?

An operator who sees the process starting to get out of control can in some cases stop the machine, make an adjustment, and continue. But the bulk of process variations cannot be brought under control by the operator alone. They are caused by flaws in the system (material, tooling, methods, machinery) that require management intervention to correct. However, by constantly identifying and eliminating these special causes of variation, operators and management working together can continuously improve product consistency.

Four Keys to Successful SOC

Today SOC at Harley is considered a success by management and by most employees. But achieving this success was far from smooth sailing. Senior management thought it had a simple strategy for introducing SOC but discovered that implementing the strategy was far from trouble-free. The strategy was to:

- Train all employees in statistical methods
- Apply statistical methods on the shop floor
- Study and reduce the process variations revealed by these techniques
- Continue to educate employees, using on-the-job training
- Encourage employees to strive for continuous improvement in the process

Simple? Far from it. Senior management had to learn some lessons the hard way.

1. First, you must win middle managers over to the SOC concept and the philosophy of continuous improvement of work processes. The whole idea that *everyone* should continuously improve the process and that operators would use statistics to understand and control a work process shook up and scared quite a few middle managers. They had an understandable fear of the unknown.

To deal with this problem, key managers were asked to attend a three-week course in using statistical methods in the continuous improvement of work processes given by the University of Tennessee. Until the first day of class, there was doubt about whether they would even attend the course. But they did, and the benefits were enormous. Not that they became statisticians or quality technicians. That wasn't the point. What was important was that they came to understand the role of SOC in the new drive for the continuous improvement of products through improving work processes and were then able to provide support for the operators once they, too, got into SOC.

2. You must be willing to invest in thorough SOC training for your operators or the program will fail. Senior management found this out when it initially limited SOC training to a two-hour orientation course. This turned out to be totally inadequate.

The first education program provided too little education and tried to educate too many people at once. Harley made a typical management mistake of playing the numbers game, focusing on how many people were going through the training instead of on how well they were being trained.

It soon became obvious that this superficial, once-over-lightly approach wouldn't work. The entire training program was then redesigned, resulting in a 20-hour in-house course that gave each employee a thorough grounding in basic SOC techniques that he or she could apply on the job. (Since then, the training has been expanded even further, and the current goal is for all employees to receive between 40 and 90 hours of training in various aspects of SOC and other problem-solving techniques.)

In line with Harley's EI philosophy, it does not use automated, computerized charting because that would take SOC out of the hands of the employee on the floor. Automated charting could turn statistical control into a button-pushing operation that would be meaningless to the operator. The way it is done in some companies, the operator generates the data and a quality assurance engineer puts it into a computer. In some cases it doesn't come back to the operator or it can't be understood by the operator. In other cases it comes back too late for the operator to take action. By having operators make their own charts, the information is immediately available, current, and understandable when they need it.

3. You must give operators posttraining support until they gain confidence in their SOC ability. Three months after the first class of employees had graduated from their SOC training, management found that about a third of the charts were not current. Obviously, there was a very high dropout rate. Reason: People simply lacked the self-confidence to use the process. When they ran into a problem, they just stopped using the process because they didn't want to appear stupid by asking their supervisor for help. To solve the problem, four hourly employees who were adept at SOC techniques were selected to be "floating coaches." This approach worked well since the operators had no embarrassment about asking their peers for assistance.

4. You must be ready and willing to respond to problems uncovered by SOC. After starting off with high expectations, many employees using SOC were turned off by the program. Reason: They would use SOC techniques to determine that a machine lacked the capability to produce parts to the required specifications, but when they communicated the problem upward, no one was ready to deal with it.

The same thing was happening with SOC that used to happen in the old days: If you had a problem you told the supervisor three times and if nothing happened, you said "they don't care" and just went on about your business. If no one responds to the problems you uncover with SOC it can become a big turn-off. Senior management agrees that if it had it to do all over again, it would begin by taking greater care in choosing the critical characteristics to chart, and then make sure there were enough people with expertise and enough technical resources to help the operators solve those problems when they came up.

Aiming for Perfection

Again, the goal of continuous improvement is to go beyond meeting engineering tolerances and eliminate variability completely—which, in turn, enables engineering to design closer to the ideal. SOC has substantially contributed to Harley-Davidson's progress toward that goal. Basically, the operator on the floor was made responsible for plotting, establishing control limits, analyzing, and reacting to any problems that occur. Giving people this responsibility has offered a challenge that many have taken up enthusiastically. Now, instead of fighting their supervisors or peers, they are fighting the process and devoting their efforts to improving it. Example: One grinder operator took his process from 200 percent off engineering specification down to 18 percent off, and now he's aiming for 10 percent.

Tactics and Techniques: Getting Suppliers Into the Act

Any company embarking on the Productivity Triad must also prepare to make major changes in its supplier relationships because the Productivity Triad won't produce results for manufacturers if their suppliers provide poor quality and delivery service.

Why Traditional Supplier Relationships Had to Go

In years past, Harley-Davidson's relationships with suppliers were like those of most other U.S. manufacturers. Top priority was to get the most competitive price. This was accomplished by frequent bidding and rebidding, developing multiple suppliers, and dual-sourcing parts—all of which, of course, created adversarial rather than cooperative relationships. It also meant building large inventories of safety stocks, just in case some components were defective, which still didn't prevent parts shortages caused by late deliveries and quality problems.

When Harley embarked on the far-reaching Productivity Triad program, it quickly became clear that the company's suppliers would have to change their manufacturing methods as well. There was no point in trying to install JIT inventory methods at Harley if suppliers, because of their lengthy, expensive setup costs, required long production runs of parts which resulted in large inventories at both their end and Harley's. The costs were simply too high: parts produced but not needed, storage of the unneeded inventory, costly inspection and counting, extra handling to move inventory around, and the risk of obsolescence.

How to Get Suppliers to See the Light

Converting your suppliers is far more difficult than converting your own plants. Many Harley suppliers thought at first that JIT was simply a scheme to keep Harley's inventories at the suppliers' facilities. Obviously, there was no point in that— wherever the inventory was kept, the cost of maintaining it would still end up being Harley's. The point, of course, was to *get rid of inventory*.

Initially, Harley made the mistake of trying to sell the JIT concept to suppliers' middle managers. Some of them were sold, but not their CEOs. *Lesson:* Take your case right to the top. If the CEO isn't willing to make the change, it won't happen!

Harley had more success when it sent a team of senior

manufacturing people to talk to *top* management at the plants of its 50 biggest suppliers. The team explained to each supplier how, by reducing setup times, it could cut its in-process inventory in half. This usually was met with disbelief, so Harley engineers would then demonstrate, on one of the supplier's own machines, how easily it could be done.

That was a start. Supplier visits were then followed by supplier symposiums held on-site at Harley-Davidson, where suppliers learned about the new manufacturing methods in more detail.

They were also invited to send their own people through Harley's in-house employee programs on problem-solving and SOC. By this time, senior management had realized that it wouldn't be enough for suppliers to adopt JIT without also converting to the whole Productivity Triad, meaning both EI and SOC in addition to JIT. The drive for quality, which is led by the JIT system, *forces* the supplier to use SOC. And none of it will work unless the supplier's employees are willing and able to make the change.

From Adversaries to Partners in Profit

The process of converting suppliers to the Productivity Triad led to some radical changes in Harley's relationships with its suppliers. Among the most important changes:

- A close working partnership between manufacturer and supplier
- Long-term agreements (2 to 3 years) with preferred suppliers, rather than traditional short-term contracts with 90-day cancellation clauses
- A focus on quality and supplier's costs, rather than on beating them down on price
- A shift to single-source suppliers rather than two sources for the same product
- Stabilized production schedules so that suppliers are not jerked around with constant changes

What's in It for Me?

Though suppliers were skeptical at first, many soon became convinced that they stood to benefit by becoming business partners with Harley-Davidson and adopting the Productivity Triad systems in their own operations. A supplier's manufacturing improvement not only assured that it would continue to get Harley's business, but also made it more competitive generally. One striking example of this was the case of a screw-machine supplier who was at about the bottom of Harley's quality and dependability list. The supplier was unresponsive to Harley's request to change—until it was told that Harley would have to take its business elsewhere unless the supplier did so. The supplier then agreed to Harley's sending two people over to work with it and run its employees through Harley's training program.

One year later, that supplier is now one of Harley's top suppliers in terms of quality and dependability—the parts arrive on schedule and go directly to the line with no receiving inspection. The supplier is now doing the same volume and mix of business but with two-thirds fewer employees. It is delighted because it is more profitable, and Harley is delighted because it has the parts quality and delivery service it requires.

The importance of providing tangible help and guidance for suppliers is underlined by another supplier's comments:

> Harley-Davidson approached us in early 1987 with requests for quotation and a new philosophy for a job shop: long-term commitments. With the potential of a lasting relationship came their willingness and expertise in helping us to achieve like goals. Specifically: Just-in-time inventory, to reduce waste in finished and unfinished products; statistical operator control, to identify and control machining problems; and employee involvement, for opening the doors of communication to hear what our people need to make better products. Some of these programs had been previously *suggested* by other customers, but only Harley-Davidson offered *direct guidance and assistance*.

Mistakes to Avoid

*Everyone was feeling their way—management and employees.
Mistakes were made for two reasons: First, Harley was implementing
unfamiliar, radically different manufacturing systems, and second,
under severe pressure from Japanese competition, Harley lacked the
luxury of time to prepare for change properly.*
   As a result:

• Senior management started EI groups with no real commitment to genuine employee involvement. The result was resentment and apathy. *Lesson: Unless management is sincerely committed to it, EI simply becomes a gimmick that won't work.*

• Harley failed to prepare middle managers for changes that threatened their authority because with survival at stake these changes had to be made quickly. *Lesson: Don't delay. Get started now overhauling your systems and preparing your managers while you still have time to do it right.*

• Harley failed to implement all three components of the Productivity Triad together. Missing was SOC. As a result, JIT and EI were not entirely successful because employees lacked the statistical tools needed to control and improve quality. *Lesson: Introduce the Productivity Triad with a coordinated plan that involves all elements—EI, JIT, and SOC.*

Above All, You Must Believe

You must *believe* and you must have a will to change. For most companies to adopt the Productivity Triad requires a virtual cultural revolution involving massive retraining. The process can be traumatic and frustrating in the beginning, and results may not be immediately apparent or performance may even temporarily decline. Unless management makes a commitment—total, absolute, and irrevocable—to seeing it through, it will fail. With total commitment, you can become a world-class competitor—the only kind of company that can expect to survive in the 1990s.

chapter 13

Strategies for Product Development and Marketing: Adapting to a Customer-Driven Era

When 13 managers found themselves owning Harley-Davidson in 1981, their most pressing problem was to get manufacturing systems under control so they could develop new, quality products. Otherwise, they would have no chance of competing with their major rival, Honda.

By 1983, the company had made great strides in improving quality, productivity, and employee relations. But it was not out of the woods competitively. Like many other U.S. firms, Harley-Davidson faced a rapidly changing marketplace. The consumer market was undergoing a profound transformation. Homogeneous mass markets were breaking up into highly differentiated segments, each with its own needs and desires.

It was the start of the "customer-driven" era. Consumers were calling the shots—and what they wanted, they got. Instead of providing just Coke and Tab, the Coca-Cola Company was dispensing a broad variety of fizzy drinks to its thirsty customers. Even traditional old Campbell Soup was experimenting with niche soups: Nacho cheese for Texas and California, creole for southern markets, red bean for Hispanic areas.

Harley-Davidson had never given its riders that kind of wide choice. But, as it has other companies, the consumer revolution forced Harley-Davidson into changing: from a company that virtually dictated what its customers could have to one that wouldn't dream of making a major marketing or product strategy move without getting direct input from those customers.

Way back, the Harley motorcycle was marketed as a utility vehicle: practical transportation that was not necessarily exciting. That theme was carried out by the bike itself, which was offered in just one color: gray. (In a momentous change in the twenties, Harley abandoned gray for . . . olive drab.) Ads depicted Harley riders not happily barreling along a country road, but delivering laundry and dry cleaning.

Once the car replaced the motorcycle as practical transportation, Harleys became more colorful. But the company still made just two or three basic heavyweight models. It got by with this narrow choice because by 1953 it was the only motorcycle maker left in the United States, and except for British brands it had no overseas competition to worry about.

Six Strategies Harley-Davidson Used to Beat Its Competition

Led by Honda, Japanese motorcycle makers established a U.S. beachhead by

- Invading the market segment that was least threatening to Harley-Davidson: lightweight bikes
- Going for high volume with low price
- Keeping prices low to further increase volume

Then, after securing their beachhead, they

- Expanded their product line with heavyweights that went head-to-head with Harley
- Went even further by marketing Harley look-alikes that copied virtually everything special about Harley machines
- Flooded the market with inventory and discounted heavily

This strategy—based on the Japanese bike makers' ability to produce excellent quality at low manufacturing costs—paid off handsomely by enabling the Japanese to take a big chunk of market share away from Harley. In a 10-year span (1973–1983), Harley's share of the 850cc-plus market dwindled from 77.5 percent to 23.3 percent, with Honda's share almost twice that at 44.3 percent.

Harley's dilemma was that improved quality and newly engineered V² engines alone could not bring back that lost market share. Yes, Harley absolutely had to lift its quality to survive at all. But even when it did so, the Japanese, with already high quality, still had a substantial edge in price.

This was the marketing challenge. Harley-Davidson could not compete on price against Honda, a company with tremendous financial resources. (Its advertising expenditures, alone, were outgunning Harley 40 to 1.) To regain market share, Harley would have to establish other market values. It chose six major strategies to accomplish this, which any company facing the same market problems and financial constraints can learn from.

Strategy 1: Define Your Niche and Stick To It

In the past, Harley had tried to repel the Japanese attack on a broad front by selling lightweight and middleweight bikes as well as its traditional superheavies. But the front was *too* broad for a small company; Harley just didn't have the firepower to beat back the Japanese giants with their superior quality, lower costs, and relentless drive for market share.

When those 13 managers bought the company in 1981, they were split into two factions with differing ideas on market strategy. One faction dreamed of challenging Honda, not only for the heavyweight lead, but in smaller motorcycles, too. The other said no, our niche is classic heavyweight machines, and that's the market we should go after.

The trouble with the first group's strategy was that when Harley tried to compete on lighter machines, it didn't have a bulletproof product because it had all kinds of quality problems with the machines. But Harley could confidently charge a premium price for heavyweights, because it had good, solid product design and an established customer base of dedicated enthusiasts. Harley also had a premium price on lighter motorcycles, but this price position was doomed to fail because these were entry-level bikes and customers wanted to spend as little as possible on something they weren't even sure they'd like.

The big-bike niche philosophy won out. With the help of styling vice president Willie G. Davidson, the company identified and exploited "mini-niches"—such as customized, touring, sport/touring, and sport/street motorcycles—in the heavyweight end of the market. The strategy worked, and Harley's share in the heavyweight niche has been zooming.

Strategic Lesson: Many U.S. companies could profit from Harley's approach. Pick your niche and concentrate on beating your competition in that niche. Find niches within the niche. That's what Harley chose to do: It now makes nothing but classic heavyweight motorcycles and it is dominating this market.

Strategy 2: Listen to Your Customers and Give Them What They Want

Although Harley had added some new models, it was still offering what one industry observer called "your plain vanilla motorcycle." Harley's major challenge was to introduce models that would attract new customers without alienating old ones. The answer it came up with was to build on the potential of the "factory custom" bike.

You Want Mint Chocolate Chip, You've Got Mint Chocolate Chip. Harley owners are strong on individualism, thus they want their Harleys to look different from everyone else's. In the past, they had bought Harley's "plain vanilla" motorcycles and customized them with all kinds of personal touches: engine chrome, custom welded handlebars, teardrop gas tank, upswept rear fender, etc. Harley's new strategy was to build some of these custom refinements right into a broad variety of models at the factory. And after buying their Harleys, owners can continue to customize them with the many Harley mechanical accessories available.

To implement this strategy required maintaining close links to the ultimate customer, the motorcycle enthusiast, because involvement with the customer is absolutely critical. With Willie G. and others, "close to the customer" is not just a slogan, it's a passion. Company officers spend almost every weekend from April to October at motorcycle events and dealerships. In their leathers and boots, they mingle with riders and talk motorcycles. They listen closely to riders' design suggestions—although they seldom adopt them literally because of technical requirements, government regulations, and other practical restrictions. What they come away with are rider preferences that enable them to design models that are different and yet maintain the authentic Harley look that riders want. The innovations are subtle rather than extreme, because Harley riders don't like radical breaks with tradition.

Harley advanced the art of factory-customizing in 1977 with the introduction of the Low Rider. But it was not until the 1980s that the factory-custom strategy came into its own and the variety of available models grew at a fast pace. Harley now produces 28 different models, up from 14 in 1981.

Advertising conveys the factory-custom strategy. It hammers away at the theme that Japanese knock-offs of the Harley look as though they had been designed by a faceless, anonymous committee, that is, they lack individuality. Harleys, on the other hand, "make a bold custom statement that is not like anything else."

The High Price of Not Listening.   Harley's factory-custom strategy—along with the improved quality of its machines—has given it an edge over its Japanese competition. The key to its success is that it listens to its customers. Company managers are unanimous in saying that listening to rider views helps Harley-Davidson avoid making expensive design and marketing mistakes.

A sobering example of how much such mistakes can cost is reported in *The New York Times* of October 11, 1988. John

Holusha describes what happened when General Motors' Buick division radically changed its Riviera model:

> When the new Riviera was introduced in 1986, it was 19 inches shorter than the model it replaced, and its chopped-off rear section resembled those on some of G.M.'s economy offerings. Sales plunged to half the previous year's level and have continued to drift downward. A redesigned model, with 11 inches added to the back end, was rushed into production for the 1989 model year. The experience caused chastened Buick managers to pledge not to repeat the mistake. "We will design cars people want, not try to teach people to want the cars we design," said Darwin E. Clark, the division's marketing director.

Buick's lesson was similar to the one that Harley-Davidson learned the hard way when it introduced its Cafe Racer model in 1977: Harley customers will not accept a motorcycle that breaks too radically with its roots. This machine, unlike anything Harley had produced up until then, was a total departure from previous stylings and customary riding positions and therefore was a resounding financial flop (even though it has its cult adherents). Since then, Harley has listened with dedicated attention to what its customers have to say, recognizing that any newly styled product may have a significantly limited sales volume until customers warm up to it. Based on this experience and customer preferences, the company has developed a product strategy of mating modern, state-of-the-art motorcycle technology with the heritage and classic designs of the traditional Harley-Davidson machine.

In addition to talking face-to-face with customers, Harley does extensive formal market research and acts on the data if they are consistent with its informal findings. Harley's marketing philosophy is that you can't know too much about your customers, so it gathers detailed information through surveys, interviews, and focus groups.

Strategic Lesson: Although Harley's marketing problems may be unusual in some ways, the principles it uses to solve them apply to most U.S. companies today. And one of those principles is: If you want to beat your competition worldwide you must listen to and understand your customers—and then, if you can, give them what they want. Operationally, this means (1) *creating* opportunities for customers to tell you what they think about your product or service and (2) taking the time to evaluate what they're *really* saying. (Above all, don't change for the sake of change. Let the customer tell you what changes are acceptable.)

Strategy 3: Differentiate Your Product

Harley is trying to sell the entire Harley-Davidson experience, not just the motorcycle. It does this in several ways. First, advertising consistently promotes the "more than a motorcycle" theme. Typical is this excerpt from the Harley catalog, which is intentionally lavish and features large, full-color photographs of the latest models on glossy paper:

> When you put your hard-earned money into a Harley-Davidson, you're getting more than a motorcycle. You're buying into a motorcycling legend. And a feeling that's impossible to put a price tag on.

This "charisma" strategy effectively differentiates Harley from Honda, Yamaha, and the other Japanese makers, whose advertising emphasizes product technology and features rather than the mystique and camaraderie of the motorcycling experience.

Harley also offers the "whole environment"—something no other motorcycle maker appears to be able to match—through the company-sponsored Harley Owners Group (H.O.G.), which it started in 1983. Strategically, H.O.G. helps keep the company close to its customers and gives them the Harley experience in a structured form. And it's another important point of differentiation from the Japanese bike makers, who do not sponsor owner clubs.

Every Harley purchaser receives a one-year free membership in H.O.G. and can continue the membership for $35 a year. For this, H.O.G.'s nearly 100,000 members receive the following:

- A bimonthly club publication, *Hog Tales*, which provides a news pipeline from Harley-Davidson to members about details of motorcycling events, new Harley products, and "exclusive" H.O.G. accessories for members only
- A six-month subscription to *American Iron*, a general motorcycling magazine
- Admission to company open houses, local and national rallies featuring name entertainment, and private H.O.G. receptions at major motorcycle events and races across the United States and Canada
- Eligibility for membership in local dealer-sponsored H.O.G. chapters that put on group rides, field meets (low-speed competition), parties, charity events, and other activities
- "Fly and Ride" arrangements provided by the H.O.G. Travel Center, for members who want to fly to other parts of the world and then tour on a rented Harley
- The H.O.G. Insurance Program, which enables members to buy insurance at competitive rates
- An emergency pickup service
- A separate rider support group for female riders and passengers that provides riding activities, training in motorcycle safety and basic motorcycle servicing, and access to exclusive merchandise

Getting Away From It All on a Harley.   A third element of selling the Harley experience might be called "live out your fantasies." There's a growing fantasy business in the United States. To escape from a humdrum workaday world where there seems to be less and less time to relax, more and more Americans are rafting down fake white-water rapids in adventure parks or spending weekends in fantasy hotels (for example, Minnesota's Burnsville Royale Hotel features one room designed to look like Lover's Lane—complete with a 1973 Oldsmobile convertible containing a neatly made up double bed).

Fantasy is becoming big business, and Harley-Davidson sees it as an additional opportunity to expand its market.

Escape from 9-to-5 does not mean just climbing aboard a Harley and taking off for a twisty road. For many it means a complete change of lifestyle, even if only for a weekend. Here's how Beau Allen Pacheco describes one Harley couple in the June 1988 issue of *Rider Magazine*:

> Glen Gerhardt from Tampa calls himself Griz, has a rakish salt-and-pepper beard, sports a stogy, wears a black vest and had brought his girlfriend Donna to Daytona. His shiny blue FX Harley is spotless. He's also a lawyer for a large multinational firm, and Donna manages a data processing firm.

Or take the "ABC Evening News" segment in 1988 that opened with a shot of what appeared to be a gang of bikers zooming down the L.A. freeway on their Harleys. In the next shot, they rumbled up to a chic Beverly Hills restaurant and trooped in. It turned out that these were all professional and managerial types escaping their high-pressure work environment by living out the Harley experience. ABC's Peter Jennings dubbed them "The Brunch Bunch." Other journalists have noted the growing numbers of RUBs (Rich Urban Bikers)—who have Harleys parked next to their Porsches and Jaguars in the garage.

Harley chic is also in. Fashion magazines feature models sporting Harley T-shirts or draped over vintage Harley bikes wearing what *Mademoiselle* magazine calls "truly cool again" motorcycle jackets. Harley-Davidson is taking advantage of this newfound popularity by placing more ads in nonmotorcycling magazines.

A substantial Harley-Davidson *Fashions and Collectibles* catalog is issued twice a year, containing a full line of functional yet well-styled leather jackets, pants, chaps, boots, and gloves for motorcycle riding, plus a large variety of "Harley" products such as toy trains, pocketknives, Tiffany-style lamp shades, dress watches, shaving mugs, belt buckles, wallets, and a choice of two aprons—one reading "Warning: I Ride Better Than I Cook!" and the other, "Relax—I Cook Better Than I Ride!"

Harley executives say these products help meet the desire of many to expand the Harley-Davidson experience from a sport to a total lifestyle.

Strategic Lesson: As one of Harley's board members, management consultant Michael J. Kami, points out, to beat your competition today you must develop products or services with individuality and something unique—whether it's charisma, quality, delivery, patents, integrity, or any other marketable characteristic.

Strategy 4: Compete on Value, Not Price

Harley-Davidson is trying to achieve cost parity with the Japanese bike makers, but that doesn't mean that Harleys will ever be able to compete with Hondas and Yamahas on price. Harley riders like metal, so Harleys have steel fenders while the Japanese models often have plastic. If they choose to do so, Harley riders are able to rebore their engines to expand the product life span, because the alloy cylinders have thicker cast-iron liners which can be rebuilt. In the customers' eyes, having this choice enhances the value of the motorcycle.

These differences cost more, so Harley deliberately offers unique features and benefits, not low price. A top-of-the-line Harley can cost $13,000. So far the company has had no difficulty finding customers to pay such prices—in recent years, it has sold every machine it can make.

Strategic Lesson: Only companies with deep, deep pockets can compete on price (price wars are *very* costly). What most companies must strive for today is a competitive edge based on value rather than price. Harley-Davidson has shown, vividly, that with this edge, even the giants with deep pockets can be beaten.

Strategy 5: Treat Your Dealers as Full Business Partners

Before 1985, Harley-Davidson didn't have the programs to help its dealers go beyond just selling and servicing motorcycles, and the results showed on the company's bottom line and on the dealers.' Although the company had made some attempts to help dealers modernize their stores, the efforts were ineffective, amounting mostly to telling them to "upgrade" their stores and sending them design manuals showing how the store should look.

Now Harley has an effective, comprehensive program design to help dealers become full-line retailers catering to the total motorcycle lifestyle. The program is successful for these reasons:

- Harley has stopped telling dealers that it is upgrading them. Understandably, dealers resent that. Instead, the company offers to help dealers improve their business volume and profits. To show how it could be done, the company conducted a pilot program with one store that demonstrated the effectiveness of modernization—for example, laying out the store in a loop design so that the customer must walk past all the displayed merchandise before getting to the purchase counter.

- Harley no longer just hands the program to the dealer and says, "Good luck." Now it plays an active role: developing the program, financing it, and helping the dealer implement it. Any dealer with a problem can call on one of the company's business-management consultants, who will spend as much time as it takes at the store to help the dealer solve the problem.

- Harley asks dealers to demonstrate their commitment to the program by investing their own money. (Redesign costs from $30,000 to $100,000.)

The program is making good progress, to the point where dealers are now selling each other on it. A direct comparison of sales gains in 1988 reveals that dealers with 6 to 18 months of sales experience after remodeling their stores show a 44.5 percent increase in sales versus a 25.5 percent sales gain for the total dealer network.

Strategic Lesson: You may make a good product, but the customer's image of your company is usually determined by contact with your dealers. That's why any marketing strategy must pay attention to how dealers sell your product.

Strategy 6: Build on Your Name

Harley-Davidson is a name that can sell all kinds of peripheral products. But until the early 1980s management did not fully recognize the potential of this market.

For many years, the company had provided its own line of motorcycle and rider accessories, but many other products bearing the company name were "bootlegged" without trademark permission by a variety of entrepreneurs, not all of them respectable. Some T-shirts, for example, had obscene, racist, and violent messages and images. Some catalogs featured "Harley" pot-smoking paraphernalia. These bootlegged products perpetuated the public perception of Harley riders as unsavory biker outlaws.

Harley-Davidson became increasingly concerned about the many people using their trademark without authorization. After winning a major lawsuit against one of the biggest infringers, Joe's MCN, and sending out countless cease and desist notices to unlicensed makers of Harley accessories, the company succeeded in regaining control of its trademark and eradicating most of the bootleg products.

To maintain control of the use of its name and to share in the financial benefits of selling accessory products, the company started an extensive trademark licensing program in 1983, based on royalties and stringent controls for the use of its name and logo. "Our licensing program protects our trademark and prevents others from using and abusing it," says Jeff Bleustein, who oversees the program (in 1985 he made a radical job switch from vice president of engineering to vice president of parts and accessories). High-quality products are assured by the standards built into the licensing agreements and enforced by a company review of every new design. Licensees themselves assist in protecting the Harley-Davidson trademark against illegal use because they, too, have a stake in preserving its distinction.

The trademark licensing program generates a stream of new T-shirt designs and other products over a wider range and at lower cost than would be possible using just Harley-Davidson personnel and capital. These products provide additional income for both dealers and the factory and help to expand the total Harley-Davidson experience.

The licensing program also allows Harley-Davidson products to reach a nonriding market through distribution in such stores as Bloomingdale's and J.C. Penney. Bleustein says, "It brings Harley-Davidson products and the Harley-Davidson name to people who might never have previously thought of visiting a Harley-Davidson dealership and turns some of them into motorcycle customers. The program gives us and our dealers priceless advertising and promotion, far beyond what we could do ourselves."

Harley-licensed products, however, cannot be sold exclusively through Harley dealers, and that's a sticking point with many of them. The company responds that licensing gives Harley dealers a greater variety of high-quality accessories to sell. Moreover, some items—such as denim garments—cannot be priced low enough to sell unless they are made in larger volumes than could be sold through the dealers alone.

Despite this, some dealers fear that selling accessories through other retailers is just the beginning and that someday other retailers will be selling Harley motorcycles as well. To ease these fears, Harley-Davidson has issued formal licensing policies assuring dealers that this will not come to pass.

Strategic Lesson: There can be no such thing as standing still in today's competitive environment. A company must play to its strength and continually pursue profit opportunities in all areas of its business.

chapter 14

Financial Strategies: Turning Around to Survive— And Thrive

After the buyout from AMF, Harley-Davidson senior management had one long-range objective: to bring the company back as the preeminent manufacturer of heavyweight motorcycles in the world. But the senior managers also had an urgent short-range objective: to stay alive financially. Although the managers didn't recognize them at the time, the signs for their even surviving long enough to achieve the long-range goals were not at all good.

At this writing, eight years later, the company has a good shot at its long-range goals. But it has had to live through a wild financial roller-coaster ride—and at several points along the way it almost came off the rails. The story of what Harley-Davidson did to extricate itself from one financial crisis after another has useful lessons for other U.S. companies.

Living With the LBO

The leveraged buyout from AMF was small potatoes compared with today's megabuck LBOs, but in 1981 it was one of the largest ever. And it was one of the most highly leveraged ever: $1 million in equity bought a $300 million company.

Another distinguishing feature of this LBO is that the Harley-Davidson buyout team got 100 percent of the deal, which rarely happens these days. Now a deal is usually packaged by an organization that specializes in acquisitions, and as a result the management ends up with only 10 to 20 percent of the equity and a new boss—the financial packager. But Harley's buyout team figured that if it had its own money in the equity, it wanted to make the operating decisions.

Harley-Davidson's total line of credit was $100 million—of which it took down $65 million at closing—from four lenders. Of that, $30 million was a term loan to be paid off in stages. The remaining $35 million was in a revolving credit account—in banking jargon, a "revolver"—and the amount available was based on a percentage of Harley-Davidson's assets, such as accounts receivable and finished-goods inventory. As mentioned in the first half of this book, the lead lender was Citicorp Industrial Credit, Inc., which held 65 percent of the loan, and three other banks held the rest of the loan: Girard Bank of Philadelphia (now Mellon East), First Wisconsin National Bank of Milwaukee, and New England Merchants National Bank (now Bank of New England). These other banks had no authority to alter Citicorp's decisions on the loan.

The Downside of Asset Borrowing

Although Harley-Davidson had some solid positives going for it—loyal customers, strong dealer network, strong in-place management team, and dedicated employees—it did not exactly meet the profile of the ideal LBO candidate, particularly because it didn't have parts that could be easily broken off and sold to pay down debt. The loan was based strictly on physical assets—and that's where Harley ran into trouble.

Asset-based borrowers are pretty much at the mercy of their lenders, and banks tend to take a tough, uncompromising position on this type of loan. Citicorp's lending formulas were extremely conservative—*too* conservative from Harley's viewpoint. As mentioned earlier, while Harley's banks would lend it only 70 percent of the manufacturing *cost* of a new motorcycle, some other lending institutions were willing to lend Harley dealers 100 percent of their *purchase price* under floor-plan arrangements. Similarly, the banks were lending the company only about 13 cents for every dollar of retail sales value of parts and accessories.

These formulas seriously restricted Harley's ability to borrow the money to keep going if it ran into trouble. And this is exactly what happened. The economy slid downward, and interest rates zoomed upward—a bad climate for selling expensive motorcycles and the worst possible climate for an LBO.

As the LBO was being finalized, the U.S. motorcycle market experienced a sharp slowdown in sales. The reasons: recession, high interest rates, and high unemployment—especially of blue-collar workers, Harley-Davidson's traditional customer base.

The company was losing market share, and it failed to cut production quickly enough. This left it with record inventories of finished motorcycles as the LBO deal closed, and dealer inventories were already too heavy. The dual problem of having to cut production to offset excess inventories *and* to cope with declining retail sales (largely because of market-share loss) was what nearly did the company in.

What Harley-Davidson Did to Survive: Three Key Strategies You Can Use

1. Play Straight With Your Lenders

In an LBO, your relationship with your bank can be adversarial or it can be cooperative. In the United States, the adversarial relationship is more common. Banks worry that borrowers aren't doing everything they should be doing to enable them to pay down their debt, while borrowers accuse banks of making things so difficult for them—with covenants and other restrictions—that they can't operate properly.

The Japanese Difference. By comparison, the relationship between the lender and corporate borrower in Japan is quite different. In *The New York Times* of October 30, 1988, Louis Uchitelle points out that Japanese banks often own a stake in the borrowing companies. That leads them to become more supportive. When companies suffer reverses or need capital to develop new products or break into new markets, the banks are willing to help by deferring interest payments or refinancing debt. The Japanese system is unlike the American system in that it assumes long-term relationships between the companies and their bankers.

Despite the less sympathetic U.S. environment, it is possible for U.S. companies to have positive relationships with their banks. It is a two-way proposition, of course, and banks must participate in this approach if it is to work.

The Trust Factor.   Without trust, it is probably impossible to avoid an adversarial relationship between bank and borrower. By being forthcoming and candid, Harley-Davidson was able to establish that trust factor with Citicorp, the lead lender, and with the other three banks. For example, when there was a problem, Harley always tried to apprise the banks immediately. Jack Reilly, Harley's first senior loan officer at Citicorp, found this a refreshing change from his negative experiences with other LBOs. From his point of view, it made his life much easier:

> With bankers, the biggest problem is when you have
> surprises and you have credibility gaps. We didn't have
> to worry about that with Harley-Davidson. What they
> told us, they delivered on. They said, here's what the
> risks are, here's what we'll deliver. There were never
> any surprises, and even in the worst of times, there was
> never a trust problem. Most companies, when they get
> into difficulties, right away the bank is the bad guy.
> Harley directed their negative vibes toward their
> competition, not their bank.

This was not to say that Citicorp didn't keep a sharp eye on its own interests. (For example, Citicorp wanted a hefty $5 million fee for meeting Harley-Davidson's overadvance needs.) So one lesson to be learned in bank relationships is that banks, like their borrowers, are in business to make a profit. They view their risks differently than borrowers view theirs. Banks are always thinking of what could go wrong and then taking steps to protect themselves. That's why Citicorp was preparing Harley-Davidson liquidation scenarios from Day One of the LBO. That's also why Citicorp tried to persuade Harley to operate just one plant, because it would be more economical, and why, in 1985, the bank wanted Harley to sell off its bomb-casing business, even though that business was making money while the motorcycle business was losing money. The bank's basic objective was to salvage the value of the loan. "What happened to Harley-Davidson was not a concern of theirs," says Rich Teerlink.

Nevertheless, an atmosphere of trust between banker and borrower can make the bank more supportive than it might be in an atmosphere of suspicion and hostility. As Harley found later, such a relationship cannot always be maintained—but the effort to establish it is always worthwhile.

2. Manage for Cash Flow, Not Net Income

Harley's senior managers quickly recognized a basic principle that is imperative for any company involved in an LBO to understand: Leverage is no substitute for a business strategy. And this business strategy must focus on generating enough cash to meet current obligations—which in an LBO can be awesomely heavy. Cash flow coverage is critical. Revco, the first big LBO to go into Chapter 11, did not learn that lesson until it was too late. It failed to gear its operations to generate cash flow and was unable to meet its debt payments.

Building Up Cash Flow and Cash Availability. Harley-Davidson had plenty of assets, including motorcycles. But you can't meet your payroll or your interest payments with assets. Confronted by this reality, Harley adopted a strategy of managing for cash flow and cash availability (meaning taking actions that make it possible to borrow more funds within the lending formula), rather than managing for reported profits.

To build cash flow the company embarked on a stringent cost control and asset-management program. Expenses were cut, staff was reduced, and inventory and receivable turns were improved. Inventory turns were the key. Harley-Davidson increased them by adopting just-in-time (JIT) inventory methods that enabled it to increase cash flow by $19 million.

To increase cash availability (when the company was already living on overadvance) required great creativity in managing cash. For example, the level of lending on finished-goods inventories was determined by month-end numbers, while the level of lending on receivables was done on a daily basis. Harley soon figured out that if it were slow in shipping motorcycles at the end of the month its inventory would go up and it could borrow more on the finished-goods inventory. And if, on the first day of the following month, it shipped all the finished-goods inventory, it could also borrow on the accounts receivable while still keeping its loan on the month-end inventory intact. This tactic helped the company through some tough periods.

Living on the Edge.   The stringent cost programs and asset-management strategies resulted in a strong cash flow improvement from 1981 to 1982. Nevertheless, Harley was still compelled to go into overadvance, borrowing more money than the bank's lending formulas stipulated. Harley had to borrow money just to keep going and, like debtor nations, to make payments on money it had *previously* borrowed. This is one of the negatives of LBOs: There's not much margin for fluctuations in the market and the economy. Whenever rates spike or business turns sour, high debt loads quickly become harder to manage. Sometimes they become impossible to manage, as Revco found out.

3. Don't Deny Your Problems—Move to Solve Them

Citicorp could have liquidated Harley-Davidson at any time. What gave the bank the right to liquidate was that by 1982 the downturn of the market and the economy had forced Harley to violate several covenants of the loan agreement, one that required it to maintain a minimum tangible net worth and another requiring it to limit its pretax loss to a certain amount.

Citicorp's first step toward liquidation would have been to cut off the overadvance. Overadvance is not something a lender bank does with enthusiasm. Every day that a collateral lender funds losses it gets in worse shape. That's when it starts thinking about alternatives: shrinking the operation further, selling it, or simply liquidating it.

Making the Tough Decisions.   Harley-Davidson's strategy to forestall any of these alternatives was twofold. One aim was to make it clear to Citicorp that the company did not consider any of these to be acceptable alternatives. Harley's senior managers were convinced that even though things looked bad, Harley-Davidson was still a viable company and could turn things around.

The second part of the strategy was to move fast on a stringent cost control and asset-management program. Citicorp was impressed by the fact that Harley management could make the tough decisions needed to keep the company going. In an October 1982 status review of Harley's account Citicorp reported the following:

- Despite drop in revenues of $12.3 million (9.5%) in the first half of 1982 compared with 1981, management reduced operating expenses from 22% of sales in 1981 to 20.8% in 1982 and improved the gross margin to 19% from 16.8% while also significantly improving product quality and reliability.
- Headcount was reduced 41.8% from 3841 on June 10, 1981, to 2235 on July 30, 1982. Salaries for those who remain were either frozen, or in the case of stockholders, reduced 12%.
- Production is now 104 units per day compared with 240 units per day last June.
- They are implementing a "material as needed" inventory program similar to the Japanese to reduce excess inventory and generate cash.
- Supplier price concession of $900 thousand annually have been negotiated and 35% of suppliers have agreed to 60-day or longer terms.
- Additional actions taken include negotiation of a contract to produce bomb casings for the government, sale of their golf-car operation for approximate $5 million, and successful introduction of the low cost ($4,000) "Brutal Sportster," well received by dealers and press.
- The combination of these actions reduced breakeven by one-third from 53,000 units in June, 1981 to 32,000 units presently.

It was only Harley-Davidson's willingness to move fast on its problems that persuaded Citicorp and the other lender banks to stick with it.

When a Banking Relationship Turns Sour

An earlier chapter told how the company's relationship with Citicorp took a 180° turn in 1984. One Citicorp team was replaced by another that took a completely different perspective on the company's prospects. The new team decided Harley-Davidson was a "leave"—meaning that the bank wanted out.

Ironically, by 1984 Harley-Davidson was on the upswing. After losses in 1981 and 1982, it edged into the black again with a profit of just under $1 million. In 1984, it did better, with a net of $2.6 million. Market share was up; it continued to improve inventory turns, manufacturing variances, and quality; and it was taking further cost-reduction steps to improve its competitiveness, pricing flexibility, return on assets, and protection against an economic downturn.

A big downside of the situation was that Harley still required overadvance financing from the lending group. As Steve Deli, managing director of Dean Witter Reynolds' Chicago office, points out:

> Loan officers don't want to stick their necks out constantly defending overadvance to their superiors. The new Citicorp team in charge of Harley-Davidson's facility decided it would be the new broom that sweeps clean. The attitude was: Harley is no good for Citicorp, so let's get rid of it.

Refinancing Crisis: How Harley-Davidson Avoided Bankruptcy

Although Harley had made contacts with investment bankers continually since 1982, in late 1985 the company had no choice but to intensify its efforts to obtain refinancing. Citicorp had made it clear that it would cut off Harley's overadvance on

November 1. If the bank stuck to that, Harley would be out of business. It had already made preparations to file for bankruptcy protection under Chapter 11.

Rich Teerlink "cold called" almost every investment banker on Wall Street and La Salle Street, and Dean Witter Reynolds approached many potential lenders. Both got flat turndowns. Despite progress on many fronts, Harley-Davidson's financial position made it less than an attractive investment. Its financial picture included negative net worth, a large overadvance position on its bank credit facility, and slim earnings following on the heels of two major loss years. And there was always the nagging question of why Citicorp wanted to pull out.

Then Steve Deli got Harley-Davidson together with Heller Financial, Inc. Heller was the only lending institution at that time that would even *consider* refinancing Harley. Heller was extremely skeptical at first, but it listened for several reasons:

- Harley-Davidson had real assets; its brand name and franchise would continue to generate sales even if its motorcycle business went under. Heller estimated the Harley-Davidson aftermarket business—parts and accessories—to be worth about $40 million.
- The company was successfully reducing manufacturing costs through advanced management techniques, showing Heller that it was making headway rather than simply being carried along.
- Market share was rebounding.
- Heller was impressed by Harley-Davidson's commitment, persistence, and confidence in being able to turn the company around.
- Harley assured Heller that Citibank was willing to take a sizable write-off on its loan.
- Heller's number two principal was a Harley rider who instantly understood the Harley mystique (in his language, "the value of intangibles"), and, as a Harley enthusiast (one senior manager believes), he tried harder to sell a difficult loan internally.

Shaping the Deal That Saved Harley's Bacon

The words of Steve Deli, who worked indefatigably to put together the refinancing deal with Heller, clearly convey the crisis atmosphere that prevailed:

> After much thrashing about, Dean Witter worked out a proposal by Heller to Harley for a refinancing agreement. Among other requirements laid down was that $5 to $8 million of loans be forgiven, that most of the other banks stay in the credit facility, and that some term debt be provided by others.
>
> We had to meet these requirements quickly because it was already November and the deal had to be finalized by the end of the year or Harley would be out of business. Journeys were made to the Bank of New England in Boston and Mellon East in Philadelphia, followed by scurrying around to seek term financing from the State of Wisconsin Investment Board—which strongly indicated a commitment would be forthcoming.
>
> On that basis, we convened a meeting of the bank group to review the proposed deal and see who would take a reduction in principal. It was an incredibly tumultuous meeting, with Citicorp having its usual phalanx of representatives. However, as Harley had told Heller, Citicorp was willing to take an $8 million reduction in principal to get out of the loan. The other three banks had enough confidence in Harley to stay in the loan.
>
> A deal was beginning to shape up—but not on favorable terms. As our negotiations progressed from a sketchy commitment to specifics, there were constant demands by Heller for more. More money put in by the other banks. More covenants. More safeguards. More ways out if the motorcycle business went downhill. More attractive terms for Heller.
>
> Our negotiating sessions were less negotiation than unconditional surrender. Heller was in the driver's seat, and we had no choice but to go along with its demands. Harley even had to give Heller the right to cut their

management compensation by 40 percent if they violated any of the many covenants.

Biting the Bullet

December 23 was crunch time. Heller had already turned the deal down once, on December 16. More concessions on Harley's part restored it to life. But when, on the 23rd, Heller turned the deal down again, the only way to revive it was to restructure the deal as a financing that was callable by Heller on 90 days' notice *at Heller's option*. This was a major blow to Harley-Davidson's future ability to survive should troubles occur. Further, Heller asked for warrants for 10 percent of the company—a device that would enable it to buy 10 percent for very little money. The new terms proposed by Heller also meant Harley-Davidson would be getting less capital at higher cost.

But Harley accepted the new deal. It had to, because Citicorp cut off overadvance on November 1 and Harley was now stretching its accounts payable. The Heller deal wasn't much of a Christmas present, but it kept Harley alive.

Going Public: How Harley Made a Run for Daylight

The Heller refinancing allowed the company to survive, but it was only an interim solution. It didn't provide long-term stability or a financial structure that Harley could count on. The loan could be called at almost any time.

There were two options. The company could refinance in the private market, with institutional investors such as life insurance companies, pension funds, or banks. By doing some long-term borrowing it could pay off part of the Heller loan and just use Heller for the revolving credit.

Or Harley could go public. That was the route recommended by Steve Deli in the spring of 1986. The reaction of Harley's senior management? Disbelief. After all, just a short three months ago the company had been one week away from bankruptcy. To go from that to asking people to buy Harley's equity on the public market was a hard leap to make, mentally.

But everyone soon realized that, looking at the present and future instead of the past, Harley-Davidson had some good selling points:

- The momentum had turned. Harley's last operating loss had been in 1982, and it now had positive cash flow.
- The company had a good first quarter, ahead of the previous year.
- It was still reducing its costs.
- Its market share was still increasing.
- It had a potential for growth that made it attractive for equity investors.
- It had a well-known name that would make the offering appealing to the retail market.

On top of that, the market that spring was active and receptive to new offerings.

Steve Deli proposed a public equity offering combined with borrowing on the junk-bond market.

Deli's objective was to raise $15 million of equity and $50 million in subordinated debt. In the end, he did 40 percent better than his projections, raising $20 million from the public offering and $70 million on the junk-bond market (payable in 1996). It was the complete opposite of the Heller deal and the Citicorp deal—no covenants, no restrictions, no formulas. All Harley had to do was make interest payments. The difference between its financial position three months earlier and at this point was like the difference between night and day.

The Guidelines Harley-Davidson Followed

When it went public, Harley's actions were guided by some basic principles that can be profitably applied by any company:

1. *Take advantage of market opportunities when you can, and don't be greedy.* It's not unusual for a company to think that if it just waits another six months the market will be higher and

it can get a better price for its offering. Harley might have done that because it could have lived with the Heller deal, difficult as it was. But if Harley *had* waited, it would not have had the flexibility, the value, and the returns it gained by going public when it did. The right thing to do at the end of 1985 was to take the Heller deal. The right thing to do three months later was to go public.

2. *Focus on increasing your financial flexibility and capacity.* There's a long-standing financial maxim that says: Sell equity when you can and debt when you must. It's true and it works. Equity capital provides you with the most flexibility and capacity because you can borrow on top of the equity. Using equity as your financing vehicle gives you lots of choices. True, there are certain advantages to borrowing when you want to raise capital. You don't have to share on the upside, you just have to pay the interest. But it makes you less flexible because you may have too much debt to borrow again the next time you are seeking capital. If you take the equity route, as Harley has, you can go either way the next time. If the market seems good for debt, you can borrow, and if it seems good for equity, you can make an offering. Harley's LBO had used up all of its financial flexibility and capacity, so its strategy was to concentrate on rebuilding them.

3. *Focus on the value you get when you borrow, not on the interest you must pay.* Subordinated debt is as close to equity as you can get without actually selling equity because there are few, if any, restrictions on your actions, and you can put senior debt on top of it. But it's expensive. Harley-Davidson found that out in 1986 when it acquired $70 million of it at 12.5 percent (when the prime was around 7 percent). The company could have balked at that. But instead of getting all wrapped up about spending an extra 1 or 2 percent, Harley looked at the value of what it was getting—and decided it was worth it.

Acquiring Holiday Rambler: How the Decision Was Made

Harley had solved a huge financial problem by going public in June 1986. Now it had a chance to catch its breath after years of living on the brink. In September, it convened a senior management meeting to develop a new business strategy that would reflect its changed capital structure.

Projections were that in December it would have $50 million in cash on the balance sheet and $70 million debt that was due in 10 years. Management decided to use that money to protect the company against future downturns.

Major strides had already been made in that direction. By reducing manufacturing costs, the company had lowered its breakeven by a third, down to around 32,000 units. But the

---

FINANCIAL STEPS TO A TURNAROUND

Here are the major financial transactions that Harley-Davidson completed on its way to recovery:

Transaction	Date	Amount of Money Involved
Leveraged buyout by senior management from AMF	1981	$81.5 million
Acquisition of $19.0 million in securities plus $4.6 million in dividends and interest owned by AMF through settlement negotiations	December 1983	$17.0 million
First public stock offering for 2 million shares of common stock at	July 8, 1986	$20,251 million
$70 million of unsecured subordinated notes		$70 million
Purchase of Holiday Rambler Corporation	December 1986	$156.7 million
Subordinated note offering by Holiday Rambler Corporation	May 1987	$70 million
Successful public offering of 1,230,000 shares of common stock by Harley-Davidson, Inc.	June 1987	$18.7 million
Successful offering of 1,225,000 shares of common stock by Harley-Davidson, Inc.	May 1988	$35.2 million

motorcycle market was mature and had been declining for two to three years. Harley's market share was growing, but that couldn't go on forever.

Problem: How to build some stability into the company to deal with downturns? Answer: Acquire another company.

This was not because members of Harley's Policy Committee believe in the merger game. They don't. In many ways, they believe that the current focus on acquisitions is misguided, that mergers don't generally create any new values and don't help to build a strong U.S. economy. Also, they believe that mergers are highly risky—sellers always know more about the risks of their business than buyers do, and often they time their sale at the peak of their company's fortunes.

Harley's senior management believes that the best way for U.S. companies to fight foreign competitors is to stick to their knitting and do what they do best through a continuous improvement process. Then they can develop a strategic acquisition policy that is complementary to their business.

That's what Harley-Davidson set out to do. It needed another business to broaden its earnings base, but it had to meet certain specific requirements.

Serendipity played a role here, because through Dean Witter Reynolds Harley discovered a company for sale that met these requirements almost perfectly: Holiday Rambler, a privately owned manufacturer of recreational vehicles in Wakarusa, Indiana.

Here's why Holiday Rambler seemed like an ideal acquisition:

• *It was in a closely related business.* Like Harley-Davidson, Holiday Rambler is a manufacturing-intensive producer of premium-priced recreational vehicles. Because of this, Harley is able to understand Holiday Rambler's engineering and manufacturing. There is no need for Harley to learn the workings of a business that is completely foreign to it, which is the case in many mergers.

• *It had a similar market.* Both Harley and Holiday Rambler are niche marketers selling their products to a specific group of enthusiasts whose lifestyles are heavily influenced by their recreational activities. Both distribute their products through a well-defined national dealer network.

• *It was an industry leader.* Holiday Rambler is the world's largest privately held producer of recreational vehicles and has a reputation for the highest quality in its field. One of Harley's guidelines in choosing an acquisition was: If you're going to acquire a company, make it the best that money can buy.

• *It was highly profitable.* This wasn't a turnaround purchase. Harley wanted a company that was already on its feet and thriving. Holiday Rambler met those specifications.

• *It had growth potential.* Like Harley-Davidson, Holiday Rambler had been gaining higher shares of its market. This growth could continue because of stable fuel prices, increased domestic travel, higher levels of disposable income, and an increase in the 45-and-over age bracket. One of the key attractions was the complementary demographics of the recreational vehicle business with the motorcycle business. Harley now has product lines that will attract people from youth through post-retirement age.

• *It was less susceptible to economic fluctuations than the motorcycle business.* Holiday Rambler sales are not greatly affected by downturns, because the company markets premium-priced vehicles which are purchased by mature consumers with relatively high incomes who are long-time enthusiasts. Interest rates are not a major factor, because a large percentage of Holiday Rambler vehicles are purchased with cash. The only potential problem, but a significant one, is the future availability of gasoline.

• *It was well diversified.* Holiday Rambler does a profitable business making specialty commercial vehicles such as delivery vans. This cushions it against the normally cyclical nature of the recreational vehicle industry.

Harley-Davidson completed the deal for Holiday Rambler on December 19, 1986. The price was $155 million, of which $35 million came from Harley equity. The remainder was borrowed against the assets of the acquired company, with no recourse to Harley-Davidson.

By the end of 1986 Harley-Davidson was a solidly financed, profitable company with revenues of almost $700 million. It had been seven days away from bankruptcy just one year earlier.

Selected Readings

Berger, Roger W., and Thomas H. Hart: *Statistical Process Control: A Guide for Implementation*, Quality Press, The American Society of Statistical Quality Control, Milwaukee, Wis., 1986.

Hall, Robert W.: *Attaining Manufacturing Excellence*, Dow-Jones, Irwin, Homewood, Ill., 1987.

Imai, Masaaki: *Kaizen: The Key to Japan's Competitive Success*, Random House, New York, 1986.

Karatsu, Hajime: *Tough Words for American Industry*, Productivity Press, Cambridge, Mass., 1988.

Kotler, P., L. Fahey, and S. Jatusripitak: *The New Competition*, Prentice-Hall, Englewood Cliffs, N.J., 1985.

Lawler, Edward E: *High-Involvement Management*, Jossey-Bass, San Francisco, 1986.

Oakland, John S: *Statistical Process Control: A Practical Guide*, Quality Press, The American Society of Statistical Quality Control, Milwaukee, Wis., 1986.

Ohno, Taiichi, and Setsuo Mito: *Just-In-Time For Today and Tomorrow*, Productivity Press, Cambridge, Mass., 1988.

Pierce, Richard J: *Involvement Engineering: Engaging Employees in Quality and Productivity*, Quality Press, The American Society of Statistical Quality Control, Milwaukee, Wis., 1986.

Pyzdek, Thomas: *An SPC Primer*, Quality Press, The American Society of Statistical Quality Control, Milwaukee, Wis., 1984.

Schonberger, Richard J: *Japanese Manufacturing Techniques: Nine Hidden Lessons in Simplicity*, Productivity Press, Cambridge, Mass., 1982.

Shingo, Shigeo: *Non-Stock Production: The Shingo System for Continuous Improvement*, Productivity Press, Cambridge, Mass., 1988.

Shinohara, Isao (ed.): *New Production System—JIT Crosses Industry Boundaries*, Productivity Press, Cambridge, Mass., 1988.

Walton, Mary: *The Deming Management Method*, Dodd, Mead, New York, 1986.

Index

Just who benefits when GM is forced to close a plant and Bosch or someone else gets all the business? In our view, two of the most uncaring things you can do to people are: (1) to give them something—whether they've earned it or not—knowing full well you'll have to ask for it back, and (2) to blow smoke up their noses (or other bodily orifices). How do you think your people see it?

MOTIVATION DOESN'T NECESSARILY FOLLOW MONEY

We submit that inordinately high wages, salaries, and unwarranted benefits not only aren't the answer, they are often a large part of the problem. Moreover, they are often used as a counterbalance or way of compensating for serious deficiencies elsewhere in the organization. Of course, an organization cannot expect to maintain esprit de corps by paying substandard salaries, but a lot of damage (and not just to the current balance sheet) can be done when people see money being thrown around. Once this occurs, pay loses its meaning. Translation: The money must have been easily obtained. They know they're not worth that much. Remuneration loses its relevance and impact, like a Christmas morning when all the presents under the tree have your name on them.

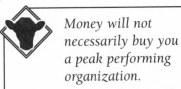

Money will not necessarily buy you a peak performing organization.

Money will not necessarily buy you a peak performing organization, either. The New York Yankees of the '80s and early '90s are perhaps a perfect example. With some of the most talent-laden rosters ever assembled on a baseball diamond (Winfield, Mattingly, Sax, et al.) and league-high payrolls, Yankee owner George Steinbrenner couldn't buy anything close to a championship. However, he did have some of those same big name players practically begging to be traded. Hmmm.

At the conclusion of the 1983 NFL season, the *St. Petersburg Times* (FL) published a study of the correlation between pay and performance for all the NFL football franchises (only 28 teams back then). Not unlike George Steinbrenner's experience, the results showed the following:

- The highest paid team in the NFL finished last.
- The lowest paid team won its division.
- The upper salary quartile produced no division winners.
- Two of the eight lowest paid teams won their division.
- Only one team in the upper salary quadrant won better than 50 percent of its games.
- The three highest paid teams finished last, next to last, and 21st.

We doubt seriously that the situation has changed much over the intervening years. In fact, we recall the 1995 Miami Dolphins and the 1996 New York Jets, both highly paid, underachieving teams loaded with expensive free-agents. True to form, the Jets had the worst record in football.

WHEN TOO MUCH WORK IS NOT ENOUGH

Launching on average a new product every month in order to maintain their lead in the field of Internet access software, the employees of Netscape work incredibly long hours. Among the company's highly motivated engineers, 70-hour weeks are reportedly the norm, with round-the-clock stints common when it gets down to crunch time. The hours have become so crazy at times that the company has actually resorted to forcing people not to come to work. (How would you like to have that problem?)

NETSCAPE COMMUNICATIONS CORPORATION

SELECTED FIRST QUARTER (JAN-MAR) FINANCIAL DATA, IN $THOUSANDS, EXCEPT NET INCOME PER SHARE

	1996	1997
REVENUES	56,121	120,241
GROSS PROFIT	47,627	104,423
NET INCOME	3,589	7,944
NET INCOME PER SHARE	$0.04	$0.09

Source: Netscape First Quarter Financial Summary, 1997.

To give their people an edge and enable them to be more comfortable (and productive) when they are at work, Netscape employees generally set their own hours, dress the way they want, and furnish their workspace just like they would their home. While some have added sofas, refrigerators, stereos, and the like, Lou Montulli, a 23-year-old Netscape engineer, has furnished his cubicle with two huge aquariums.

You may be thinking about now that this whole idea sounds fishy, and Netscape is just another high tech California company destined for a train wreck because there's no sense of discipline and the "inmates are being allowed to run the asylum." Yet, surprisingly, these also happen to be some of the same practices employed by Southwest Airlines and Hewlett-Packard for nearly 30 years.

> *The only people who work this hard are people who want to.*
> —Jon Mittelhauser – a Netscape founding engineer

YOUR PEOPLE ARE YOUR BEST COUNSEL, SO LISTEN!

Good leaders are smart enough to realize that the average employee is not likely to be completely candid with a "superior" in a strictly formal setting. Therefore, it becomes necessary from time to time to alter the manager/employee relationship in a controlled, constructive manner designed to remove all impediments to true communication. *Contented Cow* companies like Southwest Airlines, Federal Express, Rosenbluth Travel, and Disney—all detailed in the following examples—have perfected simple yet innovative methods for connecting with their workforce.

> *There's not any idea you can have [here] that people are not willing to listen to at any level. They want to help you develop it, and they'll go to any length to help you in any way they can.*
> —Soni Tron, production worker, North American Honda

SOUTHWEST AIRLINES

One of the methods employed by Southwest to keep its management staff firmly grounded in the real world, while demonstrating that they care about their people, is a program requiring top managers to regularly spend time (at least one day per quarter) working alongside their people in the field. The executives handle baggage, answer reservation lines, and other important operating-level tasks. (Thankfully, this program excludes flying and aircraft maintenance duties!)

FEDERAL EXPRESS

Like many other companies, FedEx performs an annual employee survey. But unlike other companies, they don't just ask the questions, tabulate the results, and then go back to sleep. They actually do something about those results. In other words, FedEx makes a serious effort to listen to their people through the survey results. How serious? For instance, the scores registered on the company's employee opinion survey (or SFA, for Survey-Feedback-Action) are a heavy factor in promotional decisions for managers. In fact, executive bonuses are paid only after a performance hurdle is cleared in each of three areas: Profitability, Customer Service, and—you guessed it—the Employee Opinion Survey Scores. In other words, the company could make a jillion dollars of net profit in a given year, but if their customers and employees aren't as satisfied as the shareholders, no executive bonuses.

> We've all heard the criticism "he talks too much." When was the last time you heard someone criticized for listening too much?
> —Norm Augustine

ROSENBLUTH TRAVEL

Rosenbluth Travel CEO Hal Rosenbluth conducts the surveys and a whole lot more. In addition to having a special hot-line for employees to contact him directly with suggestions or criticism,

Rosenbluth spends two days a year working with and listening to randomly selected associates. Moreover, he makes sure the company's 360-degree review program starts with him, and sponsors an "Associate of the Day" program in which any of the company's 3,000 employees has the opportunity to spend a day working alongside him or another senior executive of their choice.

DISNEY

Introducing an average of 80 to 90 new products each year, fresh ideas are absolutely crucial to a company like Disney. They recognize the need to listen and are enthusiastic about creating opportunities to hear their employees. In a 1996 speech before the Chicago Executives Club, CEO Michael Eisner detailed a playful but effective process his company uses to solicit ideas from its people. Several times each year, various Disney divisions host their own version of TV's once popular "Gong Show." Employees are encouraged to bring forward their product ideas for consideration by the company's top brass. According to Eisner, "Anybody who wants to, and I mean anybody, gets a chance to pitch an idea for an animated film to a small group of executives, which includes, among others, me and Roy Disney, our vice chairman, and Peter Schneider, head of Feature Animation. For this to work, you must have an environment where people feel safe about giving their ideas. ... Yes, we gong people if we think an idea won't work, but we tell them why and we tell them how it might be improved."[11]

To these companies it's not a program at all, but a way of life!

Clearly, the above mentioned efforts aren't rocket science—they never are—but you've got to believe that GM's Roger Smith might have had a better idea about what was wrong with his company had some comparable plan or program been in existence there. For companies like Disney and FedEx, however, you get the sense the plan or program is relatively unimportant in the overall scheme of things. In fact, to these companies it's not a program at all, but a way of life! What matters most is that this ultra-simple approach is backed up by diligent action, day after day after day. As Southwest's Vice President for People Libby Sartain puts it, "I keep telling them [her HR peers] that it's all about values and caring and treating people like you want to be treated and their eyes glaze over. They want the quick answer."[12]

> *The leader must have time to listen to his men. It is easy to look important and say, 'I haven't got time,' but each time the leader does it, he drives one more nail in the coffin of the team spirit whose life he should really be cherishing.*
> —Lincoln Andrews, a West Point faculty member under MacArthur

CHAPTER SUMMARY

1. Caring is an attitude, not a program. It has nothing whatsoever to do with sentiment, emotions, or "being nice."

2. First, you feed the troops.

3. Motivation doesn't necessarily follow money.

4. If you care about your people, you listen to them, really listen!

Best Practices:

1. Southwest Airlines' executive day at the operating level.

2. FedEx's Survey-Feedback-Action.

3. Rosenbluth Travel's employee day at the management level.

4. Disney's "Gong Show."

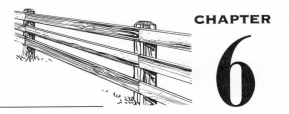

TELL 'EM
THE TRUTH

We adopted a philosophy that we wouldn't hide anything, not any of our problems, from the employees.
> —Rollin King, founder of Southwest Airlines

TRUTH OR CONSEQUENCES

Few things abound within the employment arena more poisonous than insincerities, half-truths, insidious omissions, and just plain lies. One of the principal reasons the truly great companies find themselves atop the summit of success year after year is because they go to great lengths to avoid confusing people by lying to them, most particularly, those people who are or aspire to be on their payroll. They don't lay out a bunch of Dilbert-type platitudes which they either can't or don't intend to live up to and, at the same time, they are very plainspoken and unapologetic about things they do feel strongly about.

If you care about your people, you make it a point to tell them the truth, even when (and especially when) it hurts. Good leaders make it a point to deliver bad news in an up-close-and-personal way. As Dennis LeStrange of IKON Office Solutions puts it, "People need to hear the bad news directly, from the person who made that decision, rather than read it in a memo; and they deserve to hear it early."[1]

Seeking to avoid the shackles imposed by unionism and our judicial system over the past decades, American industry—largely at the urging of human resource practitioners and labor attorneys—has adopted an overly conservative (some might call it mealy mouthed) approach to dealing with employee performance issues. The atmosphere of caution is so pervasive, in fact, that in the course of tip-toeing around possible charges of discrimination, favoritism, wrongful discharge, and the like, managers have in many cases completely lost sight of the mission at hand, namely fixing performance errors! And yet we wonder why it's so difficult to improve things like quality and productivity, and why people get so upset with us when we finally do tell them there's a problem with their performance.

MALICE IN WONDERLAND

In the 1980s, we did some work for a company we'll refer to as Giant. With nearly two billion dollars in annual revenues and an employee population near 40,000, the company was sizable indeed. However, because they were finding it necessary to terminate the services of a high number of employees for performance-related reasons, Giant's management determined that they had a problem. In one 18-month span, for example, they terminated some 986 people, not for egregious transgressions like lying, cheating, or stealing, but for doing a crummy job. Tasked by the CEO with looking into this and coming up with some answers, we began investigating the situation. We searched in all the usual places and talked to all the usual suspects—some of the "firees" as well as the managers who had done the dastardly deeds. We combed through personnel files, examined hiring practices, and did a massive search through Giant's rather sophisticated HR information system.

At some point, we learned of Giant's "Performance Review Policy," which was pretty standard, requiring formal written reviews every six months until death or termination. A staff member hammered his way through the HR system, trying to find a correlation between poor reviews and the terminations, but quickly returned with the news that there was "obviously a flaw in either the data itself or the search parameters, as no correlation could be found."

Wait a minute! We asked him to take another look at the data. At the same time, we had someone physically look at the review forms contained in the hard copy records. In the end, the conclusion was the same: There was no correlation between the reviews and the terminations. Giant managers had dutifully conducted performance reviews with every one of these 986 people in the six months immediately preceding their termination, but in only three of those cases had they actually informed the employee that they were doing an unsatisfactory job! *Incredibly, roughly two-thirds of these same people had also received merit increases in the six months preceding their termination!* We submit that, sad as it is, what was happening at Giant is more the rule than the exception. In fact, it's probably going on right now in your company. Go find out!

Now, we are not suggesting that the whole world gets up in the morning and says, "I think I'll go to work and tell a fib today." Lying is not that deliberate or direct, yet too often it seems second nature in workplace situations, just like at Giant. To be honest, it starts before the person is even hired.

LIAR, LIAR

Most managers walk around with the well-founded suspicion that people are going to lie to them in the employment interview process. Many do, to be sure. But how frequently do they receive the same in kind before the interview is even half way through. Sound familiar?

Applicant: "So what's it like working around here?"

Manager: [preoccupied with getting the wash out, the cars built, burgers flipped, etc.] "It's a great place to work. ... It's almost like family."

[Yeah, the dysfunctional sort.]

Applicant: "How will I learn the job?"

Manager: "Oh, we've got an extensive orientation and training program."

[Right, it probably lasts all morning.]

Applicant: "What are the big bosses like?"

Manager: "They're great people. They really believe in putting people first. Just look here in our annual report at what our Chairman and CEO said, 'I am confident  because I am so proud of the job being done by our more than 300,000 people.'"

[Was that before or after all the layoffs, buyout offers, and your big raise?]

But that exchange seems innocent compared to what happens once they come on board. In his book, *The Dilbert Principle*, master satirist Scott Adams has categorized what he terms the "Great Lies of Management." In a fashion similar to that employed by a popular late night TV show, here they are:

#13. Your input is important to us.

#12. Our people are the best.

#11. We'll review your performance in six months.

#10. I haven't heard any rumors.

 #9. Training is a high priority.

 #8. We don't shoot the messenger.

 #7. Performance will be rewarded.

 #6. We reward risk takers.

 #5. The future is bright.

 #4. We're reorganizing to better serve our customers.

 #3. You could earn more money under the new plan.

 #2. I have an open door policy.

and the #1 all-time great lie:

drum roll, please

 #1. Employees are our most valuable asset.[2]

The principle of "truth or consequences" is certainly simple enough. Yet it is violated on a regular basis as companies spew forth one philosophy while practicing quite another. The only thing we're suggesting is that, especially when it comes to communicating with your workforce, PR should take a distant back seat to honesty. If your company is a tough place to work, say so, and be very explicit in explaining why and how. Don't apologize for it! If your business is in trouble, say so. And for pete's sake, if an employee is screwing up, say so; that's what managers get paid for. So, either step up to the plate or go sit in the dugout!

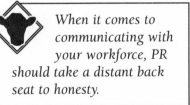

When it comes to communicating with your workforce, PR should take a distant back seat to honesty.

I didn't lie to anyone.
> —Don Shula, when asked what he'd like to be remembered for

CHAPTER SUMMARY

If you care about your people, you tell them the truth, period.

1. People need to hear the bad news directly from the person who made that decision, rather than read it in a memo; and they deserve to hear it early.

2. The whole problem with Performance Reviews is not the form, the frequency, or the lack of rater objectivity, but a lack of honesty!

3. Just like at home where we teach our children to lie at an early age ("Tell 'em Daddy's not here."), we begin early at work, before people are even on our payroll!

Worst Practice: Giant's "Performance Review Policy" (and probably yours).

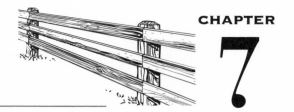

WHEN TIMES GET TOUGH

He'll sit there and listen. I mean, really listen. He's in our corner. That takes the load off. Then when you go on the football field and the man says, 'Look, I want you to run down there, catch that ball and run into that wall,' then who are you to say 'no'? You catch that ball and you run into that wall. You say, 'Okay, Coach, you were there for me; now I'm gonna give it up for you.' That's crucial.

—Michael Irvin, Dallas Cowboy wide receiver, talking about his former coach, Jimmy Johnson

IF YOU CARE, YOU'RE THERE

Perhaps more than anything else they can do, organizations and their leaders demonstrate that they care by their physical presence when times are tough. In our view, there is something of a quid pro quo involved here. Recall from the first chapter that by definition, discretionary effort is a contribution people can make if they want, but only if they want. The inclination to part with some of that discretionary effort is based, at least in part, on the individual's perception of how things would go if the shoe were on the other foot. In other words, "You're asking me to walk through fire for you? Would you do the same for me? Have you done the same for me?"

Local Heroes: Ryder's Response to Hurricane Andrew

When Hurricane Andrew roared across South Florida in 1992, thousands of homes were destroyed and tens of thousands were left homeless, including many of Ryder's 2,000 employees in the Miami area. On an institutional level, as soon as the winds subsided, Ryder—the five billion dollar commercial truck leasing and logistics giant—began making on-the-spot, interest-free loans up to $10,000 to employees who needed it, and dispatching repair crews to the homes of employees (and their neighbors!) who had been hardest hit by the hurricane.[1]

On a personal level, Ryder Chairman, CEO and President Tony Burns (whose own home suffered severe damage as well) began spending as much time personally delivering needed supplies to employee homes and helping with repairs as he did tending to corporate business. Said Burns, "I really think being a good citizen and offering opportunity to all people is not only the absolute right thing to do, it's also great business. Customers want to do business with you, and employees want to work here."[2]

Ryder System, Inc. Net income for 1991–1995

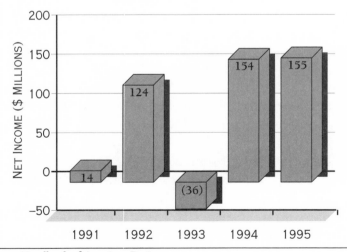

Source: Hoover Handbook of American Business

IF YOU REBUILD IT, MORE WILL COME

On the night of December 11, 1995, in the tiny town of Lawrence, Massachusetts, residents were horrified as Malden Mills, one of the town's major employers (2,500-plus jobs), saw the lion's share of its textile manufacturing capacity burn to the ground. Undaunted, Aaron Feuerstein, the mill's 70-year-old owner, vowed that "with God's help, we will overcome the events of the past 12 hours and continue to be a vital force in New England." One of the first things Feuerstein did was give each employee a paycheck, a $275 Christmas bonus, a coupon redeemable for food at a local grocery store, and, more significantly, his personal assurance that their salaries and benefits would be protected for a minimum of one month (a time frame he subsequently extended not once but *twice* as the rebuilding process wore on).[3]

> *On an institutional and personal level "Contented Cow" companies tend to do a much better job of putting their bodies and their money where their mouths are.*

Malden Mills did rebuild, and their customers stuck with them. Now Feuerstein can't understand what all the commotion was about. "I simply did a normal thing," he said. If that's such a normal thing for a 70-year-old man, why shouldn't it be for the rest of us? While some might brand Feuerstein a saint for paying out $15 million in wages and benefits he wasn't required to pay, others may consider him a fool for not taking the insurance money and running—either to his own retirement, or at least to a lower cost area in which to rebuild.

Neither is the case. Feuerstein is an astute business person capable of making incredibly rational decisions even in the presence of a still-smoldering factory. First of all, factories are typically insured for their replacement value, and any insurance payoff would likely be limited to the depreciated value of the property had he chosen not to rebuild. Second, assuming the business earned Feuerstein $20 million on its $400 million or so in revenues, he and his family would be walking away from a lot of money over the course of two or three generations had they opted out. And finally, Feuerstein has got this *Contented Cow* thing absolutely, positively figured out. With both customer and employee retention rates already hovering around 95 percent (do you suppose there's any relationship?), imagine what new heights his business might reach with a new factory and the same highly skilled, well-trained, and now emotionally turbocharged people running it.

No matter their size, both on an institutional and personal level, *Contented Cow* companies tend to do a much better job of putting their bodies and their money where their mouths are.

About 10 months after the Malden Mills fire, a similar event took place in Memphis, Tennessee, when a vicious thunderstorm took the roof off a local eatery by the name of Fred Gang's. The owner, Jack Stout, responded just as Feuerstein had done. "We're maintaining any person who was on the payroll ... at full wages, *including lost tip compensation*," said Stout. While his restaurant was closed upwards of three months, Stout did not flinch. "We've had people with us five, 10, 12 years, and some since the restaurant opened in 1976," he said. "Fred Gang's is more than a paycheck to them."[4]

> *People just want to know that somebody knows, and cares.*
> —Dennis P. LeStrange, IKON Office Solutions

PROVIDE SOME SYSTEM OF JUSTICE

Caring must occur on a systemic as well as on a personal basis. People need to feel a sense of justice and know the answer to the dreaded but almost certain question: "Where do I go with a problem?" In the words of Alan Westin, Columbia University law professor, "Corporations must do justice well internally, or have it done for them."[5] We think it's inevitable that whenever a person has a complaint or concern, something is going to happen, whether it's sanctioned by the organization or not. In those cases where there is no sponsored mechanism—or one not working properly—people will resort to what might be termed "self-prescribed remedies." In short, they'll take matters into their own hands.

Certainly from the company's standpoint, the most dangerous option employees have is to fix the problem themselves. The least visible and perhaps most effective way of doing this is by simply "powering back" a notch or two. Whenever the employees' focus of attention shifts from productive effort to worrying about their problems, the result is the withholding of discretionary effort. It's nearly imperceptible, almost impossible to manage, and, not unlike Mr. Garfield's experience with the hungry Eastern flight attendants, invariably winds up in your customer's lap.

Before you dismiss this as something that happens only at failed organizations like Eastern, consider the results of a 1996 Gallup Poll which reported that fully 25 percent of us are angry at work. Not disappointed or disillusioned—angry! Younger workers (ages 18–34) are madder than older folks (the over 50 crowd). Hendrie Weisinger, a Westport, Connecticut, psychologist offers a list, in no particular order, of what gets the American worker hot under the proverbial collar, be it of the white or blue variety:

1. harassment, sexual or otherwise
2. favoritism of one employee over another
3. insensitivity of managers
4. depersonalization of the workplace, causing employees to feel as if they're just numbers
5. unfair performance appraisals
6. lack of resources, including everything from support staff to corporate credit cards
7. lack of adequate training
8. lack of teamwork
9. withdrawal of earned benefits
10. lack or violation of trust
11. poor communication
12. absentee bosses

If you would like to see further proof, pay a quick visit to *http://www.disgruntled.com*, an internet Web site created specifically for people to vent their spleen about perceived injustices in their workplace. The fact that the site exists isn't in and of itself particularly remarkable. After all, there's a Web site for just about everything. But what *is* a little unsettling is the sheer volume of published complaints, and the inescapable fact that most of them are being penned from the workplace. (In fact, software publisher Daniel Levine has incorporated a "Boss Escape" icon which enables users to quickly shift to a screen image which more closely resembles the work they're being paid to do at the moment.) In a seemingly unending stream of letters signed: "In a Show Me State of Shock"; "Sick of the Hospital I Work In"; and "Hapless Sap," to name only a few, employees describe a plethora of vexations and troubles, many of which pertain in one way or another to the issue of job security.

While on the surface an aggrieved employee may appear to do nothing about the situation, the fact remains that people really don't forget about their perceived injustices. Rather, they file them away and accumulate others until a breaking point is reached. At which time, they escalate their demand for justice.

All too often, an employee who has moved on to a more overt plan of action will find someone else to help them with their problem. While the number of people turning to unions to accomplish this has been steadily declining for 20 years, don't count organized labor out, especially in view of moves like the AFL-CIO's decision to boost spending on organizing from $2.5 million in 1995 to $30 million in 1997.[6] Many Americans were reminded of this in August of 1997, when the Teamsters Union effectively shut down United Parcel Service for two weeks, and brought much of the commercial sector to a screeching halt.

UNION MEMBERSHIP

% OF ALL EMPLOYEES	YEAR	TOTAL MEMBERS (MILLIONS)
18.0	1985	17.0
17.5	1986	16.9
17.0	1987	16.9
16.8	1988	17.0
16.4	1989	16.9
16.1	1990	16.7
16.1	1991	16.6
15.8	1992	16.4
15.8	1993	16.6
15.5	1994	16.7
14.9	1995	16.4
14.5	1996	16.3

Source: U.S. Bureau of Labor Statistics

Meanwhile, it has become increasingly popular for people to involve other outside advocates like agents, lawyers, and state or federal agencies to get what they want. According to the latest information from the American Bar Association, there are 966,000 lawyers alive and presumably very well in the United States (34,000 of them on federal payrolls alone). That's one for every 270 persons. If a 1996 finding by the U.S. Dept. of Labor is any indication, all those attorneys have been working overtime because, since 1991, the number of suits filed for unlawful discrimination and harassment has tripled!

Stay away from the courthouse; you'll never make any money there.
—J.E. Davis, founder of Winn-Dixie Stores

FAST, FAIR AND ADMINISTRABLE JUSTICE

Contented Cow organizations realize that whenever you've got two or more people working in some common endeavor, there are going to be perceived injustices and serious problems which arise from time to time. They realize too that most people really don't want to sue their employer, join a labor union, or involve an outside agency, let alone quit their job. So, rather than waiting to be victimized by one or another of the self-prescribed remedies, they proactively install some system which tolerates and even encourages the airing and resolution of the problem, so people can get on with the business at hand.

In 1990, Dennis Spina took over the helm of one of the nation's largest propane distributors, Suburban Propane. Experiencing a decline in retail sales and margins due to eroding service and historically high prices, Suburban had nearly 8,000 extremely nervous employees, and customers defecting in droves.

Moreover, Suburban had recently acquired Petrolane, one of its largest competitors, in a heavily leveraged deal. With all these negatives conspiring against him, and in addition to being on the verge of a disastrous "heating season" (an extremely mild winter), Spina had his hands full. New to the propane business, Spina spent the bulk of his first 10 days riding with and working alongside the company's delivery drivers. That act itself should have sent a clear message to headquarters staffers and company officers, many of whom probably wouldn't have recognized one of their own delivery vehicles if it ran over them.

What came next was an even bigger shock. Spina assembled roughly a dozen of the company's "best and brightest," drawing equally from the managerial, professional, and hourly ranks. He told them essentially that there were still a lot of things about the business he didn't understand, and probably some things he never would. But one thing he did know was that the only way to resolve one of their very greatest concerns—notably for their future—was to sell more gas and find ways to deliver it more efficiently, to more satisfied customers. Continuing, he added, "And we'll never be able to do that as long as you have to spend even one minute of your precious time looking over your shoulder wondering and worrying about something bad happening to you because of the capricious act of a manager or, more probably, some unintentionally dumb corporate practice. The only thing I want you and your co-workers to worry about is doing your job the best way you know how."

Spina then instructed the group to create some sort of problem and complaint resolution mechanism that would serve as something of a safety net for Suburban employees. The only constraints he put on the project were that whatever they came up with had to be "fast, fair, and administrable." A few months later, the group emerged with an ultra-simple three-step process which they subsequently named EARS (Employee Appeal and Review System). In announcing its implementation, Spina said, "[EARS] will afford our employees the opportunity to have workplace disputes resolved in a fair, objective, and timely manner by the people who know them best. We must recognize that if an employee has a problem, then the company has a problem, and it's to everyone's advantage to get it resolved immediately, before it becomes a customer problem."

We believe EARS represents the cutting edge of corporate problem and complaint resolution procedures. After the installation of the EARS procedure, Spina commented to us, "One of the unintended benefits was that this process forced a level of introspection that made us look at some of those policies and procedures which placed our customer contact people in a position of having to explain dumb actions by the corporate bureaucracy."

DON'T EXPECT EMPLOYEES TO PAY FOR YOUR MISTAKES

Companies demonstrate whether or not they care by the extent to which they expect their people to pay for managers' mistakes. Sometimes employees are asked to give up perks they once enjoyed, which isn't always a bad thing to do, especially in light of the alternatives. But people take an understandably dim view of the matter when that sacrifice is caused by (or occurs in the face of) managerial indiscretions or extravagances.

> *Companies demonstrate whether or not they care by the extent to which they expect their people to pay for managers' mistakes.*

Consider, for example, the case of a large southern hospital. When faced with the prospect of having to lay off more than 100 full-time employees, they decided instead on an ambitious cost-cutting program, which is detailed in the following excerpt from a memo distributed to all hospital staff:

(Our editorial comments appear in brackets [].)

MEMORANDUM

As part of our Continuous Quality Improvement process [please!], we must continually look for ways to improve efficiency. This is particularly true as we move deeper into a managed care [some would say mangled care] environment. One way to do that is to reduce expenses, which places us in a better position to bid on health care contracts. [So far, it sounds reasonable.] As we receive more contracts because of lower cost pricing, we will assist in increasing the probability of stable employment for the future. [Yeah, right. We'll have to wait and see about that.]

Effective [such-and-such date], the following "expense improvements" [write that one down] will be implemented:

- Hourly shifts will be cut from 13 to 12 hours and overtime will be eliminated, saving $1.2 million.
- The five holidays for which we now pay premium overtime will be reduced to three, saving $127,000.
- The weekend differential will be cut from 30 percent to $2/hour, saving $806,000.
- The number of compensated days off for salaried employees will be cut from 13 to eight, saving us $227,000.
- The tuition reimbursement plan will be eliminated, saving $1.2 million.

The total cost savings of the above will total more than $3.5 million, allowing us to stabilize employment for 107 full-time employees.

On the surface, the memo doesn't sound unreasonable at all. It's kind of the old "let's all pull together to keep this ship afloat" idea, one which we support. What the memo left out was the $4.1 million capital expenditure in the same year for such health-improving hospital features as a new marble entranceway, expanded lobby complete with a one-million-dollar aquarium and attendant staff, and new china for executive functions.

The grumbling over the cost cuts turned to loud shouts and defections when the opulence was installed. And then a year later, after all the selective belt-tightening, a hundred more people received "unstable employment"; they were laid off. All we can say is that we're glad neither of us lives near enough this hospital to depend on it for health care. We imagine there are some pretty discontented cows running around the place. And while we're sure they're all behaving professionally, we don't even want to think about the dangerous combination of a mad cow with a needle or proctoscope!

While the eventual layoffs at the hospital may seem cruelly handled and only halfheartedly forestalled, "guaranteed employment" is every bit as unjust and unkind. Inevitably, both the individual employee (whose performance is failing), and that person's co-workers (who must carry the extra load), will get swept out the door together when the grim reaper appears. Yet companies must not be deluded by false hopes or unrealistic expectations when scaling back their workforce.

Sometimes a change of pasture will make the cow fatter.
—American frontier saying

Above all else, companies should be very careful how much faith they put in the savings projected to occur via their downsizing, re-engineering, or—insert your own code word for "layoff"—efforts. Studies by the American Management Association and others have proven conclusively that most such efforts result in no near-term improvement in operating profits, or productivity. A survey of 531 large business organizations conducted by the Wyatt Company showed that, among companies that had undergone "restructuring," only 46 percent saw any attendant increase in earnings within two years following the restructuring. Less than 34 percent of those same companies realized an increase in productivity from the layoffs, and better than half of the companies actually refilled the positions they had eliminated within a year of downsizing![7] (And we wonder why some refer to the practice as "dumbsizing.")

> *I wasn't smart enough about that [speaking of the "People Factor"]. I was reflecting my engineering background and was insufficiently appreciative of the human dimension. I've learned that's critical.*[8]
> —Michael Hammer, the "Father of Re-engineering"

Corporate Insanity

While there's not much evidence to suggest that layoffs really help, they are a trend that doesn't seem to be going away. Challenger, Gray & Christmas, an outplacement firm that keeps tabs on such numbers, reported in July of 1996 that 312,356 corporate layoffs had been announced in the first half of that year, up 33 percent over the 1995 midyear tally.[9] As we see it, there are two opposing and equally important schools of thought on the subject.

First, as the frequency and pace of change in the commercial landscape increases, companies are propelled in and out of business sectors and markets at an ever-more-rapid rate. It seems an immutable fact that the days when employees could reasonably expect to have a one-company career if they so wished are pretty much over, perhaps forever. From now on, nearly all businesses will continue to find themselves reacting to an over or under supply of labor as they relentlessly pursue "better, faster, and cheaper."

No matter how great the hue and cry is over management's obsession with the short term outlook, market forces have spoken. In fact, given that nearly everyone these days has money in the market—via a 401(k) or IRA—a Cleveland pipe fitter is just as inclined as any Wall Street analyst to raise hell when earnings don't meet or exceed targets every quarter. In an interview not long ago, Peter Lynch, former manager of Fidelity's Magellan Fund, pretty much echoed this thought. "All of us are looking for the best deals in clothing, computers, and telephone service—and rewarding the high-quality, low-cost providers with our business," he observed. "I haven't met one person who would agree to pay AT&T twice the going rate for phone service if AT&T would promise to stop laying people off."[10]

> *Worried cows don't make very productive (let alone, contented) cows.*

> *While at General Electric, I said at one time that we should be striving to have all our employees ready to go and anxious to stay. ... If workers feel their employer is keeping them employable at all times [via growth and learning], their sense of insecurity will diminish.*
> —Frank Doyle, chairman of the Committee for Economic
> Development, and retired executive
> vice president of General Electric

Second, from the opposite side of the fence, we think the extent to which employees are concerned about the prospect of *losing* their jobs mirrors inversely the extent to which they are concerned with *doing* their jobs. In short, worried cows don't make very productive (let alone, *contented*) cows. The folks you are counting on to deliver high quality goods or services to your customers mustn't be too busy worrying about their own futures to *care* (important word) about the business.

While layoffs are indeed at times a necessary event, there is a big difference between grudgingly accepting them as a final desperate act of corporate survival versus what Springfield Remanufacturing CEO Jack Stack calls "corporate insanity" (i.e., a convenient way to periodically trim a little fat). In either case, there's no getting around the fact that they are a sign of management failure. According to Stack, "You lay people off when you've screwed up, when you've guessed wrong about the market, when you haven't anticipated some critical development or created adequate contingency plans. It's a sign of how badly management has failed, and the people who get hurt are invariably those who had nothing to do with creating the problem in the first place."[11]

SOME RULES FOR "STAYING OUT OF THE SOUP"

Here are some precepts we believe will help you avoid this unpleasantness altogether, if you'll only execute them faithfully:

1. Spend 10 times as much time worrying about the *quality* of employees being added to your payroll as you do the number of them. As Machiavelli said, "The first method for estimating the intelligence of a ruler is to look at the men he has around him."
2. Adopt outrageously high performance expectations, continually "raise the bar," and on an ongoing basis, reassign or remove people who don't measure up. As you're going about this, don't allow loyalty to be confused with competence. Do it humanely, but do it! Initiate a "career change" for managers who can't or won't do this.
3. Eliminate every single systemic inducement to adding unnecessary headcount. Never, for example, tie anyone's pay, position, or perks to the number of people they "supervise."
4. After doing the first three, be as judicious about adding head-count at work as you are at home.
5. Finally, don't allow profitability or "affordability" to cloud your judgment or lower your standards on any of the above, ever.

In the final analysis, how layoffs are perceived by your work-force (and the buying public) comes down to your corporate mind-set. If it's acceptable in your organization one day to hire people "full-time," and then send them home a few months or years later—simply because you've miscalculated your requirement for labor or ability to profitably sell a product or service—then you don't care.

Some organizations are characterized by a sort of binge-and-purge personality—"corporate bulimics," if you will—caught up in a capricious cycle of staffing up and laying off to meet labor demands exactly. We are not talking about hiring temps, or a strategic decision to permanently outsource certain non-core activities. Rather, we mean those companies which routinely hire and lay off because they erroneously think it's a good way to do business. Rarely if ever do they acknowledge the consequences of the emotional upheaval visited upon the employees involved—not only those who leave, but particularly the ones who stay—and its impact on the overall health of the organization.

To be fair, we know most CEOs agonize a great deal over the decision to send some people home so that the jobs of others might be preserved. Thoughtfully and regretfully, at times they must conclude that it is the only unfortunate course of action to take.

If you DO find yourself in the unenviable position of having to send people home, there are some things you can do to make it easier on all concerned:

1. Make sure that you've first exhausted all alternative remedies (shortened workweeks, voluntary pay reductions, job reassignments, and the like). In the same vein, people who have demonstrated themselves as non-performers should be dealt with as such, in advance of any workforce reduction.

2. Get it over with quickly and at once. While "sudden death" is bad enough, the lingering variety is unconscionable. In the words of "Chainsaw Al" Dunlap, "What I keep uppermost in my mind is that if I don't release them today, I'm going to have to cut more of them in six months or a year anyway. Doing it piecemeal is a fraud upon everybody—the employees, management, and the shareholders."[12]

3. Make sure the pain inflicted on top management occurs first, and is clearly disproportionate. In Perot-type terms, the officers must bleed first, and most; or, as "Chainsaw" puts it, "Start at the top! Get rid of the corporate toys, squeeze the corporate headquarters, shrink high-priced management. The last thing you do is deal with the unions, so they know you went after real waste first."[13]
4. Don't hide anything from anybody. Your rationale for making these moves needs to be painfully evident and unassailable. Failure to make this case will fuel understandable anger, and frustration, not to mention a permanent loss of trust.
5. When it's over, say so, and mean it. Turn your attention immediately to enacting serious measures that will help you make damn sure you don't have to go down this road again.

ANHEUSER BUSCH

Not unlike others we're aware of, Anheuser Busch deserves credit for the way it has decided to regulate the numbers in its labor force. In January 1997, the nation's largest brewer, anticipating a need for a reduction in its workforce in the years to come, instituted a hiring freeze rather than layoffs. Like putting the company on a sensible diet, it is a far better response than the bingeing and purging to which the untreated corporate bulimic is doomed.

RUBBERMAID

Lately, Wolfgang Schmitt, CEO of Rubbermaid, has found himself under pressure to do something about his company's slowing rate of growth. Says Schmitt, "Sure, we could take out a lot of our people. But we could give up our future. One, we'd demotivate the people who remained. Two, they surely wouldn't have the loyalty they now have. Three, if there were any good people left, they wouldn't be here long. They'd be looking around. And uncertainty reduces risk taking."[14] Remember, this isn't a moral argument, but rather, a quest for credibility that goes directly to the hearts and minds of the people on your payroll.

The *Contented Cow* companies have figured out you cannot have it both ways. Corporation by corporation and business unit by business unit, they have defined the sanctity of long term employment prospects, what conditions they were willing to accept, and baked them into the equation. For too long, leaders have ducked these responsibilities, preferring instead to try to play the game with two completely different sets of rules. Get on one side of the fence or the other. No one is asking you to make a moral judgment, only a very practical one. So, do it!

ZAPMAIL

It is important to realize that disaster and extinction are not the same thing. FedEx proved this point in the mid-1980s when faced with the prospect of losing roughly half its business to electronic document transmission—the company launched its ill-fated ubiquitous fax service known as ZapMail. Not one to do things in a small way, FedEx spent over a billion dollars developing the technology, getting satellite transponder time, and hiring a dedicated workforce to sell, maintain, and deliver the service.

Despite some pretty sophisticated planning, what the company didn't count on was the space shuttle *Challenger* disaster, which severely constrained satellite transponder availability; the effects of the AT&T breakup on the ability to get dedicated land lines; and the sheer explosiveness of facsimile growth. These developments spelled the demise of ZapMail. When they finally 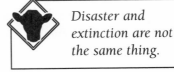 *Disaster and extinction are not the same thing.* pulled the plug on the project, FedEx found itself with a lot of expensive gear and about 1,300 people it absolutely, positively didn't need.

Amid all the consternation associated with shutting down the service, one seemingly all-important subject—layoffs—was never even broached. Based on a commitment founder Fred Smith made to his employees years earlier, the company promised never to send anybody home unless the very survival of the whole enterprise was at stake. Every single member of the defunct Zap-Mail division was offered a job elsewhere in the company. In the end, some took the offer, and some didn't, but it was their choice. According to Smith, "We reorganized and absorbed virtually every person into the workforce. The financial loss related to Zap-Mail was substantial and probably could have been mitigated against if we had given 1,300 people two weeks notice. But the decision was management's, and every one of those people had worked tirelessly to make ZapMail work. ... There was no way we weren't going to make good on our no-layoff philosophy."[15]

> [Layoffs] never entered our minds. Our philosophy very simply is that it is a very short-term thing to do. If your focus is on the long term, the well-being of your business and its people, you don't do it.
>
> —Herb Kelleher

RHINO FOODS

One of the best examples we've seen of dealing with a temporary overstaffing situation comes from tiny six-million-dollar Rhino Foods, a Vermont-based specialty frozen dessert, ice-cream novelty, and ice-cream ingredient manufacturer. In the spring of 1993, the job security of Rhino's 60 employees was seriously threatened by an unexpected drop in sales and a simultaneous increase in operating efficiency.

Rather than fold his hand or attempt to deal with the problem alone, Rhino President Richard Foos asked his employees to come up with a solution. Within three weeks, members of the company's Overcapacity Task Force came back with a novel yet downright business-like solution. Through the Employee Exchange Program, as they called it, Rhino workers would be farmed out to work at neighboring companies in the Burlington area which were experiencing temporary employment demand. Working only with companies which shared a common business philosophy and employment practices, Rhino provided its people with benefit and seniority continuity, in addition to making up any loss in wages. (Companies participating in the program included outfits like Gardener's Supply Co., and Ben & Jerry's Homemade, Inc. of nearby Waterbury.) Employees whose interim jobs paid more than their regular ones were allowed to keep the difference. Since successfully navigating through these troubled times, Rhino's sales and earnings have reportedly grown somewhere around 600 percent.

RHINO FOODS

	1990	1993
EMPLOYEES	13	60
SALES	890,000	6,000,000
SALES PER EMPLOYEE	68,462	100,000

Source: Foundation for Enterprise Development, 1997.

I feel that in general terms it (the HP way) is the policies and actions that flow from the belief that men and women want to do a good job, a creative job, and that if they are provided the proper environment they will do so.
                                                —Bill Hewlett, HP co-founder

CHAPTER SUMMARY

1. If you care about your people, you're there when times are tough.

   Best Practices:

   1. Ryder System, Inc. and Hurricane Andrew.

   2. Aaron Feuerstein rebuilding Malden Mills.

   3. Fred Gang's is "more than a paycheck."

2. Provide some system of justice. If you don't, someone else will do it for you.

   Best Practice:

   Suburban Propane's EARS Program.

3. Don't expect your employees to pay for your mistakes.

   Best Practices:

   1. Rhino Foods' Overcapacity Task Force.

   2. FedEx's handling of employees from its failed ZapMail project.

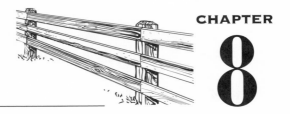

TAKE CARE OF THE LITTLE THINGS

I enjoin you to be ever alert to the pitfalls of too much authority. Beware that you do not fall in the category of the little man with a little job, with a big head. In essence, be considerate, treat your subordinates right, and they will literally die for you.
— Major General Melvin Zais, U.S. Army

WHERE EVERYBODY KNOWS YOUR NAME

Whether you like the man or not, Jimmy Johnson has demonstrated an uncanny knack for winning in the NFL. His two Superbowl victories less than five years after entering the league obviously were impressive enough credentials for Miami Dolphins team owner Wayne Huiezenga to hire Johnson to replace the legendary Don Shula—the winningest coach in the history of professional football.

Prior to his arrival in Miami, Johnson pointed to some really basic things that coaches, managers, and CEOs ought to be doing, but in many cases aren't. Like just getting to know your players' names, for instance. According to Johnson, "Some coaches bring their rookies into camp and, though they might know their first and second round picks by name, take the approach with the lower round picks and free agents that 'I'll learn his name if he makes the team.' What some don't understand is that whether a player makes the team might hinge on something as subtle as whether you know his name and whether you treat him as an individual that you care about, with talent you believe in."[1]

To us, (and perhaps to you as well) it seems totally absurd to be taking up time and space even mentioning this, except for one thing: It happens! As a case in point, one of our clients, an otherwise exceptionally well-run multi-billion dollar firm has for years experienced turnover in excess of 50 percent within its 3,000-plus member direct sales force. The turnover figure for newly hired reps (less than six months of service) exceeds 70 percent. Because of the high body count, company insiders have openly admitted that "we don't really bother getting to know them all that well because they're not going to be here very long." Better look inside your own organization for signs of similar attitudes.

> *Whether a player makes the team might hinge on something as subtle as whether you know his name and whether you treat him as an individual that you care about, with talent you believe in.*

We call them "little things" because in the overall scheme of things, that's exactly what they are. They're no big deal—to you. But quite often, they are of huge importance to the employee(s) concerned, and can absolutely mean the difference when it comes to whether or not someone is really going to extend themselves for you and your organization.

Among *Contented Cow* companies, examples of the personal touch abound. Here are a few of our favorites: Art Seessel, president of Seessel's Supermarkets (a Memphis-based regional grocery) regularly took time to send personal congratulatory notes to his employees for their "off-hours" accomplishments. One such note went to David Dettelbach, a part-time produce clerk, congratulating him on his high school athletic accomplishments. For years, Lucille Packard (widow of HP's David) personally shopped for and bought small presents commemorating employee weddings and childbirths. Dennis LeStrange, of IKON

Office Solutions, personally sends birthday cards to each of his 1,300 employees. In each case the message is clear: They see their respective employees as more than merely a pair of hands sorting produce, assembling printers, or fixing copiers.

THE NEED TO HAVE (SOME) FUN

Earlier we talked about the incredibly long hours logged by Netscape engineers ("When Too Much Work is Not Enough"). Since its inception, the entire software industry has been notorious for its workaholic standards. We suspect a problem may develop if such extended workdays have in fact become the "unwritten rule" (even if you can shoot billiards in the lounge). It will be interesting to see if dwelling in your office will become part of the job description, or whether future generations of software engineers will revolt.

In the meantime, late 1996 labor and employment figures for northern Florida showed a negative 3 percent unemployment rate for the area's computer programmers.[2] Statistically, that means every computer programmer in the region had a job, and 3 percent of them were *moonlighting*. Imagine that. Are we talking an employee's market, or what? So it's not surprising that David Graham, CEO of Jacksonville's InTuition, Inc.—the student loan servicer—was nervous about his company's ability to retain its top-notch technical employees during a 15-month, make-it-or-break-it conversion to all new software and hardware. When it was all over, however, the project was such a resounding success that it won the 1996 Project Management Institute's *Project of the Year Award*. Graham rewarded those responsible not only with a substantial bonus, but more to our point, with a gala dinner at an elegant yacht club. "We work hard," says Graham, echoing a theme voiced many times by Southwest's Herb Kelleher, "but we have to have fun."

We heard about the need to have some fun from lots of people in successful companies. Betty Kahn, of Chicago-based Crate & Barrel, a retailer of home furnishings says, "This is a partying company. We do a lot of group eating."[3] And it's not just at special events that the atmosphere of fun seems to make a difference. If you know anything about retail sales jobs, you know the associates at Crate & Barrel aren't working in retail to get rich quick; they're there because they're having fun.

Often the work and the fun are hard to distinguish between. Crate & Barrel managers are notorious for doing things like tying a lottery ticket or a couple of movie passes to the handle of a broom for the benefit of the first person to pick the thing up and use it. This kind of thinking is par for the course at Crate & Barrel, a standout in both employee and customer satisfaction in the specialty retail market.

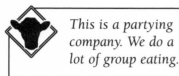

This is a partying company. We do a lot of group eating.

RANDOM ACTS OF GRACE AND KINDNESS

Thong Lee, former laundry worker and now a bartender at the Seattle Marriott, will likely never forget the day that his boss, Sandy Olson, shut down the hotel's laundry for an entire day so the whole staff could attend his mother's funeral. Today, Lee proudly proclaims that he "puts on this uniform, just like an NBA player."[4]

In their absolutely delightful book, *NUTS*, about Southwest Airlines, authors Kevin and Jackie Freiberg offer an example on a somewhat grander scale. It seems that one day, Southwest Executive Vice President Colleen Barrett called into her office an employee who recently had been featured in some "not so glowing" customer letters. When asked if everything was okay, the employee apparently broke into tears and proceeded to describe a recent painful divorce, a custody battle over a 3-year-old child, and on top of that, an insurmountable $1,800 legal bill. A few hours later, the employee received an envelope with nothing but her name scrawled on it, and $1,800 in cash drawn from Colleen's personal account. Her reaction, aside from many subsequent years of loyal service? "At what other company could you walk in thinking you're fired and walk out feeling loved, listened to, and really cared about?"[5]

CHAPTER SUMMARY

In the final analysis, it's frequently the "little things" which demonstrate whether or not you care. Little things like:

1. Just knowing people's names!

2. Making the effort to call attention to things which are important to people, like their birthdays, anniversaries, and accomplishments outside of work.

3. Knowing when to have some fun!

4. Regularly committing random acts of grace and kindness, on your own time, with your own money, and by sticking your own neck out for people.

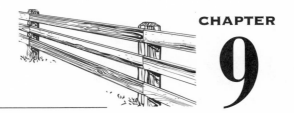

A Case for Some Useful Benefits

Everything has changed but for the way we think.

—Albert Einstein

All in the Family

In the majority of American households today, both Mom and Dad go off to work for at least 40 hours a week. But wait! What happened to the woman who used to stay at home and do all the stuff that has to be done in the house? The cleaning, the laundry, taking care of sick kids, waiting for the exterminator or the oven repair guy, the grocery shopping, and, oh yeah, the cooking? Well, her position has been eliminated, but not the duties. So just as in corporate America, everybody has to pitch in and do the extra work in their spare time.

The term *Work/Life Balance* has been used to describe these changing patterns of human behavior, and that term works well for us. Lots of people out there want both. So many, in fact, that if you don't do some things to attract these people, your competitors will get them, the good ones at least. Ellen Galinksy, director of The Families and Work Institute, a non-profit research organization in New York, says that companies which respond to the need to adapt work to people's lives will win workers' loyalty, and with that, a competitive edge.[1]

We have all seen many programs that come under the heading of Work/Life. We think the programs are far less important, repeat, *far* less important, than having a clear understanding of what you wish to accomplish with respect to those workers who also happen to have a life. It means looking at the changing reality of your employees' lives away from the workplace. Why? You do it because you want to continue to be productive under a whole new set of rules and realities. In fact, we don't really even like the term "family friendly," but prefer the more accurate "family responsive." If you have to do things differently now to be successful in response to the role of today's family, then it makes sense to do them.

> *The programs are far less important, repeat, far less important, than having a clear understanding of what you wish to accomplish.*

Before you institute any of the programs or practices we'll describe, however, make sure you have some clearly defined Work/Life goals. We think a good Work/Life program, or system, should be designed to:

- Improve productivity.
- Attract the best people for the jobs you need done.
- Increase retention.
- Improve customer service, period.

Whenever considering any family-responsive measures, it only makes sense to do a business case analysis, comparing the costs with the benefits of the proposal. Don't use other people's data; do the analysis yourself, based on your own situation.

It may be hard to quantify the benefits of family responsiveness, but there are plenty of successful companies which have both quantifiable and anecdotal evidence that have convinced them they were doing the smart thing for the success of the enterprise:

• First Tennessee Bank, for example, found that supervisors rated by their employees as family-responsive retained employees twice as long as the bank average and kept 7 percent more retail customers. This, the bank says, contributed to a 55 percent profit gain over two years, to $106 million.[2]

• Fel-Pro, a Skokie, Illinois, gasket maker, reports that employees who take advantage of its family programs were more likely to participate in team problem-solving, and nearly twice as likely to suggest product or process improvements.[3]

• Aetna Life and Casualty cut in half its resignations by new mothers when it extended its unpaid parental leave to six months, and saved a million dollars a year in hiring and training expenses.[4] (The Families and Work Institute found that absenteeism for those using work/life benefits was 50 percent less than that for the workforce as a whole.)[5]

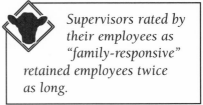 *Supervisors rated by their employees as "family-responsive" retained employees twice as long.*

• Boston-based John Hancock Financial Services says its family programs save the company approximately $500,000 each year in reduced turnover and absenteeism.[6]

AVERAGE LENGTH OF EMPLOYMENT SERVICE IN YEARS

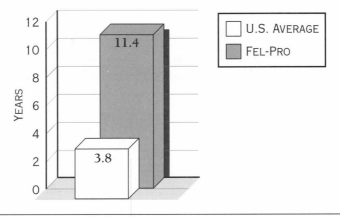

Source: Fel-Pro, U.S. Bureau of Labor Statistics.

While there are many interesting practices among the family-responsive policies adopted by American organizations, we'd like to look at four of them:

- Flextime
- Telecommuting
- Job-Sharing
- Child care accommodations

FLEXTIME

In the least structured flextime programs, people work about 40 hours a week. It doesn't matter which 40, as long as they get the work done. Other flextime plans are more rigid; they simply are not bound by the traditional 8–5 time frame. For instance, you may work from 6:00AM to 3:00PM, or from 10:00AM to 7:00PM.

For some workers, especially those with school-age children and a spouse, flextime provides a major convenience, and for many companies, it requires practically nothing to accommodate. It's probably the least costly of the practices we looked at. As with all of these practices, having it on the "menu" and actually making it available to people can be two very different things.

Despite its apparent simplicity and nominal cost, this practice sends a very powerful signal. As David Packard pointed out (HP was among the first companies in the U.S. to use it), "To my mind, flextime is the essence of respect for and trust in people. It says that we both appreciate that our people have busy personal lives and that we trust them to devise, with their supervisor and work group, a schedule that is personally convenient yet fair to others."[7]

TELECOMMUTING

Somewhat of a misnomer, telecommuting isn't commuting at all; it's staying at home, in your bathrobe if you like, and working by way of technology. Millions of workers telecommute regularly, according to Telecommute America, the non-profit group assembled to study and promote the practice. In 1996, 25 percent more Fortune 1000 corporations offered telecommuting arrangements than had made them available in 1995, but Telecommute America is quick to point out that telecommuting is not for everyone. It seems to work best when the job is one in which the employee is compensated on the basis of results, not activity, and when the worker is highly Committed already.

Salespeople and computer programmers make up the largest segment of the regular telecommuting population. (Translation: "We have rented out your office or cubicle to someone else."), but other professions are joining the fray every year. Temporary telecommuting arrangements have worked well in cases of a new mother easing back into work after childbirth, or during periods of partial convalescence following illness or surgery. Some people telecommute only occasionally, like when a child stays home sick, or during severe weather. In these cases, it can be very productive to be set up for telecommuting so that employees can take advantage of it should the need arise from time to time.

Telecommuting is not only a nice benefit to offer workers whose jobs and whose temperaments can handle it, it can also save big bucks in office overhead, and offer real gains in productivity. And that's what interests us. When the claims staff of the Hartford, Connecticut, office of Aetna Life and Casualty began telecommuting, the company recorded a 30 percent increase in the number of claims processed annually.[8]

Beware the perils of telecommuting, though, and they are worth considering. Such arrangements can clearly pose a threat to teamwork. The work of telecommuting groups has to be managed differently. Telecommuters and their managers have to make deliberate efforts to communicate clearly, since it probably won't happen on its own. Another danger involves overlooking outstanding talent or performance just because you don't see the person in the office very often. Though formidable, these considerations are far from insurmountable.

AETNA – TOTAL REVENUE

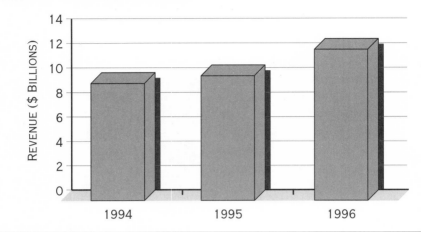

Source: Aetna Annual Report, 1996.

JOB SHARING

Though not yet very popular, job sharing offers real benefits to both employers and employees who take advantage of it. In job sharing, (usually) two people simply split a regular full-time job. Each partner works slightly more than half the week to allow for some overlap and hand-off time. In the U.S., many job sharers are people who would simply opt out of the workforce if job sharing were not available. Companies that use job sharing often do so as an important and viable alternative to losing good talent.

You might say, "Nobody would really leave a job because of an inflexible work schedule." Think again. At the Chubb Group of Insurance Companies, a 1991 work/family needs analysis determined that of 7,800 U.S. employees, 60 percent were in dual-career families. About 50 percent had child or eldercare responsibilities, and another 20 percent anticipated having such responsibilities within three years. Almost one-third of employees who left the company in that year said in exit interviews that they did so to help them balance their work and family lives.[9]

Here's one example of how job sharing works. We have a friend who, along with a job sharing partner, is the head librarian in a large city library. She works 22 hours a week, all day Monday and Tuesday, and until 2:00PM on Wednesday. Her job sharing partner arrives each Wednesday morning at 11:00, and works out the remainder of the week. From 11:00AM to 2:00PM on Wednesday, partner #1 "hands off" any tasks and information partner #2 needs, and then the other hand off usually happens by phone over the weekend.

As good as job sharing might sound, it is the least used of the four practices we looked at. While 74 percent of employers represented on The Conference Board's Work-Family Roundtable offer job-sharing, less than 1 percent of their employees participate, a survey of the 155 companies shows.[10] The biggest problem seems to be the subtle, unwritten resistance of managers, and the intangible political downsides. We have to wonder if this isn't a little like the age-old mystery of the tree falling in an unpopulated forest. If you offer a benefit, and no one takes it, is it really offered?

Job sharing isn't for everyone. In fact, there are probably more jobs that wouldn't qualify than those that would. But consider this scenario: You have a really great employee whose job is well suited to job sharing and he or she wants to job share. The job sharing arrangement is disallowed, either explicitly or implicitly, by sending the message that this would be career suicide. Therefore, the person decides to leave. Who's better off?

CHILD CARE BENEFITS

No other family-responsive practice is more complicated than that of child care. Some companies offer referral services, a practically free, and frankly, not very valuable service to employees. Others are on the opposite extreme, and operate on-site child care facilities. Most fall somewhere in the middle by offering child care subsidies at nearby facilities. Whatever your organization decides to do about child care, if anything, you should be mindful of the cost of doing nothing.

The Chubb companies became concerned about the fact that 50 exempt employees had left the company between 1992 and 1993 because of child care issues. Chubb knew that in its industry, it cost 97 percent of salary to replace the average employee. In the case of exempt employees, the average replacement cost was estimated at 150 percent of salary. On the basis of this data, it cost Chubb more than $3 million to replace the 50 exempt employees who left the company in 1992 and 1993 for child care reasons.[11]

And those who stay employed, but are constantly grappling with child care problems, are probably costing you even more than those who leave. According to Dun & Bradstreet, the annual cost to U.S. businesses of time lost through a breakdown in child care arrangements is about $3 billion![12] Nixon, Helms, and White in the *Journal of Compensation and Benefits*, report that about 5,000 U.S. parents reject work each *day* because they cannot find adequate or affordable child care.[13] If the job engine of a strong economy continues to roar, driving the unemployment rate further south, this will become even more of an issue.

One way companies have addressed the problem is by building and operating on-site child care facilities. For the eighth consecutive year, SAS Institute Inc., the Cary, North Carolina, software developer we mentioned earlier, has been recognized by *Working Mother* magazine as one of the "100 Best Companies for Working Mothers." Inclusion on the 11th annual list was based in part upon its family-responsive practices, including on-site child care. "Women comprise almost half of our workforce so we are very sensitive to issues specific to women in the workplace," said David Russo, vice president of human resources for SAS Institute. "SAS continues to set the pace for catering to the needs of employees engaged in both pursuing a career and raising a family."[14]

With employee turnover at 4 percent, versus an industry average of almost 20 percent, SAS Institute must be doing something right. Since its founding in 1976, the company has become the world's ninth largest independent software company, growing 526 percent in the last 10 years alone, and consistently wins honors for being a company full of *Contented Cows.*

But is on-site child care always the answer? Not necessarily. Construction of a new child care center is expensive, usually half a million to a million dollars, and you'll need a steady supply of at least 75 children to make it break even, says Marguerite W. Sallee, CEO of Nashville's Corporate Child Care Management Service Inc.[15] Besides, if you're not in the child care business, you really should outsource the management of the center. Moreover, child care experts warn that on-site child care is often the only alternative considered, and then often rejected because of the cost and impracticality of the proposal.[16] In many cases, further probing has discovered that flexible hours or part-time arrangements were of more value to employees than a big fancy child care facility.

GO ASK YOUR PEOPLE

Flextime, telecommuting, job sharing, on-site child care. These are four programs that can make a difference. IF they are seen as valuable by your employees. IF they reduce stress, turnover, hiring, and training costs. IF they allow your employees to serve your customers better. But don't limit your thinking to those areas.

You will have more success with family responsiveness if you ask and expect employees to take responsibility for their own family issues, and then partner with them to provide ways to address the needs of the family. Companies which opt instead to take responsibility for all their employees' family choices will both fail at it and live to regret *their choice*.

Ask your employees, "What are you struggling with all the time? What would make your life easier? So much easier that it would enable you to make a substantially greater contribution to what we do here?"

Chubb asked questions like these and, as a result, came up with a solution to "Snow Days" at its Warren, New Jersey, headquarters. Several days each winter, schools would be closed for weather reasons, but businesses, including Chubb, were going strong. On these days, Chubb allows parents to bring children ages 5 to 12 to work. Caregivers supervise the children from 8:00AM to 5:00PM in training and conference rooms. Activities include arts

CHUBB INSURANCE GROUP

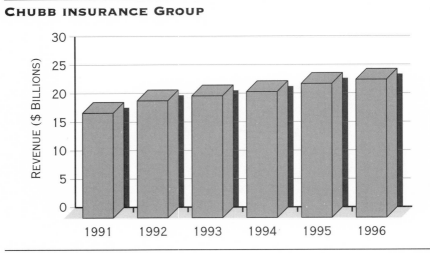

Source: Chubb Insurance Group.

and crafts, reading, physical play in the company's fitness center, and board games. With virtually no cost to the company, parents pay a one-time registration fee of $25, plus $15 per day per child. The daily fee includes morning and afternoon snacks.[17]

STARBUCKS: BUSINESS-MINDED BENEFITS

Since opening its first store in Seattle in 1971, Starbucks Coffee has grown to more than 1,200 stores and kiosks as of this writing (see Figure 9.1). Named one of *Fortune's* 100 Fastest Growing Companies in 1994, the company has experienced truly meteoric growth in both sales (650 percent) and earnings (900 percent) since going public (SBUX) in 1992. Chances are you've seen their mostly young, part-time workforce in action, serving up everything from a cup of plain black coffee to a "for-here, double-tall decaf, non-fat, no-whip amaretto mocha." It may be that the Starbucks "baristas," as they call their counter workers, pull their shots of espresso with such energy and animation because of some atmospherically generated caffeine high present in their storefront cafes. Or, it may be because they are simply pumped

FIGURE 9.1
STARBUCKS COFFEE COMPANY STORE LOCATIONS

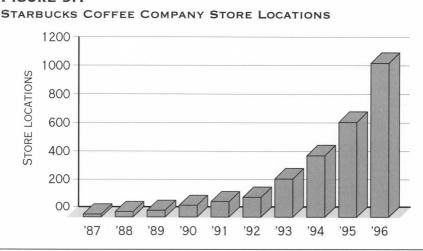

Source: Starbucks, 1997.

about working there. Part of the reason may have something to do with their exceptional benefits package.

As we pointed out earlier, there's no commercial wisdom in the notion that "more is better" when it comes to employee benefits. But at Starbucks, according to Senior Vice President of Human Resources Sharon Elliott, the benefits plan (which includes, among other features: health, dental and vision care, stock options, a 401(k), vacation, and a weekly pound of coffee), "more than pays for itself."[18]

In the fast-service restaurant business, employee longevity averages somewhere in the vicinity of four months. By comparison, the average Starbucks barista is on the job one and a half years, with more than a few staying for up to nine years. And those who stick with it can amass a respectable fortune, not from the $6–$7 an hour in base pay, but from "Bean Stock," the company's innovative employee ownership plan. An employee who stays at Starbucks for five years or more can accumulate enough stock to make a down payment on a house. Says Corey Rosen, director of the National Center for Employee Ownership, "That can make a difference for the rest of their lives."[19]

At least three features are worth noting about the benefits plan at Starbucks:

• Given the company's heavy dependence on a largely part-time workforce and the desire to retain skilled baristas, Starbucks apparently sees some wisdom in treating their part-timers like "real people" when it comes to benefits eligibility. (After a 90-day waiting period, both full and part-time employees are eligible.)

• Perhaps the most novel aspect of their approach to benefits is that the plans were designed not by some guy with a green eye shade in lower Manhattan, but by the employees themselves. As Howard Schultz, president and ceo (all Starbucks titles are lower cased) explains, "Since our partners are the ones who use, and are most affected by the health-care plan, asking them to help develop a tailored plan was the only way to achieve our goal."[20]

• Finally, and surprisingly, given the plan's origin, employees pay one-third of the cost, with the company contributing the remaining two-thirds. Consistent with the theme of this book, good benefit plans are a shared obligation, not a gift. (That which costs me nothing has little value.)

(Almost) Everything Under One Roof

Your workplace may have a cafeteria, even a bank, or some other little conveniences to keep you from having to go offsite for life's daily routines. Here are a few simple adjustments that have made a big difference for the *Contented Cows* who dreamed them up.

• Do you have a car repair facility onsite where you work? You do if you work at the "Taj Mahal," as EDS's Plano, Texas, World Headquarters is affectionately known. The compound's garage, along with its bank, store, day care center, and dry cleaners save employees tons of time over the course of a year, and it makes them more present, literally, on the job, and more productive.

• Pharmaceuticals maker Rhône-Poulenc Rorer offers a multitude of on-site services—including a shoe repair service, dry cleaners, car servicing, jewelry repair service, floral service, shuttle buses and vans, and a 400-square-foot company store—designed to allow employees to tend to errands without leaving

RHÔNE-POULENC NET INCOME

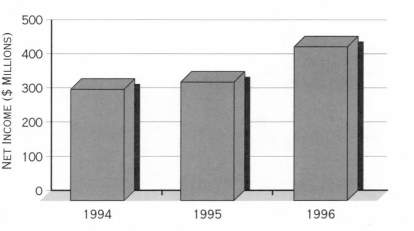

Source: Rhone-Poulenc, 1996 annual report.

work. The company has found that employees stay at work longer if they don't need to rush out to do errands.[21] Makes sense to us.

• PepsiCo offers "concierge" services to help employees with errands and tasks that need to be done during the workday—such as getting an oil change, lining up an evening babysitter, or contracting for house repairs. The employer has found that by taking care of these tasks (which were once handled by the "housewives" of a bygone era), it can help employees keep their minds on their work. As a result, PepsiCo has a more focused workforce.[22]

• Take-home meals provide another example of doing something smart to make life just a little easier for people. Retailer Eddie Bauer, enjoying annual sales growth of 20 percent, and drug maker Rhône-Poulenc Rorer, both keep the company cafe open late to prepare individual or family meals for harried employees to take home.[23] (P.S. It's also not a bad way to supplement the bottom line of what is typically a money-losing operation.)

• At Fel-Pro, the first shift runs from 7:24AM to 3:54PM. Why such an odd schedule? A company-commissioned study of the traffic patterns in the area of the plant found that this schedule would enable first-shifters to shorten their commute times and help them avoid traffic hassles. The result? A marked decrease in lateness and an increase in productivity and effectiveness.[24] We never said it took an Einstein to figure out these things.

CHAPTER SUMMARY

If you care about your people, you provide benefits which are truly beneficial—to you, to them, and to your bottom line. You recognize, for example, that the family is changing. If you respond in ways that help people care for their families, they can be more productive.

1. Four ways to be family-responsive are to provide:
   - Flextime
   - Telecommuting
   - Job-sharing
   - Child-care options

2. Before launching into any kind of benefit, find out what people want. Go ask 'em; don't assume! Do a business case analysis. Do your own homework. Make changes for business reasons, not good corporate PR.

Best Practices:

1. SAS Institute's on-site child care.
2. Starbucks Coffee's benefits and stock ownership plan for both full- and part-time employees.
3. Fel-Pro's commuter-friendly shifts.
4. On-site personal services at EDS and Rhône-Poulenc Rorer.

SECTION FOUR

CONTENTED COWS ARE ENABLED

$$\left(\begin{array}{c}\text{Enabled – To provide with the}\\\text{Means or Opportunity}\end{array}\right)$$

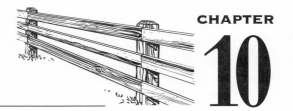

EMPOWER THIS!

When the systems, structure, policies, procedures and practices of an organization are designed and lived out so that employees genuinely feel they come first, trust is the result.
—Jackie and Kevin Freiberg, *NUTS*

THE RECENT ETYMOLOGY OF A BUZZWORD

In August of 1979, I first used a word in a speech in New York that I had never heard used within the context of employee relations. However, over the last 18 years, the use of that same word in the business lexicon has reached virus-like proportions. In the process, the term has taken on a life (and many new definitions) of its own. Sadly, as is too often the case with any product, image, or even a humble word which somehow makes the journey from obscurity to ubiquity, we see entire books, seminars, tapes, lectures, T-shirts, and ballcaps devoted to it. There's nothing wrong with that, except for the fact that with every mindless repetition, its meaning gets hopelessly muddled, if not lost altogether. The word?

Empowered.

The reason for discussing empowerment is even more crucial now than it was in 1979. Even as managers rush around doing whatever they do to "empower" their people, many are headed entirely in the wrong direction. Your people may not really need "empowering" at all. Think about it. They know how to find their way to work. For the most part, they not only know what their jobs are, but also the best ways of doing them. Management professor Henry Mintzberg offers an analogy. "Consider," he says, "a truly advanced social system: the beehive. Queen bees don't empower worker bees. The worker bees are adults, so to speak, who know exactly what they have to do. Indeed, the queen bee has no role in the genuinely strategic decisions of the hive, such as the one to move on to a new location. The bees decide collectively, responding to the informative dances of the scouts. ... What the queen bee does is exude a chemical substance that holds the system together. She is responsible for what has been called the *spirit* of the hive."[1]

> *What employees really need is for managers to stop standing on their necks long enough to let them DO their jobs!*

Our experience has shown that what most employees really need is for managers to stop standing on their necks long enough to let them DO their jobs! In short, what they need is for us to stop *disempowering* them.

A pivotal concept of those remarks back in 1979 was that successful organizations went to truly great lengths to ensure that they were hiring only those who were "qualified" for the position in question, and equipped by virtue of temperament, ideology, and attitude to be successful and content within the organization.

With that vital first step established, it was then equally important to ensure that these spanking new, highly qualified, and motivated troops were equipped with the "whys and wherefores" of the organization, and firmly pointed to a target. "Crack troops" don't tolerate standing at parade rest or aimlessly wandering very well. In fact, they become dangerous, both to themselves and those around them.

In order to be truly effective, we've got to make sure our people are totally and completely equipped to do their jobs and then (and only then) get ourselves (and the organization) out of their way! Stand aside and let them work!

We're not about to suggest that getting people to assume additional responsibility is easy. It's not. Some folks (and this isn't confined to the lower echelons) *like* being told what to do. But the real problem as we see it is that too many managers enjoy satisfying that wish. And because they enjoy it, they're good at it. They start by hiring people who *need* to be told what to do, and then tell them in every way imaginable that they don't want them to think or take responsibility. Requiring people to take responsibility for their work and allowing them to define and solve problems requires them to amend, among other things, both their roles, and, once again, their expectations.

> *We've got to take out the boss element.*
>
> —Jack Welch

IDENTIFYING FOUR TYPES OF MANAGERS

In their letter to shareholders published in the company's 1995 annual report, GE Executive Officers Jack Welch, Paolo Fresco, and John Opie crystallized the problem we're attempting to pinpoint:

> *It was at Work-Out sessions that it became clear that some of the rhetoric heard at the corporate level—about involvement and excitement and turning people loose—did not match the reality of life in the businesses. The problem was that some of our leaders were unwilling, or unable, to abandon big-company, big-shot autocracy and embrace the values we were trying to grow. So we defined our management styles, or "types,"* and how they furthered or blocked our values. And then we acted.*
>
> *Type I [the Contented Cow] not only delivers on performance commitments, but believes in and furthers GE's small-company values. The trajectory of this group is "onward and upward," and*

---

* Coincidentally, GE's "types" correspond to descriptions historically used in bovine classification. (See J. Albright, op. cit.) Hence, these "cow-nterparts" are included in brackets [].

the men and women who comprise it will represent the core of our senior leadership into the next century.

Type II [the Slow Milker, Chronic Kicker, or Finicky Eater] does not meet commitments, nor share our values—nor last long at GE.

Type III [the Fence-Breaking Explorer] believes in the values but sometimes misses commitments. We encourage taking swings, and Type III is typically given another chance.

Type IV [the Boss Cow]. The "calls" on the first two types are easy. Type III takes some judgment; but Type IV is the most difficult. One is always tempted to avoid taking action, because Type IV's deliver short-term results. But Type IV's do so without regard to values and, in fact, often diminish them by grinding people down, squeezing them, stifling them. Some of these learned to change; most couldn't. The decision to begin removing Type IV's was a watershed—the ultimate test of our ability to "walk the talk," but it had to be done if we wanted GE people to be open, to speak up, to share, and to act boldly outside traditional "lines of authority" and "functional boxes" in this new learning, sharing environment."[2]

ONE BAD APPLE CAN SPOIL THE WHOLE BARREL

Hundreds of contenders abound in the wings, waiting to accept the accolades and financial rewards associated with *Contented Cow* stature. But many of these companies fail to progress beyond the "wannabe" stage, precisely because of a few, or maybe just one, of the aforementioned Type IV managers. The efforts of the legitimate *Contented Cow* managers are severely diluted, if not obliterated, by these few "bad apples."

Look around. Maybe you're feeling pretty smug about the contentedness of your workforce in general, but do you notice a pocket of your organization with uncharacteristically high turmoil and turnover? It's possible they're still making their numbers. But it *might* be worth taking a closer look.

In more than one company we've examined, we've seen the valiant efforts of lots of well-intentioned leaders completely overshadowed by one or two Boss Cows. But, because they were achieving short-term results, albeit at the expense of people in their areas, it was tough for anyone to summon the courage to do anything about it.

It's not just the damage these Type IV's do within their own departments. Greater destruction by far occurs elsewhere in the organization, when people see this type of behavior tolerated or even encouraged. There seems to be a mixed message that sounds like this: "Our people are our most important assets. Really, they are. And our practice is to treat people in ways that will motivate them to stellar performance. We realize we've got one or two managers around here who don't get it. That's okay, because they're turning in the needed results right now. If you're not under their control, don't worry about them. Just be glad you don't work for them. If you do happen to work for them ... well ... it's a free world."

That just won't work. The glaring inconsistency involving even just a few will undermine and mitigate the valiant efforts of the majority. Once again, it is an all-or-nothing proposition. You're either Committed or you aren't. Remember, this is not a quest for the "moral high ground." It's just plain good business, and if there is any doubt, go back to Chapter 1 and revisit GE's financials.

If upon looking around, you discover a couple of these folks in your organization, you owe it to them (and everyone else) to be very clear about about your commitment to these principles. If they choose not to sign on, cull them from the herd, now. Do it professionally and humanely, but do it!

GIVE PEOPLE BACK THEIR WORK

As currently viewed, empowerment is something which is bestowed on those whose boxes on the organization chart are south of our own. Consistent with this plantation mindset, if it were not granted to them, they wouldn't have it. Now, contrast that with some situations where workers truly *do* have a high degree of influence (control, if you will) over their work and the work environment. Three that come readily to mind are those involving physicians, commercial airline pilots, and professional basketball players. In all three cases, the workers are well empowered already, with no thanks to either a manager or any sort of empowerment program.

Do you really think, for example, that a Delta Air Lines pilot needs special empowerment from the chief pilot (or anybody else at Delta) to request a different altitude to avoid some thunder cells, or that your doctor needs additional empowering from a hospital administrator to order a chest X-ray? Or, can you imagine Chicago Bulls coach Phil Jackson calling a special practice or a timeout during a game for the purpose of empowering Michael Jordan, Scottie Pippen, or (heaven forbid) Dennis Rodman to pass the ball, take a shot, or run a different play than the one which had been called? Of course not, and the reason is that whatever empowering is going on took place long ago, when it was baked into the person's job.

> *No profit grows where is no pleasure ta'en. ...*
>
> —Shakespeare

CHAPTER SUMMARY

1. Stop trying to "empower" your people. You'll only drive them (and yourself) crazy trying to figure it out. It's far easier and more beneficial to find those things which serve to *dis*empower them (dumb policies and procedures, managerial behaviors, etc.) and eradicate them. Do it with a vengeance!

2. Hire people who truly want to take responsibility for their work, then get out of their way!

3. Painful as it may be in the short run, either convert the "Boss Cows" to a new style of management or help them find a new job ... preferably with a competitor.

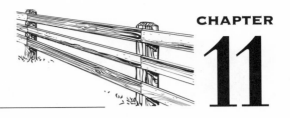

ENABLED EMPLOYEES ARE INCREDIBLY WELL TRAINED

*To try to build an organization against weakness frustrates the purpose
of organization.*

—Peter Drucker

WHY YOU CAN'T GET A PILOT'S LICENSE BY MAIL

Take a look inside the cockpit (er flight deck) of a modern jet-
liner. At first glance, one can't help but be astonished by all the
instruments—the gauges, computers, screens, levers, dials, and
the like. How the men and women who call that place their office
keep it all straight is, in and of itself, a miracle.

However, for our purposes, what you in fact see up there is
considerably less important than what you *don't* see, namely a
supervisor or manager. Instead, there are two, maybe three people
who, due to the vagaries of crew scheduling, probably don't know
each other very well, but they do know exactly what their job is,
and they know how to do it.

For those who need a numbers fix about now, consider this.
Pound for pound, in terms of the ratio of "worker bees" per man-

ager, commercial airline pilots are among the most productive employees you'll find anywhere. Typically, for the major commercial carriers, the number of crew members per manager is in excess of 100:1. Compare that to the span of control ratio in your (or most any other) business!

So how did they reach such levels of efficiency? Well, it's true perhaps that the airlines do enjoy an advantage insofar as being able to state the mission and goals for their flight crews in a simple, succinct fashion. The mission, for example is pretty clear:

> *Fly this plane and its passengers from New York's Kennedy Airport to Atlanta's Hartsfield Airport.*

So, too, the goals:

> *Do it safely, and as efficiently as possible.*

Sounds simple, right? But consider that there are probably a million things that could happen to that aircraft between New York and Atlanta. Therefore every single crew member who straps-in up front must be trained to deal with any eventuality.

Mind you, it's not that the airlines necessarily *want* to spend exorbitant amounts of time and money to ensure that their aircrews are trained to this degree of proficiency. Rather, they know they have to, because without it nobody in their right mind would get on the plane. Moreover, they are compelled by law to meet certain safety requirements. The problem with our more earthbound organizations is that we don't have anybody or anything scaring us enough to make us do it.

Many companies fund training efforts when times are good, then either slash or eliminate them entirely when times get tough. *Think for just a moment about the sheer stupidity of this concept: We have an earnings problem, so we're going to work our way out of it by "dumbing down" the organization with less skilled, less competent people! Now the only problem will be to find dumb customers to purchase our goods and services and even dumber investors to buy our stock!*

TRAINING EXPANDS THE MEANING OF PROFESSIONALISM

So where is it written and why is it that just because they don't wear labcoats, epaulets, or attend Harvard, a waitress, machinist, sales clerk, assembly worker, or anyone else cannot or should not be viewed and treated as a professional, with all the attendant rights, privileges and, yes, responsibilities? In a sense, what we're advocating is that if you really want to maximize your employees' level of contribution, you treat them the same way the hospital does its doctors, the airline its pilots, the law firm its lawyers, and so forth—as *professionals*.

The pursuit of professionalism throughout an organization means, among other things, a commitment to training. One organization that doesn't cheat in this regard is Hewlett-Packard which, according to co-founder David Packard, spends upwards of a half-billion dollars annually—a sum which equates to nearly 2 percent of revenue—training its 98,000 employees.[1]

> *If you really want to maximize your employees' level of contribution, you treat them the same way the hospital does its doctors, the airline its pilots, the law firm its lawyers, and so forth—as professionals.*

USAA, the San Antonio based auto insurer, is a believer as well. Under former (1969-1993) President Robert McDermott, a retired Air Force brigadier general and former dean of the Air Force Academy, the company invested massively in employee training (as much as 3 percent of revenues). Judging by a 146-percent increase in the asset/employee ratio between 1985 and 1994, we'd say their ROI from this type of investment isn't too shabby at all.[2] And, since 1970, they've successfully lowered their employee turnover rate from 40 percent to 6 percent![3]

An investment in knowledge always pays the best interest.
—Ben Franklin

How much training could it possibly take to prepare a Starbucks barista to take the counter at one of the coffee chain's cafes? Would you believe 24 hours of formal classroom training, and 25 to 30 hours of practical onsite training?[4] To pour coffee?! No, but to learn to "call" the order using precisely the right syntax, to brew the coffee, pull shots of espresso, steam milk with varying fat content, and to learn "cup management," a mnemonic mechanism which uses the position of the cup and its handle to signal to the person preparing the drink exactly what was ordered. Never knew it was that complicated? Well, it is. And if you pride yourself, as Starbucks does, in providing an exceptional experience for the customer, you can increase your chances for success by providing exceptional training for those on the front line.

In 1995, the American Society for Training and Development conducted a survey to determine the amount of money (as a percent of payroll) that companies were spending on training. As indicated by the following graph, a majority of respondents (58 percent) were spending somewhere between 0 and 1.5 percent of payroll on their training efforts, and about a quarter of them were somewhere above 1.5 percent.[5] While one could make the argument that many appear at first glance to be seriously underfunded, at least by comparison to companies like HP and USAA (which are reportedly in the 2–3 percent of *revenue* range), the thing that shocked us the most about the study results was the fact that 16 percent of the respondents didn't even know what they were spending![6] (see Figure 11.1) *Do you?*

THE HIDDEN COSTS OF IGNORED TRAINING

Let's look for a moment beyond the direct and obvious benefits. What is the cost of *not* providing needed training? More to the point, what is the cost of incompetence in any part of your organization? To be sure, there are direct costs. You pay an added price for re-work, lost customers, and yes, the cost of additional supervisors to run around looking over the shoulders of your motivated but marginally competent troops. But we believe there is a cost far greater and more debilitating than any of these, and

FIGURE 11.1

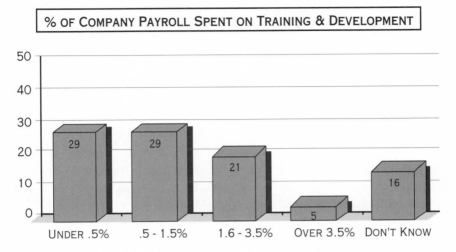

% OF COMPANY PAYROLL SPENT ON TRAINING & DEVELOPMENT

it has to do with what happens to the psyche and performance of your employees when they don't feel particularly competent, or confident in their ability to do something.

How many times in your life, usually in a customer interaction (where you're the customer), have you had a sales clerk, reservationist, waiter, or any employee for that matter, start the transaction with the words "I'm new at this. ..."? (*By the way, how would you like to hear those same words from your neurosurgeon as you're being wheeled into the operating room?*) In making that pronouncement, what that person really is saying to you and, more importantly to themselves is, "I'm probably gonna screw this up, so please be patient and understanding with me." And if a person *thinks* they will screw something up, guess what? They will! Moreover, if they screw it up this time, how confident are they going to be the next time? Your potentially contented, productive employee just became a very demoralized one, and for good reason. As Jimmy Johnson points out, "The coach or manager's job is to make the player feel as good about himself as he can possibly feel, all the time. You'd think every coach, manager, and CEO in America would understand this by now."[7]

Make no mistake about it. People who are proficient in their jobs and who *know* they will be competent enough to handle the difficult tasks ahead feel confident about themselves and stay calm and poised in on-the-spot crises. As a result, they perform better than an employee who never got a lesson in the basics.

WALKING, TALKING CATALOGS AT CRATE & BARREL

Have you ever been to a Crate & Barrel, the home furnishings store? If so, you may have been surprised at how much each of their sales associates knows about every item in the store's vast inventory. That's because they do an incredibly good job of equipping each of their people with detailed knowledge about everything they sell. One of Crate & Barrel's top priorities is keeping salespeople fully informed of every available product. A new item hits the shelf only after associates have "read all about it," and for the really big lines and complicated items, each store receives a *Video Information Bulletin* which is required viewing for everyone in the store. Says C&B's Betty Kahn, "They have to know the product, so they can sell it."[8]

AN INTELLIGENT LEARNING PROCESS

It's no surprise or coincidence that FedEx, GE, and Southwest have some of the most admired (and emulated) corporate universities in the world. Of far greater importance than the bricks and mortar behind these institutions is the level of personal commitment displayed by their respective CEOs. Each, for example, regularly makes time to visit the classroom, and, beyond merely waving the flag, participates meaningfully in the learning process. Anyone who has ever witnessed new managers jousting with Fred Smith in the "U," or Jack Welch in "the pit" at Crotonville knows there is some serious learning going on.

Without a doubt, the *Contented Cow* companies are deadly serious about the issue of training, an attitude that goes well beyond the amount of money they spend doing it, the impressiveness of their truly first rate learning facilities, the breadth of course offerings, and the like. Instead, we think what makes them special is that despite the success they've enjoyed or how big they may have become, they have not lost sight of one of the most fundamental precepts in the whole employee relations arena: The person who started work for them this morning is as close to a model employee as they're ever going to get. And unlike so many others who no doubt recognize the same thing, they actively (fanatically might be a better word for it) DO something about it.

While we have talked about orientations as an opportunity for employers to establish open, two-way communication with new hires from the outset, we cannot overemphasize the fact that orientations are primarily for training. Like many companies, Disney requires every single employee—no matter what their station in life—to attend a comprehensive new employee orientation (Disney Traditions). But the similarity ends there, because the focus is not so much on telling people where to find the paper clips, having them fill out forms until their fingers ache, or introducing them to dozens of new people who will likely be forgotten by lunchtime. Instead, they make sure the new cast member is carefully introduced to the company's traditions, philosophies, and a very different way of life—the Disney way.

Rosenbluth Travel, the giant travel agency, flies every newly hired Travel Sales Associate to its Philadelphia headquarters for an orientation. There the focus is on the company's beliefs, history, values, and goals. Following the orientation, the TSA's are then immersed in a comprehensive six to eight week training program before they are turned loose on paying customers.[9] How long do your managers and new hires spend with this process: an hour, maybe two?

Faced with problems that are becoming all too familiar, Marriott found it necessary to redefine the parameters of the traditional orientation, especially when faced with the question, "Where does training begin?" Heavily dependent upon low-wage workers (many of whom are recent immigrants from places like Bosnia and China, or fresh from the welfare rolls), the company has baked a lot of reality into its training regimen.

Marriott recognized that there were some rather elementary things—like speaking English, basic literacy, parenting (*that's caring for kids, not creating them*), work etiquette, and problem solving—many of their people needed to learn before teaching them how to do their job even became relevant. While some may argue that they've crossed the line into a whole new social order, Charles R. Romeo, director of employee benefits for ConAgra, puts it another way: "The burden is on us, not on the employee, to change. For many of us, that's a new recognition."[10]

TRAINING TO PROFICIENCY: A WRONGHEADED APPROACH

Let's make an important distinction here. Spending a ton of money on training is *not* the issue. In fact, relative to the ROI for their training dollars, many organizations spend entirely too much time and money on training, either because they mistakenly view it as the answer for every performance or behavioral problem, or they've somehow been sucked into accepting the notion that training to proficiency (i.e., no wash-outs) is the way to go. Sadly, in many cases, it represents nothing more than throwing money at the issue, a practice which is unfailingly stupid.

THE FAA: BLIND IN ONE EYE?

The Federal Aviation Agency (FAA) presents something of a case in point. In the past, newly hired air traffic controllers would all report to the organization's training academy in Oklahoma for their initial training and certification. Those who—with a reasonable amount of instruction over a reasonable period of time—couldn't pass muster went home to seek their fame and fortune elsewhere. At some point this practice was amended in favor of a train-to-proficiency approach, and the end result is that now nobody ever gets sent home or, as our friend Alex Nicholas calls it, de-selected. Instead, you wind up with a situation where people who would have washed out under the old system are *still* in training and on the job years later, and every day must have their work carefully overseen by an experienced controller. A competent employee ends up babysitting an inept one, making them both, at best, marginally productive; and both are making the same money!

Generally, this type of situation seems to arise either from some misguided thinking about the nature of the employment relationship, or because the training organization doesn't want to stand up and be held accountable for its efforts. We are firm advocates of taking pains to ensure that people are proficient in required job skills for the life of their job tenure. We're equally fervent in the belief that there is a point at which you realize "this dog won't hunt."

As very frequent flyers, we take considerable comfort in knowing that commercial aircrews are not only well trained, but that they must regularly (every six to 12 months) demonstrate their capability via a proficiency test. Pilots (and flight attendants) who don't pass those checks are grounded until they can. Sadly, we don't have the same confidence in the air traffic control system on which those pilots depend.

 There is a point at which you realize "this dog won't hunt."

TRAINING UP A (DESERT) STORM

Prior to the start of hostilities in the 1991 Gulf War, General H. Norman Schwarzkopf kept his troops out in the desert for what seemed to many like an eternity. And it wasn't simply because he was waiting for the last diplomatic efforts to fail. They were there to train.

Of course, the U.S. Armed Forces had not gone out in the street and simply drafted the first half-million people who happened to be standing around. In the main, General Schwarzkopf's command consisted of well-equipped, professional soldiers who had already undergone months, if not years, of training. Many had experienced combat before. But it was important to the general not just to ensure that his soldiers were ready, but to get them to the point where *they* knew they were ready.

According to Schwarzkopf, the fact that his troops were a lot better equipped than their adversaries was nearly inconsequential. In an interview with David Frost shortly after the war, the general theorized that if the armament situation had been reversed, his troops would *still* have won as clearly and convincingly as they did, due largely to the psychological advantage. Nor can one underestimate the importance of the troops' knowing that Schwarzkopf had not whiled away the months in a cushy rear area waiting for the ground phase to begin; he had endured the desert with them.

VISIBILITY MATTERS

All too often, a company decides to send people to a training program without first securing the buy-in of the organization's leadership. Like it or not, people want to know that the training course they're taking time to sit through is as important to senior management as it is supposed to be to them. Often that means senior management needs to sit through the same program as everyone else, not in their own condensed mini-versions, but right alongside all the others.

There should be no executive parking spaces when it comes to training. They must participate enthusiastically and, perhaps most importantly, they need to demonstrate the skills they expect everyone else to learn. Commenting on his participation in a 60-hour training class alongside other Rubbermaid employees, CEO Wolfgang Schmitt said, "I had to visibly be a part of it. People look to see if you just talk about it or actually do it."[11]

Not long ago, we conducted a workshop in Coaching Skills for a group of plant managers and superintendents for Florida Power Corporation. The session was conducted in a company training facility in the small town of Crystal River, about 100 miles north of the company's St. Petersburg headquarters. The vice president who brought us in, George Marks, underwent the training along with all of his direct reports. George's personal presence and participation in the training wasn't lost on anybody.

His willingness to be observed in a new situation—a vulnerable, "untrained state"—was appreciated by the other class members.

A few months later, George decided to bring us back to provide the same program for the next level of employees below his direct reports. Although he had already completed the training, he thought it was important to put his stamp of support on the program for this group. However, the scheduling that worked best for the attendees wasn't convenient for him. This particular day, he had an important budget meeting back in St. Petersburg, but because he thought it was important enough for him to kick off the training session, he took a company helicopter from St. Petersburg to Crystal River early that morning.

At 7:45AM, he landed at a small airport a half mile from the training site, then drove over to kick off the training program by telling the assembled group of the benefits he had realized since taking the course. After his talk, he and a Crystal River colleague got in a car and drove south to St. Petersburg. He made a 200-mile round trip to deliver a 10-minute message. What the employees gleaned from seeing their vice president standing in front of them and knowing the effort it took for him to be there was far more important than any single thing any of us said that day. The message had been sent, loud and clear: "This is important. It's so important that I went through it before you did. I'm using it, and now I want and expect you to do the same."

By contrast, we conducted several training sessions for a large Midwest manufacturer. Due to the conspicuous absence of any member of senior management throughout the entirety of this effort, we often heard the question, "If this is so important, where are they?" Months later, an informal survey of those who attended indicated that only a few people were using the skills we covered in the course. It's possible the senior officers didn't really need to be there for their personal benefit but, as we've heard so many times before, perception is reality. To us, it's a little like the difference between the parents who *send* versus *accompany* their children to church.

A QUICK SELF-EXAM

Sadly, companies seldom go to the trouble of ensuring that the training efforts they've paid for have actually taught their people anything. Here are some questions we believe you should ask:

1. Have you established and do you train to minimum proficiency standards?
2. How must trainees *demonstrate* proficiency, both on an initial and recurrent basis? We're not just talking about skills training, either. Don't let anyone try to tell you that learned skills and acquired knowledge can't be reliably demonstrated. (While we're on the subject, why is it that no one ever flunks a corporate training program? Are both trainers and students *really* that good?)
3. What follow-up measures do you have in place to ensure that people have actually *learned* something from a training effort, and that they intend to use it?

One of our clients has implemented a simple but effective tool to work on this one. After a training class (which he and his entire senior management team usually attend first), his people receive a letter which asks them to describe for him in writing not only what they've learned, but how they intend to put it to use. (see below)

Dear _____:

You have just completed a two day XYZ Skills Workshop sponsored by our company. My hope is that the workshop was a success, and that you are coming away armed with new skills which you can put to use.

My purpose in writing is to reinforce the expectation that the acquired skills/methods do, in fact, need to be put to use. Put simply, you and your fellow participants were provided this developmental opportunity because of the belief that it would lead to more productive and satisfied managers and work units.

Within the next week, I would like for you to provide me a brief (2 pages or less) written summary as to:

- *What you learned;*
- *How you intend to apply it in the course of your every day job;*
- *What I (or other members of our management team) can do to support you in this regard;*
- *How, when, and by what means you plan to measure the relative success of these efforts.*

Sincerely,

John Q. President

4. Who pays for the training?

Some would argue that it makes no difference, as in the final analysis it all comes out of the same wallet anyhow. We disagree vehemently. If a training offering arrives as a gift of the Training Department or somebody else's cost center, it's not viewed with nearly the same seriousness as it would be if each department or workgroup were required to fund it themselves. Better yet, why not require each employee to personally budget (and account for) their *own* development expense?

5. Finally, and perhaps most importantly, what are your training priorities?

Sounds like a stupid question, but most organizations don't have a clue. Instead, they approach the subject like a family of four in a Chinese restaurant: "Let's have one from column A, one from column B, etc." And just like the Chinese meal, when the food shows up, people eat what they like and don't eat what they don't want. The problem with this haphazard approach is that it

Why is it that no one ever "flunks" a corporate training program?

guarantees you'll spend more than you should, and you'll never get full or, in business terms, reach the critical mass which is essential to getting some return on that investment. If, for example, customer service training for front line employees is a priority, then every single front line customer contact employee ought to get it. No exceptions and no free passes! If leadership training is a priority, then every single leader ought to get it. No exceptions there, either! Just think about it. How would you like to get on an airplane knowing that the captain and first officer had opted out of their emergency cockpit procedures class?

CHAPTER SUMMARY

Training is a vital part of the enabling process, and is a competitive advantage. Fully 90 percent of the $30 billion or so spent annually on training is spent by only 0.5 percent of all U.S. companies, with much of that being wasted. You must:

- treat training as something other than a luxury
- link it tightly to your business strategy
- know how to organize and deliver it
- set clear ROI expectations (individual as well as organizational)

Best Practices

a. New Product Training at Crate & Barrel.
b. New employee orientation at Disney and Rosenbluth Travel.
c. Marriott's non-traditional "real world" curriculum.
d. Leadership development at GE, Southwest, and FedEx.

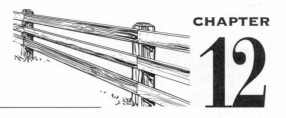

ENABLED EMPLOYEES ARE TOOLED

$$\left(\begin{array}{c}\text{Tooled – To equip with the} \\ \text{means for production}^1\end{array}\right)$$

In any competitive situation, a chief duty of leadership is to minimize the impact of unexpected conditions and distractions on the team in combat. This demands the trained eye, awareness, and judgment of the leader if the troops are to prevail on the battlefield.

—Pat Riley

TOOLS, NOT RULES

We've said this before, but it's so important, we're going to say it again: Organizations don't become *Contented Cows* purely on the strength of their employee relations practices. All of your policies, methods, systems, and procedures have an impact on your workforce in some way. So come on, broaden your concept of what makes a cow contented! It does no good to go out and hire talented people who fit well within the organization; get them all fired up about the voyage; equip them with a capable leader; and train the stew out of them, if forces within your organization's *system* are going to frustrate or prevent them from performing.

What we are talking about is analogous to going out and spending a half million dollars to build an Indy car, another half million to get a backup car, hiring a top-name driver and pit crew, paying for months of practice, then about 30 minutes before the race, sending your crew chief out to put a governor on the engine. While none of us would *plan* to do something this stupid, we somehow manage to pull it off on a fairly regular basis. We do it through policies that are just plain dumb; systems that treat intelligent people like they're complete morons; and cultures which ensure that no mistake goes unpunished.

BE CAREFUL WHAT YOU INCENT; YOU'LL LIKELY GET IT!

At the risk of offending some of our friends in the compensation profession, most pay systems suck a big egg. They are not only broken, they make no sense. They not only fail to incent people to do their best, but in many cases, actually induce them to do a poor job.

Perhaps the most obvious example is paying someone according to how much time it takes them to do something—a notion which in nearly every case is fundamentally bankrupt. Anybody who registers an I.Q. can figure out very quickly what they need to do to make more money under such a time-based arrangement, and it's not in your customers' or stockholders' interest for them to do it. So why in the world do we pay people that way? Some would have you believe that it is required by law. Not true! Companies like Worthington Industries and Chaparral Steel have known this fact for a long time; their employees are all salaried.

Be especially careful in defining what it is you motivate people to do, because that is exactly what they're *going* to do. Sears was reminded of this in the early '90s when, as the result of a new pay scheme for its automotive service people, they wound up with a public relations nightmare when the company was accused of systematically defrauding car-repair customers by making unneeded repairs.[2]

Conversely, Lincoln Electric, the Cleveland-based manufacturer of electric motors, has enjoyed immense success over its 100-plus year history, due in part to its unique piecework pay system which rewards employees for doing exactly what they're supposed to be doing. By the way, they are also afforded the opportunity to earn well in excess of area wages and to manage their own work (the foreman to worker ratio is reportedly in the neighborhood of 1:100).

All organizations would do well to scrutinize with a healthy dose of suspicion the job evaluation systems they use to determine the relative worth of each job—principally of the managerial and professional variety. Most are based on some version of a point factor system which gives credit for things like the knowledge and skill required to do the job, and the level of accountability that goes with the position. This seems a perfectly rational and reasonable approach until you consider the outdated 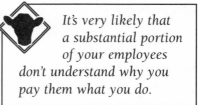 *It's very likely that a substantial portion of your employees don't understand why you pay them what you do.* means by which something like accountability is usually gauged—the size of the individual's budget and the number of people reporting to them. Here again, the goals of the organization (be more productive, effective, etc.) and those of the individual (make more money) become completely incongruent, and, over time, we know which one is going to win out.

This same argument can also be made in other areas. Based on a fairly traditional model and some rather curious logic, many organizations furnish their employees with a finite number of "sick days" each year. The intent is that these days will be used as income protection when the person is, due to unavoidable illness or injury, unable to come to work. But people feel compelled to use up their allotment of days each year, regardless of whether or not they are actually ill.

Let's compare this to two different approaches a bank could take to protect its customers against overdrafts. One approach would be for the institution to provide each customer with an additional $1,000 each year, with the caveat that the money only be used to protect against overdrafts. (We've got a feeling we know how this scenario would play out.) Or, they could advise credit-worthy customers (would they really want any other kind?) that, within reason, they would temporarily cover account overdrafts. However, the bank warns that if the customer abuses the privilege, they will have to revise the relationship, or terminate the agreement.

Companies which take this latter approach with the issue of sick days, like Chaparral Steel and FedEx, are beginning to experience significantly fewer unscheduled absences. In some cases, they are reporting unscheduled absence rates of less than 1 percent of scheduled work days versus a mean of around 1.6 percent for all employers.

Now let's assume for the moment that you've managed to get most of the dumbness out of your pay and benefit systems; that you're no longer paying anyone (including your accountant and attorney) on an hourly basis; that you're not paying people who should be cooperating with one another to compete; and that everyone's got a substantial portion of their pay at risk. We're home free, right?

WRONG! Because it's very likely that a substantial portion of your employees don't understand *why* you pay them what you do or what exactly it is they must do to make more. And they certainly can't appreciate the linkage between their reward system and the organization's overall performance (assuming there is one).

A case in point: In April 1996, the board of directors of Delta Air Lines approved a generous stock option program for their employees, granting them, on average, the right to purchase approximately 300 shares of DAL over the next 10 years.[3] The decision was based on the perceived need to generate a higher level of goal-congruence between DAL and its employees, and to pump up sagging morale. That's all well and good, except for one thing. It has now been well over a year since the program was approved, and most of their people know nothing about it. Of the 50 or so randomly selected DAL employees we spoke with, roughly 30 knew nothing about the program at all, and *none* of them were able to explain it!

THE PROPER USE OF BONUSES

We know a fellow who runs one of the largest independent Honda auto-repair garages in America. The business is growing and thriving mainly because (get this) customers love them! Anyhow, at the end of his first full year of leadership, our friend John wanted to share some of the spoils with those who had helped make a good year possible. Despite his partners' wishes to the contrary, he instructed the company accountant to cut a generous bonus check for each employee, hoping that it would strengthen the link between individual and corporate interests.

Unfortunately, the ink was barely dry on the back of those checks when John called us with bad news. His people were no more attuned to the company or its customers than they were *before* the bonuses. He still had a contingent that came to work late every day, others who wouldn't lift a finger to help a co-worker, and, worst of all, he was seeing a noticeable decline in the performance of some of his better people.

So what was at the root of all this? Well, it seems that some of the better performers were miffed that they had fared no better than others who, by virtue of their lackluster performance, already had one foot on a banana peel. And, more importantly, no one really understood what the bonuses were for in the first place! In the final analysis, John had not only pumped a sizable chunk of his net income down a dry hole, he had actually managed to make things worse!

Sadly, this same saga is played out every day as ESOP's, 401-(k)s, profit sharing plans, and a variety of shorter-term performance incentives fail to work as well as they should because people don't understand them. The answer isn't to abandon these devices as a means of encouraging maximum effort, but rather to first ensure that they are sensibly and simply designed, and then to take the time and expend the effort necessary to ensure that people understand and appreciate them. Remember Peter Lynch's point from Chapter 4. Get out your crayons!

Still, if well-designed and implemented, incentive programs can bring productivity gains worth far more than the outlay. InTuition's David Graham credits part of his company's turnaround to an incentive bonus and profit sharing plan. Designed to be awarded for both individual *and* team performance, the team component is especially powerful. If one team member sees another slacking or doing something that will adversely affect the company's profits, he or she will exert the necessary peer pressure to correct things. "Hey, that's my bonus you're messing with!" they're likely to say. The collective efforts of all the members of the team, who know precisely how the bonus is figured, is a great motivating force.

Our advice is to keep incentive programs fresh, and relevant to the desired performance by making sure everyone knows exactly what and where the target is. "You've got to tweak them [incentive plans] from time to time," Graham cautions. "Don't let them grow stale. After a while, they lose their incentive value and start to be viewed as an entitlement."[4]

HELP NOT HINDER

Contented Cows go to great lengths to develop and implement not only policies, but procedures and support systems which are designed to make heroes (not scapegoats) out of their employees, most particularly those who serve on the front line.

Marriott discovered an example of this in some of its hotel property restaurants. It seemed that the wait staff on the breakfast shift was spending something like 70 percent of their time doing things other than waiting on tables. When they investigated the situation further, they found their waiters and waitresses frequently having to spend time in the kitchen doing things like picking up orders, making toast, and rummaging through the freezer for new containers of juice while their customers were left wondering why the coffee refill was taking so long. Today, as the result of reworking the support system at some Marriott properties, *the servers never even have to enter the kitchen*. The culinary staff takes care of all food preparation.

MARRIOTT INTERNATIONAL, INC. OPERATING PROFIT

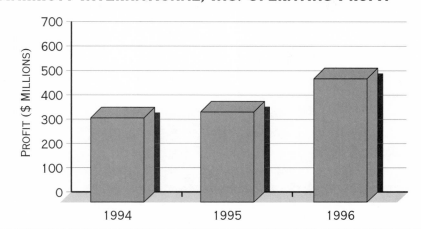

Source: Marriott International Annual Report, 1996.

When a meal is ready, the kitchen beeps the server and a runner delivers it to the table for presentation by the server.[5]

OVERBOOKED ON THE INTERNET

Contrast Marriott's handling of their problem with the first great cyber-fiasco of the internet industry. You know the one we mean: America Online. In December of 1996, AOL switched to an unlimited usage plan with most of its eight million subscribers. The only trouble was that the company failed to prepare—to equip itself—with adequate capacity to handle the switch from measured to unlimited service. And so millions of subscribers found it impossible to sign onto the system except in the dead of night. This was, as one analyst put it, like selling 10,000 tickets to a concert in a hall that only seats 800.

How would you like to be an AOL telephone customer service representative in the midst of this debacle? All you can do is sit there with egg on your face and take it—endure every call—because, you know what? Every one of those angry customers is right.

NO SALE ON COLD TURKEY

Two weeks before Christmas one year, the microwave oven in my house started malfunctioning. Now, I don't know about your place, but that's about the last thing we want to live without during the holiday season. So I called 1–800–949–7185, home of the people whose repair vans are emblazoned with the words "We Service All Major Brand Name Appliances No Matter Where You Bought Them," and whose yellow-pages ad proudly states, "Free Service Call When We Repair."

After the usual identification process with the telephone representative, I stated the problem: Something was causing the microwave to arc and burn up the turntable support. She said they would be able to come out the next day and repair the oven, and that the service call would be free, unless I chose not to have the repairs made. I indicated that was fine, but made a special point of telling her that the technician needed to be sure to bring at least a new turntable support since, for all intents and purposes, that part was toast.

Around 8:30 the next morning, the technician called to verify that someone would be home and let us know that he would arrive between 10:30AM and noon. Great! I reminded him that, at a minimum, he would need to bring a turntable support for the microwave.

The technician arrived as scheduled and immediately diagnosed the problem: "Your turntable support is defective and it's causing the thing to arc." In that moment, I was feeling pretty good for having correctly guessed the cause of the problem. I figured I'd be a hero to my family when they got home because the microwave would be fixed—Wrong! The next words out of the technician's mouth were, "I don't have that part on the truck so may I use your phone to see if we have it in stock?" My chin dropped.

Making the call he should have made four hours earlier, the technician was promptly put on hold for an eternity by his own parts department. When he finally got through, it was only to find out they didn't have the part, would have to order it, and even if they put a "rush" on it, I'd be "looking at a minimum of seven–10 days with no micro." I indicated that was a bit more cold turkey than I was interested in eating, and with the technician still standing in the kitchen, picked up the phone, called the manufacturer, and ordered it myself—with a four-day committed delivery. After hanging up the phone, I turned around and the technician presented me with a bill for $40. "What's this?" I sputtered.

"Well, you refused the repair."

"No, I didn't refuse the repair; you didn't do what both you and your telephone rep were asked to do, and as a result, couldn't and didn't repair anything." Now, don't get me wrong, the fellow was very nice. In fact, while he was waiting for the parts people to wake up, we had a most enlightening conversation about what it's been like working for Sears. He was a 14-year employee and a happy camper. When asked what he liked most about his job, he responded, "They don't put any pressure on you." No, I thought to myself, they don't, but I'm about to. Following a very civil conversation in which he agreed that he could see my point, the man indicated that it wasn't up to him to tear up the invoice. Now what's wrong with this scenario?

First, the technician bears some responsibility for not acting on the information he was given at 8:30AM. Beyond that, his employer (the "softer side" people) utterly failed him, and every other repair person they have on the streets by:

1. Not backing them up with a parts ordering process which would prevent them from sitting around forever in a customer's home with a phone stuck in their ear.
2. Not trusting a 14-year employee who drives around in a $20,000-plus company vehicle equipped with at least some parts and equipment with enough latitude to make the decision on a lousy $40 repair charge.

The reflexive thing to do would be to recommend some empowering for this guy. But that's really not what's required at all. If anything needs to be empowered, it is his *job*. It should be redefined in broad enough terms that it requires him (and everyone like him) to do more than just show up when he's supposed to, be polite, and make an honest effort to repair an appliance. Rather, it should be his job to first fix *me*, the customer, and then do whatever it takes to get the appliance squared away. There is a big difference.

The moral of my micro experience: As you continue trying mightily to get your people to take ownership for their jobs and make customers their own, you've got to realize that the *only* way that's going to happen is by enabling them to succeed. Otherwise, it's going to be business as usual. It will continue to be *your* job and *your* customer. And the employee will continue to "just fix microwaves."

NO-FAULT MAIL ORDER

Now, contrast that example of a disempowered appliance repairman on a house-call with an enabled computer repair technician on the phone a thousand miles away. I placed an order in January 1995 with Mac and PC Connection*, the mail-order computer people in Marlow, New Hampshire. I was delighted when an express delivery truck showed up the next day with a box containing my new computer system. Everything was great until I booted up and the screen started flickering, and kept flickering. Within two minutes of placing a call to the company, I was speaking with Ann, a repair technician, who walked me through some basic diagnostics and one rather simple repair attempt. It didn't work.

At this point Ann apologized for my problem (even though she didn't make the computer), and asked if it would be okay if they shipped a replacement to me that evening, for delivery the next morning. "Don't you need to check with somebody before you ship me another $2,500 computer, particularly since you won't even have this one back yet?" I asked. She responded, "No

---

* Since its founding in 1982, PC Connection has brought mail order out of the dark ages. The company has won PC World's "World Class Award for Best Mail Order Company" an unprecedented six times, and was named by the Boston Computer Society as "Best All-Around Company" in the entire computer industry. They are New Hampshire's largest private employer.[6]

sir, I can see you've done business with us for a while, and that won't be necessary at all. I'm just sorry you had the problem. As soon as you're able, pack up the defective machine, call us, and we'll have it picked up."

Wanna make a bet which employee went home happier that night, and which companies' business prospects are brighter?

THE MEANING OF MISTAKES

3M is a *Contented Cow* which knows a thing or two about making mistakes. With 50,000 different products on the market, and an internal requirement that 30 percent of each year's sales must come from products less than four years old, they've undoubtedly experienced lots of missteps along the way. They realize that the relentless pursuit of innovation is anything but a straight path.

In "Philosophy of Management," a paper published in 1941, former 3M President William L. McKnight explained the company's approach. *Those men and women to whom we delegate authority and responsibility, if they are good people, are going to want to do their jobs in their own way. ... Mistakes will be made, but if a person is essentially right, the mistakes he or she makes are not as serious in the long run as the mistakes management will make if it is dictatorial and undertakes to tell those under its authority exactly how they must do their job. Management that is destructively critical when mistakes are made kills initiative, and it is essential that we have people with initiative if we are to continue to grow.*[7]

MISTAKES MUST ABSOLUTELY, POSITIVELY NOT GO UNPUNISHED

We said early on that we're not holding the *Contented Cows* out as models of perfection. Occasionally they, too, step in some cow chips. Our impression, though, is that they are very fleet of foot at recognizing and learning from their mistakes.

An example: Throughout much of the '80s, the nature and characteristics of the average package tendered to FedEx changed. Packages became smaller, lighter in weight, and, in ever increasing numbers, contained vital correspondence rather than goods and materials. The company responded beautifully with the successful marketing of the now ubiquitous FedEx Letter. However, with the dizzying growth in letter volume came some new and different operating problems.

One of the more vexing problems resulted from the size and dimensions of the Overnight Letter envelope (as it was then known) and its propensity for getting lost in the back of the company's delivery vans. As they went about the process of picking up packages throughout the day, the company's couriers would return to the van, put the freight in the back, and drive off to their next stop. Over the course of the afternoon, these loose packages—and in particular the Overnight Letter envelopes—had a nasty habit of sliding around and finding their way into small crevices in the cargo section. This made them invisible to the couriers when they unloaded the truck at the end of the day.

The net result was that the overlooked letters remained in the van overnight (or perhaps several nights) before being discovered, and customers in increasing numbers weren't getting what they had paid for. At the time, the company had somewhere in excess of 30,000 couriers and carried approximately one million packages per night, roughly half of which were Overnight Letters. It doesn't take a rocket scientist to figure out that the potential magnitude of the problem was huge, and that on any given day, a lot of packages were practically begging to be misplaced!

Despite all the things they've done well over the years, FedEx management reacted in an uncharacteristically shortsighted manner. Taking the position that these overlooked packages were obviously the result of a careless or uncommitted workforce, their solution was to impose formal, written disciplinary action in any (and every) situation where a package was overlooked. The warning letters soon began to pile up by the hundreds, giving birth to new expressions "leave a letter, get a letter" and over time, these reprimands actually became something of a status symbol. In the eyes of many couriers, you were nobody unless you had at least one written warning.

But it was no laughing matter because, in the process, a lot of otherwise good employees lost their jobs due to an accumulation of warning letters. (FedEx believed in the three-strikes-and-you're-out approach). Moreover, the overlooked-package problem not only didn't get better, it got worse! Some couriers may or may not have been lazy, but they certainly weren't stupid. With foreknowledge of exactly what would happen if they ever did discover an overlooked package in the back of their van, many took direct measures to ensure that no such package was ever discovered. It wasn't until the company backed off the *every mistake will be punished* approach and began actively soliciting courier ideas that this problem started getting solved.

> *The hustlinest team makes the most mistakes.*
> —John Wooden, legendary UCLA basketball coach

GOOD-FAITH MISTAKES VS. ERRORS OF THE HEART

Our research and experience suggest that the *Contented Cows* (including FedEx) have done a better-than-average job of reducing the level of fear within their organizations. *Contented Cow* companies, like Hewlett-Packard, reduce fear by putting in place systemic measures to minimize the possibility of arbitrary treatment; by taking a longer view of the expected length of the employment relationship; and by permitting (and even encouraging) their people to actively experiment *and* make some mistakes.

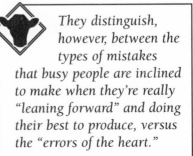

They distinguish, however, between the types of mistakes that busy people are inclined to make when they're really leaning forward and doing their best to produce, versus the "errors of the heart" where a person has knowingly violated one of the organization's core precepts. In the latter case, they don't suffer sinners very well. In fact, they don't tolerate them at all. David Packard made it known early on that anyone (repeat, anyone) who violated HP's ethical principles in order to increase short-term profits would be fired, without exception.

"I Don't Have Bigots On My Payroll"

The same can be said for FedEx's Fred Smith. At one point in the late '70s, during the company's peak growth years, a station manager was having a difficult time getting a bill paid by the accounts payable department in Memphis. At the time, *everyone* in the company was having trouble getting bills paid because there still wasn't a lot of money floating around, and development of the corporate infrastructure (A/P, A/R, Payroll, and the like) lagged the revenue systems by a wide margin.

During the course of a phone conversation with an A/P clerk, the manager apparently uttered a racial epithet. Word of the incident quickly reached Smith, who reportedly picked up the phone, called the manager personally, and asked him if he had indeed made the remark. The man was big enough to admit that he had, whereupon Smith informed him that, "It sounds to me like you're a bigot, and I don't have bigots on my payroll." Click.

CHAPTER SUMMARY

Tooling is, in effect, the process of ridding your organization of success inhibitors—those things which serve as barriers to people either doing the right things, or doing things right. Some examples:

- Policies that are antiquated or just plain dumb.
- Practices that frustrate rather than support personal effort.
- Systems (e.g., pay) which encourage or even reward people for doing the wrong things.
- Failed communication methods which guarantee that nobody understands anything!

1. You must discern between good faith mistakes and "errors of the heart."

2. Make sure your pay and incentive systems are not only well designed, but also well communicated.

   Best Practices:

   a. Salaried Workforces at Worthington Industries and Chaparral Steel.
   b. Lincoln Electric's "piecework pay system."
   c. InTuition's Team Incentives.
   d. Marriott's redesigned table service.

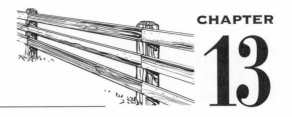

ENABLED EMPLOYEES ARE TRUSTED

People below the acme of the corporate pyramid trust those on top about as far as they can throw a Gulfstream IV, with shower.

—Alan Farnham

In *Fortune's* December 1989 issue cover story, Alan Farnham detailed in an all-too-sobering way what he terms the Trust Gap that is eating away at corporate America. The article focused on employees' general mistrust of their management. It just as easily could have focused on the other side of the trust equation, namely the degree of trust organizations were vesting in their people. Think about it. ...

In their private lives outside of work, your employees are heads of families, civic leaders, army reserve officers, mortgage holders, and a host of other things. Day in and day out they somehow manage to feed themselves and their families, pay their bills on time, stay out of jail, and behave normally by most reasonable standards. In short, they tend to be rather competent individuals with a clear picture of the difference between right and wrong.

Why then, when at work, must they face a continual barrage of not-so-subtle signs of our mistrust in them as individuals? Institutionally, we seem to find new ways every day to treat them like children, or worse. Not so, you say? Well, consider this: If you offered to pay a neighbor's child to pick up some groceries for you at the store (say, a couple of steaks, a loaf of bread, a carton of eggs, and some *Contented Cow* Milk), when they returned with the groceries would you:

- ask to see their time card, signed by a parent or supervisor,
- check their odometer readings and the price tag on each item,
- read them your eight-page policy on grocery purchases,
- march them through a metal detector at your front door,
- double count your change,
- demand a receipt?

We didn't think so. Now, if you're not going to ask for such an accounting from the kid down the street, what reason is there for requiring it of someone who has presumably passed your panel interview process, had their employment and criminal references checked, completed a personality profile, and successfully peed in a bottle? *After all, this is someone you have an opportunity to observe working for eight hours a day.*

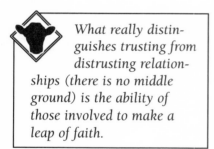

> What really distinguishes trusting from distrusting relationships (there is no middle ground) is the ability of those involved to make a leap of faith.

Trust. Integrity. Call it what you will. But whether it's as a customer, supplier, or employee, it is one of the key factors which differentiates the *Contented Cows* from the also rans. In our view, what really distinguishes trusting from distrusting relationships (there is no middle ground) is the ability of those involved to make a *leap of faith*. They must believe that each is interested in and committed to the other's welfare, and that neither will act without first considering the impact on the other.

NORDSTROM TRUST—AS SIMPLE AS IT GETS

Nordstrom, the Seattle-based department store, has become synonymous with legendary customer service. Something must be working, because in a cutthroat industry with competitors entering (and exiting) the market almost every day, this company enjoyed a 139 percent rate of sales growth from 1987 to 1995.[1] Patrons keep coming because what everybody says about Nordstrom is true—they have outstanding customer service (and fine merchandise as well).

One clue as to how they're able to get their 42,000 employees to render such outstanding service can be seen in the *Nordstrom Employee Handbook*. We've reproduced the complete and unabridged text below:

WELCOME TO NORDSTROM

We're glad to have you with our company.

Our number one goal is to provide outstanding customer service.

Set both your personal and professional goals high. We have great confidence in your ability to achieve them.

Nordstrom Rules:

Use your good judgment in all situations.

Please feel free to ask your department manager, store manager or division general manager any question at any time.

Nordstrom[2]

Unlike so many of the rest of us, Nordstrom apparently believes they made the right choice at the outset—by hiring adults with some modicum of good sense and judgment. The handbook, which allows them to treat their people as mature, competent professionals, is simply an extension of that faith.

REAL GOOD FAITH BARGAINING

In January 1995, the pilots of Southwest Airlines signed an unheard-of 10-year contract with the company. The contract was remarkable not only because of its length, but also the fact that it froze wages for the first five years in exchange for stock options. Said Southwest Executive Vice President Gary Baron, "To me, the bigger thing was the level of trust that had to exist between management and the employee group. … It's not just the money … they signed a contract which froze work rules in place for that 10-year period because they believe that we are willing, if things change dramatically, to change something if it needs to be changed."[3]

Trust tends to be based as much on the personal (i.e., manager-employee) relationship as it is on the policies and practices of the institution at large. Even in organizations where some very bad things are going on, one can still find pockets of high morale and productivity. In some respects, it may be similar to the underpinnings of motivation long understood and taught by the military. Chiefly, the notion that when push comes to shove, people don't fight for the flag, or mom, or apple pie; they fight for the guy who's standing next to them. Their trust is based not on symbols or feelings, but reality.

RETHINKING THE BREAK ROOM

Trust is demonstrated in so many small, seemingly infinitesimal ways. At SAS Institute, for instance, they apparently believe that "well-fed cows give better milk." Every floor of each of the 18 buildings on its sprawling Cary, North Carolina, campus has a well-stocked break room with a veritable cornucopia of stuff to eat and drink. Everything from crackers to M&Ms, all paid for by the company.[4] Everyone is trusted to consume only what they want. There's nothing to stop someone from shoving three boxes of Cracker Jacks in their bag and schlepping them home for those nights when they've got the munchies. Well, maybe there is. Perhaps it's the fact that they're trusted not to.

Remembering a former job, SAS Institute co-founder and President Jim Goodnight recalled, "We had guards at the door every day. We had to sign in. You'd go down the hall and put your quarter in the machine and get a cup of coffee out. A lot of those things I found somewhat offensive." Determined to create a different type of organization, Goodnight maintains, "If you do right by people, they'll do right by you."[5]

Let's not be naive. There are some untrustworthy characters out there, and a few others who, for whatever reason, just don't get it. For those, our advice is simple. Get rid of them, NOW, or whenever and wherever they pop up. The answer is *not* to try to bring them into line by enacting dumb policies and other measures which do little more than frustrate the efforts of hundreds of capable, hard working, honest people who are simply trying to get their work done. It just won't work. The only thing you're going to get from spending precious time and energy building bigger and better mousetraps is smarter mice. Or, as FedEx founder Fred Smith is fond of saying, "We're not going to lower the river—we can only raise the bridge."

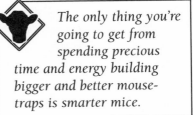

The only thing you're going to get from spending precious time and energy building bigger and better mouse-traps is smarter mice.

HP's David Packard recounted just such an example from his work at GE in Schenectady in the '30s. "The company was making a big thing of plant security. GE was especially zealous about guarding its tool and parts bins to make sure employees didn't steal anything. Faced with this obvious display of distrust, many employees set out to prove it justified, walking off with tools or parts whenever they could. Eventually GE tools and parts were scattered all around town, including the attic of the house in which a number of us were living. In fact, we had so much equipment up there that when we threw the switch, the lights on the entire street would dim."[6] In later years, Packard and HP co-founder, Bill Hewlett, took pains to ensure that their company learned from GE's mistakes by insisting that lab storerooms remain unlocked. Said Packard, "The open bins and storerooms were a symbol of trust, a trust that is central to the way HP does business."[7]

A Gold-Medal Effort

Just prior to the 1988 Olympic Winter Games held in Calgary, Canada, an official of the Dutch Olympic Team went to his local FedEx Account Executive in Amsterdam with a problem. It seemed that team officials had somehow failed to file the necessary registration papers with the IOC, and unless the documents were delivered in Calgary by midnight the following day, the team would be denied the opportunity to participate in the Games.

While FedEx service is good, the A/E knew that the very best they could do at that time with a westbound trans-Atlantic package was going to take one day too long, so he took it upon himself to purchase a plane ticket and personally deliver the important document. He didn't ask anyone's permission, he just did it.

Now some might argue that what this young man did was terribly wasteful. And if the only thing taken into account was this one transaction, they would be right. After all, he had spent a couple days of his time and several hundred dollars of the company's money on a package that might have been worth $50 in revenue. But that's not the point. It wasn't then, and it's not now.

What *is* important is that when faced with the opportunity to solve a customer's problem, he acted. Over the course of his career, this fellow will no doubt have hundreds of opportunities just like this one. Armed with the reassurance that his boss and the company have faith that he will do the right thing, he'll continue to act in the customer's interest, and, in the vast majority of cases, he's going to get it right.

[Southwest Airlines founders Rollin King and Lamar Muse] allowed employees to do whatever it took to get the job done. They didn't stand over us with a whip and say, "I want this done this way."[8]
—Dennis Lardon, Southwest Airlines director of flight attendants

TRUST KEEPS THINGS RUNNING UP TO SPEED

A central message flashing insistently from all the *Contented Cow* companies has to do with speed. At FedEx, it's the very essence of their business. As founder Fred Smith is accustomed to saying, "All we are is a 550-mile-per-hour warehouse." Southwest runs circles around its competition by being able to open a station in a new city faster than anyone else and turn its planes in less than half the time it takes competitors. GE's Jack Welch frequently comments, "If you're not fast, you're dead." 3M's insistence on coming out with massive numbers of new products at an ever increasing rate is another good example.

Speed is no accident, and it can *only* be accomplished by a workforce which is free to act because they are trusted, rather than having to ask for permission all the time. Motivated people move faster.

In his book, *Moments of Truth*, Jan Carlzon points out that employees must be afforded unquestioned authority to act in the customer's behalf. If they must stop to seek permission, more often than not, the opportunity will be forever lost. More important even than the immediate impact on the individual customer is the long term effect those situations have on the employee involved.

Lands' End tells its 3,500 employees that "they can do whatever they think they need to do to take care of a customer." In a similar vein, they do not restrict employee access to their giant warehouse via security guards, ID badges, and all the usual stuff. Says President and CEO Mike Smith, "Our culture is a critical part of who we are. It's our competitive advantage. If we maintain that, we'll be successful. If we lose it, we become a different company."9

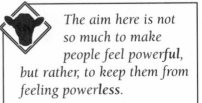

The aim here is not so much to make people feel powerful, but rather, to keep them from feeling powerless.

The aim here is not to make people feel power*ful*, but to keep them from feeling power*less*. When a person feels prohibited from using their own judgment, their sense of responsibility for

LANDS' END NET INCOME PER SHARE

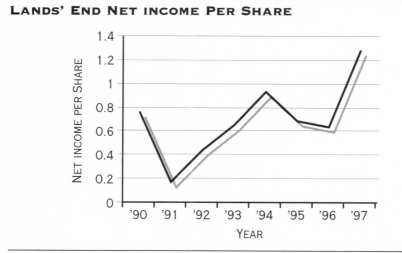

Source: Lands' End Financial Report (unaudited), First Quarter, 1997

the situation around them quickly evaporates and the not-my-job syndrome takes over.

Even tiny amounts of discretionary authority will ward off the energy sapping helplessness and despair that people feel when they find themselves dominated by forces beyond their control. This represents anything but a soft-touch management approach; it fosters greater rather than lesser expectations of people. Allowing the lions to manage their own den is a far cry from asking or expecting them to run the whole zoo!

RAISE DISCRETIONARY AUTHORITY AND SPENDING LIMITS

One of the first areas to look at is the amount of discretionary authority you vest in your employees. Get them involved (as Hewlett-Packard has done) in the hiring process, not as mere bystanders, but as decision makers. Better yet, put them in charge of it. Involve them in promotional decisions, most particularly those involving front-line management positions. Put them in charge of manpower scheduling. Permit them (no, *require* them) to be personally involved in and responsible for some spending decisions. Levi Strauss, for example, has been known to involve its forklift drivers in the purchasing of new forklift trucks.

At a minimum, afford them unquestioned authority (literally) to commit an amount of resource equivalent to at least one week's pay to improve their ability to do their jobs, or to satisfy a customer. Managers (or team-based units) operating with their own cost center or P&L should have at least four to five times that much discretionary authority.

Steve Wynn, CEO of Mirage Resorts, takes it even further. "We tell our people, 'If you see a hotel guest with the tiniest frown on her face, don't ask a supervisor, take care of it. Erase the charge, send the dinner back, don't charge for the room.' "[10]

Not unlike Southwest and Suburban Propane (under Dennis Spina's leadership), companies which demonstrate high levels of trust frequently see trust reciprocated on a massive scale when employees instruct their unions to accept less restrictive work rules, or they throw the union out altogether.

If you assign people heavy responsibilities, that implies confidence in them, and belief in their ability to deliver the goods. Such a move stimulates their desire to prove your faith is well-founded.[11]

—Price Pritchett

MAKE THAT IN SMALL DENOMINATIONS, PLEASE

In *INC* Magazine's September '96 issue, Editor George Gendron passed along an all-too-real corporate horror story. It seems that a distinguished looking man wearing jeans visited a bank branch one day. He was advised that the person who needed to assist him with his transaction was unavailable, and that he should return at a later time. Upon getting this news, he asked the teller to validate his parking receipt. When he was told "no, the validation can occur only in conjunction with a transaction," he rather firmly asked that it be done anyhow. Again he was rebuffed with the explanation that it was bank policy "only to validate parking for customers who had a transaction with the bank." At this point, the man satisfied the bank's requirement for a transaction by withdrawing the million or so he had on deposit.[12]

This teller must have demonstrated *some* intelligence when she was hired to work for the bank, right? What turned this person into a complete idiot between the day she was hired and the fateful day the man wanted to do business with the bank? A lack of trust, embodied in and promulgated via an unintentionally dumb corporate policy. Why do costly lessons this simple have to be learned and relearned every day?

If you're unwilling to give credence to the employer/employee covenant by taking this important step, then by all means save your time, money, and breath. Go out and hire dummies whenever your company has a job vacancy, pay them as little as possible, and don't even think about training them—just hire a supervisor to stand guard over every two to three people.

Powerlessness corrupts. Absolute powerlessness corrupts absolutely.
—Rosabeth Moss Kanter, Harvard Business School

CHAPTER SUMMARY

Trust is the habit of letting go, really letting go, Without trust, you will be doomed to an unacceptably slow pace. It is neither one-dimensional nor negotiable.

1. Do away with systemic signs of distrust (eg; policies, probation periods, time clocks, locked supply cabinets, etc.).

2. Dramatically increase levels of discretionary authority.

3. Remember, the aim is not to make people feel power*ful*, but to keep them from feeling power*less*.

4. Deal swiftly (and harshly) with those who "break faith," but do it individually.

Best Practices:

a. Southwest Airlines long-term pilot contract.

b. Steve Wynn's (Mirage Resorts) blanket approval to fix the customer's problem.

c. Open access at Hewlett-Packard, Lands' End.

d. SAS Institute's complimentary break room.

e. Nordstrom's employee handbook.

Employees with integrity are the ones who build a company's reputation. Working for the Coca-Cola Company is a calling. It's not a way to make a living. It's a religion.[13]

—Roberto Goizueta

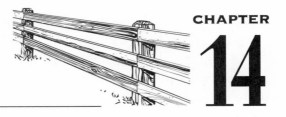

WHEN THE COWS COME HOME

(SPECULATIONS ON THE NEAR FUTURE)

At Southwest, the internal customers—the employees—are treated just like the external customers expect to be treated. Most of the time I would rather be at work than at home or doing other things.
— Kara Harris – Southwest Airlines Reservations Agent

THE CONTENTED COWS ... WHAT NEXT?

We've put a little pressure on the six *Contented Cow* companies (and a lot more on ourselves) by holding them out as beacons for others to follow. Their reputations are what they are, and we happen to think they're well deserved. Yet, will they and their shareholders continue to enjoy the advantages they've created? Will they continue to live up to and redefine what it takes and what it means to be a *Contented Cow*? Only time will tell.

Not long ago, I spent about half an hour with a fellow named Steve. For years, he has been the "greeter" at my local Wal-Mart, the same store where I met Lisa in pursuit of the watch battery. Typical of many of the company's greeters, he's a retired gentleman augmenting his pension by working at Wal-Mart. As a senior citizen who has been around the block more times and learned a lot more than most of us, I was interested in getting his perspective on the company, both as a place to work and a place to do business.

In general, Steve gave the company favorable reviews on both counts. "It's still a great place to work," he said, "but you know, it's just not the same." When pressed for some clarification about what he meant, he added that in recent years he had seen a number of subtle but, to him, significant signs of change, and not altogether for the better. "For the most part, it's little things," he said, pointing to a section of floor which should have been cleaner, and then to a couple of burned out ceiling lights. "Mr. Sam wouldn't have liked that."[1]

To Steve and other Wal-Mart associates we talked with in different stores, there were signs of erosion they attributed to the passing of the baton that occurred after Sam Walton's death. But, in fairness to Wal-Mart CEO David Glass, there will never be another Sam Walton.

FedEx is no more immune than Wal-Mart—*or any other company*—to the inexorable decline that can and will begin the very moment they take their eye off the ball. Unlike at Wal-Mart, FedEx founder, Chairman, and CEO Fred Smith is still very much alive, well, and in the driver's seat. Yet, his company is also showing signs that some of the bloom may be coming off the rose. Since 1989, FedEx has experienced an inordinate rise in management turnover, much of it at senior levels. Some, no doubt were pushed, but many weren't.

Several insiders we know have suggested that the company's defining values (expressed by the People-Service-Profit moniker) have been allowed to get a little out of sync. Many have cited as a case in point the all-too-public acrimony associated with the decision of FedEx pilots to unionize. Given his fondness for the crew workforce, this move had to have pained Smith greatly. Some have blamed this turn of events on the company's 1988 decision to acquire Flying Tigers, a company with its own storied (and radically different) culture. Regardless of the reasons, if and when FedEx starts to "lose it," the effects will be felt "in the streets" long before they're noticed "on the street." Your courier will lose a step or two and a little bit of his smile; the phones won't get answered until the fourth or fifth ring; and the trucks won't be quite as clean. You'll know.

THE PATH AHEAD

To become *Contented Cows*, companies must realize that just as *they* have choices, their employees (particularly the better, more skilled ones) do, too. The new rules of the game have been set, and now it's only a matter of time before everyone learns how to play, and play it to their advantage.

Employees will adjust, for example, to their new-found responsibility for their work, careers, and future, and that's good. It's about time. But those organizations that can't resist returning to their paternalistic ways, or won't furnish their folks the information they need to make valid decisions about their future, will face real difficulty. Any parent who has watched a child go from the teen years to adulthood knows precisely how this goes. We must either continue to change the nature of the relationship, putting it on ever more adult-type footing, or watch helplessly as they run off and leave *us*.

We will soon evolve to having three, maybe four different classes of employees, each with varying degrees of connectedness to the organization, and totally different pay and benefit schemes. Who winds up in what class of job, and for how long and under what conditions will be a choice made as often by the employee as it is by the organization. And, lest there be any doubt about it, that choice will be made for selfish reasons.

The implications of just-in-timing and the externalization of the workforce will be profound. To the extent that we find ourselves employing contractors, temporary workers, or part-timers in *core* activities, we must find new ways of harnessing or positioning their effort as a distinct competitive advantage. Otherwise, everyone winds up working for Manpower and, along with things like loyalty, dedication, and willingness to part with discretionary effort, the advantage goes away.

NO MORE BIG BROOMS OR SILVER BULLETS

Managers have received a break over the past several years. The "big brooms" of downsizing and rightsizing have enabled us to gracefully disguise the firing of non-performers and malcontents.

We were able to push them out the door with everybody else, and do it with a lot less commotion and unpleasantness than if it had happened on a case-by-case basis. But the big brooms are becoming silent. Thankfully, Lean and Mean has pretty well run its course. There aren't too many companies left with a need to undergo the kind of radical restructuring we've seen over the past decade, and besides, Al Dunlap has got a job now (*just kidding, Al*).

Given the heightened criticality of *everyone* on our payroll, we must do a much better job of facing up to performance issues. Performance appraisal and the whole PIP process will become of paramount importance. Let's face it, this is something we've done a miserable job with in the past! The Deming crowd would have us believe that we should just do away with the process; but with all due respect, they're wrong. It's an issue far too important to simply shrug our shoulders and run away from. We've got to figure it out, and do it sooner rather than later.

Professional basketball coach Pat Riley dealt with the subject head on in his book, *The Winner Within.* "Avoiding the solution of a tough, miserable problem is not discretion. It's cowardice. And it's robbery. Because as long as a serious problem goes unsolved, no team, no person can exploit its full potential. Any coach who doesn't kick the complacent ass on his team will wind up kicking his own before long."[2]

WHAT FOLLOWS THE GOLD WATCH AND GOLDEN HANDCUFFS?

Managers will have to work harder than ever to make their organizations attractive places to work. We can't just announce the end of job security, for example, without explaining what we'll put in its place. If we can't or won't offer security, we're going to have to offer real challenge, and *lots* of freedom to pursue it. The good news is that people really *do* thrive on challenge and achievement, both of the team and personal variety. But it's going to be up to us to invent the game and erect the scoreboard.

We applaud the fact that many corporations have gone to great lengths to get their people feeling like owners. That's what it's all about. Quite a few have pursued a path of actually making them owners via stock options, grants, and the like. That's even better. But as in the example mentioned earlier involving Delta, few have communicated it very well. And even fewer have bothered to clearly articulate anything about the vagaries of the market and the occasional effects this little thing called gravity has on it. Many of us have already experienced first hand the diminishing motivational ROI one gets from "under water" stock options. What makes us think our people will feel any different?

While we needn't build an entire town as Milton Hershey did, the issue of benefits must be resolved. As the Committee for Economic Development's Frank Doyle pointed out, "Neither we nor our workers can well afford the incongruity between having a more flexible workforce and our antiquated benefit structures."3 Moreover, in the case of healthcare benefits in particular, we must be mindful that we're within a few short years of having an entire generation of baby boomers starting to fall apart physically at an ever-increasing rate; and all this at a time when more and more of them will be without any health coverage. Whether those people are "real employees" in the traditional sense, contract workers, or something else, is immaterial. As Robert Owen figured out, if they're sick, hurt, or busted up, they can't work!

So What About You?

In as compelling a way as we know how, we've tried to illustrate the distinct and valuable advantages of treating people right. If nothing else, maybe what we've done will confirm for your head what your heart has known all along. With just the 12 companies we chose to profile in the *Contented Cow* comparison, one group ended up with 10 extra "zeros" behind their net income figures, along with a sizable revenue growth advantage. How much more incentive do you need?

It is our fervent hope that some of the facts or ideas we've communicated will become a cause for action. But if you intend to change some of your managerial behaviors, or perhaps your outlook or assumptions—even in a small way—do it with a sense of urgency. Don't wait. Time is not your friend.

Yet, you must be deliberate. You can start by taking a no-nonsense, clear-eyed look at the way you are operating now—no copping out or scapegoating. To those who would say, "But geez, I can't really do some of these things until my boss plows the way," or "our system just won't let me, ..." we say BULL. Find a way! Go ahead without them! The truth is you can start making a difference in your company right now, without anyone's help or permission.

And just what is your company or business, anyhow? It's not the name over the door. It is not a brand, a logo, or nameplate. It isn't the products you make or services you sell. Nor is it a ticker symbol, a bank account, or a piece of paper your attorney filed in Delaware long ago.

Instead, it's the people who will (or won't) show up for work tomorrow morning, and the attitude they bring with them when they pass through the gate or front door. It's their ideas, their sweat, their emotions, their energy. It's their expectations of you and their faith in you. It's both what they are, and what they can become.

It's people who individually and collectively, but not always consciously, decide whether to:

- walk with a spring in their step or to shuffle their feet,
- smile at customers even when they're having a bad day themselves, or, to eat the customer's lunch,
- use the tools you've provided with purpose and conviction, or, take those tools home and put them in the attic,
- show up early and stay late, or, hit the snooze button, roll over, and call in sick,
- walk through fire for you, or, merely hang on well enough to avoid getting fired by you,
- say, "I can help," as opposed to, "that's not my job,"
- find a way to do it better, faster, and cheaper, or, simply settle for "good enough,"
- make something great happen here, or vote with their feet.

Again, it's a matter of choice. Yours, and then theirs. Good luck and Godspeed.

Contented Cows DO Give Better Milk!

A CALL FOR CONTENTED COWS

We assume that some of you were attracted to this book by its premise and its title, and because you share a real interest in organizations that subscribe to the *Contented Cow* philosophy. We also think that the *Contented Cow* companies we've chosen to highlight are but a fraction of those organizations that have achieved financial success by treating employees well.

Do you feel your company deserves to be counted among the ranks of *Contented Cows*? If so, let us hear from you. Keep in mind, our purpose is to look at companies that recognize the commercial wisdom of treating people in certain positive ways, not those which are into social or humanitarian heroics. So, we're not looking for examples of corporate altruism, but stories of companies that have profited by creating a great place for people to work.

This is not a forum for those who are unhappy with the places they work. These stories abound, and you can hear them almost anyplace working people gather to talk, including the Web site we mentioned in Chapter 7: www.disgruntled.com.

We intend to continue our research into the whole notion of *Contented Cows* and corporate profits. If you'd like to contribute, please contact us, and do it soon.

Thanks in advance for your help.

Contented Cow Partners, LLC.
7847 Glen Echo Road, North
Jacksonville, FL 32211
904-720-0870 phone
904-725-8242 fax
http://www.contentedcows.com
e-mail: stories@contentedcows.com

NOTES

INTRODUCTION

1. Peters, Tom, *Thriving on Chaos* (New York: Knopf, 1987), p.286.
2. Pascale, Richard Tanner, *Managing on the Edge* (New York: Simon & Schuster, 1990), p.14.

CHAPTER 1

1. Fisher, Anne B., *Fortune,* March 4, 1996, p.95.
2. Levering, Robert; Moskowitz, Milton; Katz, Michael, *100 Best Companies to Work for in America* (New York, Plume, 1984, 1985, 1993).
3. Fisher, Anne B., *Fortune,* March 4, 1996, p.F2–F7.
4. Lieber, Ronald B., *Fortune,* December 9, 1996, p.107.
5. ™Carnation Company (Nestle), used with permission.
6. Peppers, Don and Rogers, Martha, *The One to One Future* (New York, Doubleday, 1993), p.34.
7. Wright, Frank Lloyd, *An Autobiography,* second edition (Duell, Sloan and Pearce, 1943).
8. Lasorda, Tommy, *Fortune,* July 3, 1989, p.131.
9. Garfield, Charles, *Second to None* (New York, Avon Books, 1992), p.204.
10. Levering, Robert; Moskowitz, Milton; Katz, Michael, *100 Best Companies to Work for in America* (New York, Plume, 1984, 1985, 1993), p.114.
11. *Fortune,* May 12, 1997, p.106.
12. Ibid.
13. trans. Wilhelm, Richard (Ger.) and Baynes, Cary F. (Eng.), *I Ching or Book of Changes,* (New York: Pantheon [Bollingen Series XIX] 1950).
14. Engels, Frederick, *Socialism; Utopian and Scientific.*
15. Lieber, Ronald B., *Fortune,* December 9, 1996, p.107.

CHAPTER 2

1. Thomas, Roosevelt, *Beyond Race and Gender* (Amacom, New York, 1991), p.14.
2. Albright, J., *Improving the Welfare of Dairy Cows Through Management* (Business and Management, 1982).
3. *The Washington Monthly,* June 1986.
4. Organ, Dennis, *Business Horizons 38, no.3* (May–June 1995).
5. Ibid.
6. Ibid.
7. Ibid.
8. Ibid.
9. Ibid.

10. Ibid.
11. National Institute on Aging Study, 1973.
12. Organ, Dennis, *Business Horizons,* May–June 1995.
13. Ibid.
14. Cathy, Truett, *It's Easier to Succeed Than to Fail* (Oliver Nelson, Nashville, 1989), p.70.
15. Johnson, Jimmy, *Turning the Thing Around* (New York, Hyperion, 1993), p.180.
16. Marriott, J. Willard, "Money, Talent, and the Devil By the Tail," *Management Review,* January 1985.
17. Reicheld, Frederick F., *The Loyalty Effect* (Harvard Business School Press, Boston, 1996), p.105.
18. Ibid, p.110.
19. Roosevelt Thomas, interview by author.

CHAPTER 3

1. Smith, Fred W., speech at Rhodes College, February 25, 1988.
2. Mercer Management Consulting survey.
3. Pacetta, Frank, *Success,* May 1994, p.64.
4. Neuborne, Ellen, *USA Today,* December 23, 1996.
5. Garfield, Charles, *Second to None* (Avon Books, New York, 1992), p.201.
6. Neuborne, Ellen, *USA Today,* December 23, 1996.
7. Carlzon, Jan, *Moments of Truth* (Ballinger, Cambridge, MA, 1987), p.3
8. Ibid, p.95.
9. Families and Work Institute survey.
10. David Graham, interview by author.
11. Ibid.
12. Stack, Jack, *The Great Game of Business* (Doubleday, New York, 1992), p.57.

CHAPTER 4

1. Aguilar, Francis J. and Arvind Bhambri, "Johnson & Johnson, Harvard Business School Case #384-053,4."
2. *Los Angeles Times,* December 16, 1996.
3. *USA Today,* December 23, 1996.
4. Sherman and Tichy, *Control Your Destiny or Someone Else Will* (Bantam, New York, 1993), p.245–46.
5. Freiberg, Kevin and Jackie, *NUTS* (Bard, Austin, TX, 1986), p.49.
6. Johnson, Jimmy, *Turning the Thing Around* (Hyperion, New York, 1993), p.189.
7. Lynch, Peter, *Beating the Street* (Simon & Schuster, New York, 1993), p.27.
8. Packard, David, *The HP Way* (Harper Business, New York, 1995), p.126.
9. Didinger, Ray, *Game Plans for Success* (Little Brown & Company, Boston, 1995), p.181.
10. Carlzon, Jan, *Moments of Truth* (Ballinger, Cambridge, MA, 1987), p. unnumbered.

CHAPTER 5

1. "Business Secrets of Tommy Lasorda," *Fortune*, July 3, 1989, p.131.
2. Garfield, Charles, *Second to None* (Avon Books, New York, 1992), p.123.
3. Angela Perry, interview by author, Delta Air Lines seven-year flight attendant, met on flight #1662: July 13, 1996, seat 4-A.
4. Follett, Ken, *On Wings of Eagles* (Morrow, New York, 1983), p.63.
5. *Fortune*, October 28, 1996, p.28.
6. *Fortune*, May 3, 1993, p.37.
7. Ibid, p.36.
8. Ibid, p.41.
9. *Fortune*, October 17, 1994, p.55.
10. *Fortune*, May 4, 1992, p.58.
11. *Selling Power*, September 1996, p.64.
12. *USA Today*, May 16, 1996.

CHAPTER 6

1. Dennis LeStrange, interview by author.
2. Adams, Scott, *The Dilbert Principle* (Harper Business, New York, 1996), p.51.

CHAPTER 7

1. *Sky Magazine*, January 1997, p.101.
2. Ibid.
3. *Fortune*, November 11, 1996, p.201.
4. *Memphis Commercial Appeal*, December 17, 1996.
5. Westin, Alan F., and Feliu, Alfred G., *Resolving Employment Disputes Without Litigation* (BNA Books, Washington, DC, 1988).
6. Worsham, James, *Nation's Business*, June 1997, p.17.
7. *Wall Street Journal*, December 16, 1993, p.67.
8. *Wall Street Journal*, November 26, 1996, p.1.
9. *Business Week*, February 24, 1997, p.30.
10. *Worth*, June 1996, p.89.
11. *INC Magazine*, May 1996, p.21.
12. Dunlap, Al, *Mean Business* (Random House, New York, 1996), p.174.
13. Ibid, p.170.
14. Loeb, Marshall, "How to Grow a New Product Every Day," *Fortune*, November 14, 1994, p.270.
15. Smith, Fred W., speech at Rhodes College, February 25, 1988.

CHAPTER 8

1. Johnson, *op. cit.*, p.190.
2. *Jacksonville Business Journal*, April 7, 1997.
3. Betty Kahn, interview by author.
4. *Business Week*, November 11, 1996, p.111.
5. Freiberg, Kevin and Jackie, *NUTS* (Bard, Austin, TX, 1986), p.49.

CHAPTER 9

1. Galinsky, Ellen, *Business Week,* September 16, 1996.
2. Ibid.
3. *Compensation and Benefits Review*, January–February 1995, p.41.
4. *Best's Review, Property and Casualty Insurance Edition*, June 1996, p.16.
5. *Compensation and Benefits Review*, January–February 1995, p.41.
6. *Best's Review, Property and Casualty Insurance Edition*, June 1996, p.16.
7. Packard, David, *The HP Way* (Harper Business, New York, 1996), p.137.
8. *Best's Review, Property and Casualty Insurance Edition*, June 1996, p.16.
9. *HR Magazine*, May 1996, p.104.
10. *Training*, November 1994, p.12.
11. *HR Magazine*, May 1996, p.104.
12. Ibid.
13. Nixon, Judy, Helms, Marilyn, and White, Charles, "What Companies are Doing About Child Care," *Journal of Compensation and Benefits*, January–February 1993, p.17.
14. David Russo, interview by author.
15. *HR Magazine*, October 1994, p.79.
16. Ibid.
17. *HR Magazine*, May 1996, p.104.
18. *Human Resource Executive*, March 1996.
19. Ibid.
20. Starbucks press release.
21. *Compensation and Benefits Review*, January–February 1995, p.41.
22. Ibid.
23. Ibid.
24. Bollier, David, *Aiming Higher* (Amacom, New York, 1996), p.230.

CHAPTER 10

1. Mintzberg, Henry, *Harvard Business Review,* July–August 1996, p.63.
2. GE 1995 Annual Report, p.3.

CHAPTER 11

1. Packard, David, *The HP Way* (Harper Business, New York, 1996), p.135.
2. *Hoover's Company Profile Database* (The Reference Press, Inc., Austin, TX), p.4.
3. Reicheld, Frederick F., *The Loyalty Effect* (Harvard Business School Press, Boston, 1996), p.119.
4. Alford, Henry, *New York Magazine,* May 23, 1994, p.58.
5. ASTD survey, *Workplace Visions* (Society for Human Resource Management, November–December 1996).
6. Ibid.
7. Johnson, Jimmy, *Turning the Thing Around* (Hyperion, New York, 1993), p.189.
8. Betty Kahn, interview by author.
9. http://www.fed.org/uscompanies/labor/n_z/Rosenbluth_International.html (p.1)
10. *Business Week,* November 11, 1996.
11. *Fortune,* October 18, 1993, p.67.

CHAPTER 12

1. *Merriam-Webster's Collegiate Dictionary* – tenth edition (Merriam Webster, Springfield, MA, 1993), p.1,243.
2. *San Francisco Examiner,* June 11, 1992, p.1.
3. *Delta Air Lines Proxy Statement* (September 16, 1996), p.26–27.
4. David Graham, interview by author.
5. *Fortune,* October 3, 1994, p.114.
6. http://www.pcconnection.com/about/fact.html.
7. McKnight, William L., "Philosophy of Management," 1941.

CHAPTER 13

1. *Hoover's Company Profiles*, March 20, 1997, p.4.
2. Nordstrom Employee Handbook.
3. Freiberg, Kevin and Jackie, *NUTS* (Bard, Austin, TX, 1996), p.107–108.
4. *Sky Magazine,* October 1996, p.40.
5. Ibid.
6. Packard, David, *The HP Way* (Harper Business, New York, 1996), p.136.
7. Ibid.
8. Freiberg, Kevin and Jackie, *NUTS* (Bard, Austin, TX, 1996), p.41.
9. *Training Magazine,* October 1996, p.95.
10. *Fortune,* March 4, 1996, p.98.
11. Pritchett, Price, *Firing Up Commitment During Organizational Change* (Pritchett & Associates, Dallas, TX).
12. *INC,* September 1996, p.11.
13. *Network News*, A publication of the Coca-Cola Company, April 1997.

CHAPTER 14

1. Wal-Mart Associate, interview by author.
2. Riley, Pat, *The Winner Within* (Putnam, New York, 1993).
3. Doyle, Frank, The Committee for Economic Development, New York, *loc. cit.*

INDEX